CAMBRIDGE
HISTORY OF POl

MW00583970

SIDNEY
Court Maxims

CAMBRIDGE TEXTS IN THE
HISTORY OF POLITICAL THOUGHT

Series editors

RAYMOND GEUSS

Lecturer in Social and Political Sciences, University of Cambridge

QUENTIN SKINNER

Professor of Political Science in the University of Cambridge

Cambridge Texts in the History of Political Thought is now firmly established as the major student textbook series in political theory. It aims to make available to students all the most important texts in the history of Western political thought, from ancient Greece to the early twentieth century. All the familiar classic texts will be included but the series does at the same time seek to enlarge the conventional canon by incorporating an extensive range of less well-known works, many of them never before available in a modern English edition. Wherever possible, texts are published in complete and unabridged form, and translations are specially commissioned for the series. Each volume contains a critical introduction together with chronologies, biographical sketches, a guide to further reading and any necessary glossaries and textual apparatus. When completed, the series will aim to offer an outline of the entire evolution of Western political thought.

For a list of titles published in the series, please see end of book.

SIDNEY

Court Maxims

EDITED AND INTRODUCED BY

HANS W. BLOM

ECO HAITSMA MULIER

RONALD JANSE

CAMBRIDGE
UNIVERSITY PRESS

Published by the Press Syndicate of the University of Cambridge
The Pitt Building, Trumpington Street, Cambridge CB2 1RP
40 West 20th Street, New York, NY 10011-4211, USA
10 Stamford Road, Oakleigh, Melbourne 3166, Australia

First published 1996

Printed in Great Britain at the University Press, Cambridge

A catalogue record for this book is available from the British Library

Library of Congress cataloguing in publication data

Sidney, Algernon, 1622–1683
Court maxims / Algernon Sidney: edited and introduced by
Hans W. Blom, Eco Haitsma Mulier, Ronald Janse
p. cm. – (Cambridge texts in the history of political thought)
Includes bibliographical references
ISBN 0 521 46175 8 (hc). – ISBN 0 521 46736 5 (pb)
1. Political science – Early works to 1800. 2. Monarchy. 3. Republics.
I. Blom, H.W. II. Haitsma Mulier, E.O.G., 1942– . III. Janse, Ronald.
IV. Title. V. Series.
JC153.S5   1996
321.8'6'01 – dc20   95–40703 CIP

ISBN 0 521 461 75 8 hardback
ISBN 0 521 467 36 5 paperback

Contents

Preface

In recent years, republican political thought has attracted much scholarly interest, in particular as an outcome of the publications of J. G. A. Pocock. Although the Anglo-American branch of republicanism has predominated in this line of scholarship, other varieties have not escaped attention, especially under the influence of the likeminded writings of Quentin Skinner on republican liberty. The concomitant publication of modern editions of pivotal texts, like those of Neville and Moyle, Harrington, and recently of the *Discourses on government* of Algernon Sidney, confirm this tendency. Sidney's *Court maxims*, written some twenty years before the *Discourses*, has never had an edition either contemporary or modern, and was only recently saved from perennial oblivion by the Oxford historian Blair Worden, who discovered it in Warwick Castle in the 1970s. Written in 1664–5, during his stay in Holland, this manuscript is of the greatest importance for the study of the international ramifications of seventeenth-century republican thought.

The editors express their gratitude to Blair Worden for his encouragement. Jonathan Scott deserves our recognition for his generous consent to hand over the assignment of the edition, and above all for the great support discussions with him as well as his unsurpassable biography of Sidney so abundantly provided. Thanks are also due to the staff of the Warwickshire County Record Office and to John Hogan of the University of Warwick for their generous assistance during the process of transcribing the manuscript.

The manuscript, which is now part of the Greville of Warwick Castle archive (reference CR 1886/unnumbered) is owned by and located in the Warwickshire County Record Office. We kindly acknowledge the permission of Christopher Jeens, County Archivist, Warwickshire County Record Office, to publish this edition.

Ronald Janse has prepared the transcript and the annotations. Hans Blom and Eco Haitsma Mulier wrote the introductory material. The final result is a collective one.

Note on the text

The manuscript is known to us from one copy only. This is now part of the Greville of Warwick Castle archive (reference CR 1886/ unnumbered) and owned by and located in the Warwickshire County Record Office. Its 211 pages are not in Sidney's own hand, but by two different copyists with corrections in again two other hands. The first 96 pages must date from the late seventeenth century and could possibly have been copied by Sidney's friend and one-time host Benjamin Furly (1636–1714), merchant, quaker and man of letters in Rotterdam. The second part is in eighteenth-century handwriting, possibly prepared at the request of the second earl of Warwick, who may have made some of the corrections. Although much more legible than the first half, it has unfortunately been bound slightly too tightly. Consequently a few words had to be interpolated, as accounted for in the footnotes.

This first edition is not a scholarly one. It intends to present a readable text. To that purpose names and other references have been modernized and standardized, and modern punctuation provided. The original division of paragraphs has been retained, exceptions being made where paragraphs would run on too long.

Although it has been argued that the original order of the chapters of the manuscript has been tampered with by the copyists, we have refrained from following Scott's suggestions to re-order them. For purposes of reference, the page numbers of the manuscript are given in the margin of the text. Although in the second part the numbering restarts, it has been numbered through to prevent misunderstandings. This conforms to the practice adopted by Scott.

Abbreviations have been extended and interpolations, required by the intended readability of the text, are added between asterisks. Moreover, the often incorrect Latin quotations and titles have been checked where possible, corrected where necessary, and translated in the footnotes. Modern translations have been followed where available. In cases where a Latin quotation could not be traced in the text referred to by Sidney, an indication is given of the passage Sidney may have had in mind, preceded by 'Reference to'. The quite freely paraphrased quotations from the Bible have been left unchanged, but their references are provided. Additional historical information on Sidney's ample use of ancient, modern, and contemporary history is given in the footnotes, as well as clarifications of his allusions to and paraphrases of political thinkers. For all Sidney's often remarkable opinions, we have abstained from adding qualifying or correcting comments. Footnotes are provided on the first occurrence in the text of the annotated item.

Introduction

Three crucial elements influenced Sidney's political writings: his extraordinary career, his bold character, and no doubt his particular cultural background. *Court maxims, discussed and refelled* was written while Sidney was in his forties and experiencing a large measure of adversity during his self-inflicted exile to the Continent. Sidney intended this text to unite English republicans, and possibly their Dutch counterparts as well, into an effort to re-establish the Commonwealth in England. But it would be inappropriate to look at it as just a 'work of propaganda' (Blair Worden, 'The commonwealth kidney of Algernon Sidney', *Journal of British Studies*, 24 (1985) 1–40, p. 10). A remarkably uncompromising text, it contains 'a more complete exposure of the assumptions behind, and the tensions within, Sidney's thought as a whole' (Jonathan Scott, *Algernon Sidney and the English republic, 1623–1677* (Cambridge, 1988), p. 7) than his later *Discourses concerning government* which, in more direct response to the actual circumstances of the 1680s, was to be published in 1698. The *Court maxims* abound with classical and biblical references, side by side with machiavellian themes and reverberations of Sidney's own education as a squire, providing the context for his view of English history and the nature of politics. The tragedy of the *Court maxims*, however, was that its author was already in the process of losing ground as a politician among English exiles on the Continent because of his abrasive character, while the shifting political situation made its publication inappropriate and left it gathering dust in the archives for more than two centuries.

Algernon Sidney was born in 1623 as the second son of the second earl of Leicester. His mother was a Percy, her father being the earl of Northumberland. Algernon's great-uncle was Sir Philip Sidney, the famous soldier, poet and humanist, who in 1586 died fighting the Spanish army during the siege of Zutphen in the Dutch republic. Algernon's family background was an ancient aristocratic one, his father's family having risen in Tudor times, that of his mother during the Middle Ages. Algernon's father had collected an important library at his house Penshurst in Kent, and his interest in classical and renaissance culture is well known. Unlike his elder brother Philip, Algernon inherited his father's bent for scholarly and literary activities. Moreover, he definitely showed his family's distinctively vehement and quick-tempered nature, which regularly brought him into quarrelsome conflicts of all kinds. However, Algernon also continued the family's ancient political and military tradition. In 1636, after a short embassy to Copenhagen, his father had been appointed ambassador to Paris where his sons received a great part of their education. In addition, Algernon may also have studied at the huguenot Academy in Saumur. In 1641, Charles I appointed the earl of Leicester lord lieutenant of Ireland, and Algernon joined under the command of his brother in the violent suppression of the Irish uprising. As a younger son of noble birth he had little choice but to follow a military career. With the tension between king and Parliament rising rapidly during these years, Algernon decided to join the parliamentary army and in 1644 he was heavily wounded in the battle of Marston Moor. In opting for the parliamentary side, Algernon did not share his father's political indecisiveness, for reasons unknown to us.

In 1645 Sidney was appointed military governor of Chichester and in the next year he obtained a seat in Parliament. He stood firm in defence of Parliament's position against presbyterian attempts to reform the parliamentary army. Subsequently he was appointed governor of Dover, but did not hold that position for long, because parliamentary activities were to take up most of his time. Unwavering against compromises with the king, he nevertheless also opposed the radicals and denied Parliament, whether purified or not, the right to sentence the king, which attitude brought him Cromwell's enmity. Although it is unknown whether he took the required oaths on the new government following the execution of Charles I, Sidney nevertheless continued to sit in what by then had become the Rump

Parliament. Ending his governorship of Dover by way of conflict, his role in politics cannot have been unnoticed, although he did not attend Parliament very regularly (Worden, 'Commonwealth kidney', p. 7). Sidney now started to associate with a political grouping around Henry Neville and Thomas Chaloner, both members of befriended families predisposed to republican ideas who shared an ethos of resistance to the growing power of Cromwell's army. From 1652 onwards, Sidney was a devoted republican and became a member of the Council of State. As a senior government figure for Irish affairs, he outlined legislation for the purpose of the colonization of Ireland, and also took part in the project to integrate Scotland into the Commonwealth. Most remarkable was Sidney's involvement in the foreign affairs of the Commonwealth. Together with his political friends he promoted an aggressive policy, culminating in the outbreak of the first Anglo-Dutch war in 1652. This foreign policy was more informed by economic interests than by the apocalyptic puritanism of the preceding years, and the previous political ambition of a union of protestant nations was replaced by a head-on attack on England's commercial rival, symbolized as a Carthage to be destroyed by a new Rome. But 1653 saw Cromwell disperse the Rump Parliament by armed force, and during these proceedings Sidney himself was physically threatened. From then on, Sidney regarded Cromwell as the incarnation of the vices of monarchical power and tyranny.

As a result, Sidney retired to his family estates in self-imposed internal exile. He set out to settle the family's financial affairs but without much success and his attempts in this direction led to a deterioration of his relationship with his father and elder brother alike. Amidst these events, he sat down to write a treatise *Of love*, glorifying love as a platonic quest for beauty. Cromwell's death, however, and the subsequent removal of his son from the Protectorate left Sidney free to retake his seat in the restored Rump Parliament. By the following month he was already leading the embassy to Scandinavia to restore peace between Denmark and Sweden. These countries were struggling for the exclusive control of the Sound, but England's interests required that it have some influence on the final settlement of this question too. The Dutch had interests similar to those of England and they sought to promote them by sending their navy. Now Sidney's embassy entered the field and practised the principles of gunboat diplomacy (Scott, *Sidney and the English republic*, p. 129). Not in the least disturbed by the subtleties of diplomatic practice, Sidney managed in particular to irritate Charles X Gustavus of Sweden. He did not improve matters by his famous inscription in the new visitors' book of the University of Copenhagen: 'Philippus Sidney, manus haec inimica tyrannis, ense petit placidam cum libertate quietem' (this hand, hostile to tyrants, seeks by the sword the tranquil peace of freedom) (see also A. C. Houston, *Algernon Sidney and the republican heritage in England and America* (Princeton, 1991), p. 34, and note 76), reference made to his famous great-uncle Philip as well. This not only gave Charles X something to chew on, but the newly restored English king Charles II was also acquainted with this impertinence by his court. So Sidney was less than eager to return to England. His pride forbade him to request mercy, or to concede any mistakes, as the king demanded. Moreover, he strongly doubted his safety even if guaranteed.

Thus seventeen long years of exile became his lot. Three years were spent in Rome, where he frequented the papal court, its learned cardinals and clerical nobility. In 1663 Sidney was prompted into action by his financial problems and also by the unsettled situation in England, by the execution of the regicides as well as that of his former combatant Vane, and by the first signs of religious persecution. Sidney's impatient and surly mode of conduct alienated his companions in distress whom he met during his incessant travels through Switzerland, Germany, the Spanish Netherlands, and the Dutch republic. More than once he felt the threat of the royalist assassins. It was during these years that Sidney must have written the *Court maxims*, in which the English defeat off Guinea by the Dutch admiral De Ruyter at the end of 1664 is mentioned (177 MS, p. 175), but the outbreak of the second Anglo-Dutch war on 22 March 1665 is not. One may surmise that Sidney wrote this tract in order to promote his project of launching a joint attack on England. The Dutch grand pensionary Johan de Witt, however, turned his proposal down; he was probably afraid of possible adverse consequences for the Dutch republic in the case of a failure. Nor were Sidney's compatriot republicans eager to make common cause with the Dutch, among other reasons because the Republic had recently not prevented the abduction of three regicides from Dutch territory.

Sidney spent much of this period in Rotterdam with the learned English quaker Benjamin Furly, who may have introduced him to Dutch intellectual circles. A last attempt was made, by the intermediary of the French ambassador to the Republic, to engage the recent Dutch ally Louis XIV in an invasion of England. Although the king provided a small sum, Sidney's subsequent offer to lead French troops into England was declined and the project came to nothing. This was the temporary end of Sidney's political activities among republican exiles. He withdrew to the huguenot southern part of France, from where he made frequent, protracted trips to Paris. His contacts with French aristocratic families who had only just lived through the Fronde intimate the social milieu sought by this extraordinary republican.

Sidney, however, could not acquiesce to continued exile. In 1677 he obtained a permit to take care of his financial estate in England and to visit his father. But this visit brought serious complications to Sidney's life. He was imprisoned for debt for some months and became involved in endless legal proceedings with his brother about their legacy. These purely private matters were overshadowed by political ones, however, in the wake of the crisis in the government of the royal minister Danby and the discovery of the Popish Plot. According to Sidney, Danby was the prime culprit in the new policy of religious and political repression, while the Popish Plot was a scheme to promote Charles's catholic brother James to the throne. Putting financial support by the French ambassador to use, Sidney strove to weaken the growing bond between the Orange and Stuart dynasties, as he had done fifteen years earlier by writing the *Court maxims*. He repeatedly, but unsuccessfully, attempted to get elected to Parliament, and took part in several projects to exclude James from the succession. In *A just and modest vindication of the proceedings of the two last parliaments*, written jointly with William Jones in 1681, he contested the right of Charles II to dismiss the last two Parliaments.

It was at that time that Sidney most probably started writing his famous *Discourses*, a forthright rebuttal of Sir Robert Filmer's *Patriarcha* published in 1680, but written more than forty years before. Sidney did not just intend a point-by-point rejoinder to Filmer's argument on patriarchal government. His targets were evidently to promote a revolt in England, to re-establish the credibility of

Parliament after its virtual abrogation by Charles II, and to urge the obligation of the people to undo or kill its tyrant. It is not, however, known beyond doubt whether Sidney actually was involved in the Rye House Plot to kill Charles. But we are reasonably sure that he played a role in the attempts of the Whigs to stage a general uprising in England (Worden, 'Commonwealth kidney', p. 12). Thus, while John Locke was in the process of articulating his principles of revolution, as an elaboration of the political thought of the Interregnum, in Sidney's *Discourses* another defence of the old cause was at hand. On 26 June 1683 Sidney was arrested and an accusation of high treason brought against him. Parts of the *Discourses* were seized and used in court as proof of his treacherous behaviour, although he denied authorship. An insecure government was determined to eradicate its enemies, and the unlovely treatment of Sidney by Chief Justice George Jeffreys was only to be expected under these circumstances. His defence, which Sidney undertook to deliver himself, suffered from his characteristic verbosity and was curtailed again and again. The death sentence was imposed, and notwithstanding others' attempts to obtain clemency for him, his execution followed on 7 December 1683.

The *Court maxims* addressed a particular audience and had a particular political purpose. The 'godly English', predestinarians and excited millenarians of the mid-sixties as well as the more sedate Restoration dissenters, had to be inspired to act together with other opponents of the Stuarts, including if possible the Dutch. For this very practical reason, Sidney went a long way in his defence of religious and political liberty. Drawing on the language of liberty characteristic of the international world of learning, rather than restricting himself to its local English variety, his tract thus reached a high level of abstraction uncommon for an ordinary pamphlet. He opted for the dignified literary form of the dialogue, following an ancient genre established by Plato and Cicero. Had Sidney's inspiration been found in the Italian renaissance or in his reading of Lipsius? At times his character showed when his zeal for the right cause made him forget authorial distance and fall into vehement and worldly language.

Fifteen dialogues present us with fourteen maxims of the court, as discussed by Eunomius, the commonwealthsman, and Philalethes, 'a moral, honest Courtier and lover of state truth'. The latter naively expounds the schemes of the absolute monarch to put people and country to his own, private use. Situated in a shady garden, the two debaters meet after working hours and continue till late at night, adjourning the discussion once or twice to another day. Their argument develops along the following lines.

Philalethes requests Eunomius to recount the ancient 'virtue and piety' unknown to him as a courtier who is aware only of raging self-interest. Eunomius replies that the English people are discontented with the king, who has cheated them during the Restoration with the help of courtiers and bishops. Rebutting the argument that God established monarchy from the first family onwards, Eunomius explains that government by one man is no necessity. Republics are prosperous and parliamentary monarchies are also known to have thrived. A king ought therefore to be maintained only in so far as men's interests require it. This had been the practice in England's own history. Nevertheless, in republics a more profitable use of power is to be found. There we see come to fruition the principle that God gave man reason so that he could establish civil society and live happily. In republics the 'variety of nature in the individuals [is] rendered useful to the beauty of the whole'. By 'the work of a prudent lawgiver ... [e]veryone, in his own way and degree, may act in order to the public good and the composing of that civil harmony in which our happiness ... does chiefly consist' (19 MS, p. 23). Only by subduing his vices does a man stop being a slave and encounter happiness in this virtue, as Aristotle said, since thereby he finds the freedom that embraces justice. Hereditary kingship produces only vice and hatred, and runs against the principles of reason. Even worse are women on the throne, as exemplified by the rule of Elizabeth, leading to the rise of the Stuarts. Indeed, the Old Testament shows that the Jewish people was already ruled by a mixture of aristocracy and democracy, at times even without a king, or at any rate the king was elected by the patricians.

In present times, however, kings scheme to make the nobility weak and effeminate and turn them into shameless flatterers at court, whereas the ancient nobility, whose heroic exploits under the Plantagenets still call forth so much admiration, is reduced to impotence. The people do not fare any better. They live in poverty and without a say; trade is obstructed. This is a far cry from the situation in the

Dutch republic where exactly the opposite is the case. In the present English monarchy, everybody is made to depend on the king. In particular, the bishops are the monarch's staunchest supporters. They who should watch over their flock instead help the king to rule people's consciences, which while in itself unacceptable also drives men out of the church. Religion is a godly gift, not to be imposed by the hangman. One should remember the example of the Dutch: Spain lost out completely when it attempted to dictate their religion. Unjust violence ought to be countered by just violence: 'whoever acts unjustly breaks the common pacts by which human society is established' (86 MS, p. 101). Should not Canterbury be withstood as Rome once was? '[E]very man having a rational and natural right of disputing what is uncertain, and of not receiving it till convinced that it's a certain truth' (91 MS, p. 107). But now we see the king employing his lawyers to suppress everybody by means of purposely complicated laws. The essence of civil societies, however, is justice for all members, to be guaranteed by laws which in the last instance originate from God and nature. If political laws simply followed from reason, one would need only to consult Plato (111–12 MS, p. 123). Here, a difference has to be made between the matter and form of laws. There is every reason to be afraid of oppressing factions 'favouring the private interest of one or a few men to the prejudice of the commonwealth' (121 MS, p. 130). The prerogative of kings in England is a case in point, and seems to repeat the history of the Roman empire with its caesars and favourites. The original godly inspiration of the laws is lost, the preservation of society is in peril, and '[w]e may be every day questioned for our liberties, estates, or lives' (122 MS, p. 131). The appointment of good lawyers in the chief magistracies of the body politic is prerequisite as a remedy: 'If there be anything called law which is unrighteous, they seek to abrogate it. They redress what is amiss, explain what is obscure, and supplement what is defective' (140 MS, p. 145). But under the present monarchy this is not to be expected. It is tyranny 'being the centre where all corrupt and filthy interests do meet, ... being the greatest cause of misery unto man ... The glory of a tyrant is like that of the fruits which are said to grow near unto the lake where Sodom stood. They are beautiful to the eye, but are nothing save rottenness, poison, and noisome vapour' (146–8 MS, pp. 150–1). Tyranny is evil and will deserve God's wrath. '[R]eason dictates, Scripture denounces, and the spirit explains ... that whatsoever government is unjust, cannot be permanent' (147 MS, p. 150).

The next five dialogues discuss England's foreign policy. England's true interest is not to follow the lead of Louis XIV, the king of France, however admirably the latter rules his country (154–5 MS, p. 158). An alliance with France would be full of danger and facilitate the latter's drive towards a universal monarchy. Rather than incite to war against the Dutch republic, as the English king is scheming to do to the detriment of Dutch wealth and in order to promote William of Orange to the stadholderate, a union of protestant nations should be envisaged. The United Provinces may resemble 'a vast building of loose stones' (173 MS, p. 173), yet they nonetheless enjoy liberty and prosperity from their trade and necessity will always bring out the Dutch in their defence. But reasonable as such a union would be, it is 'contrary to the interest and maxim of tyrants' (178 MS, p. 176). We now witness Charles II favouring the Catholics, who under his father killed thousands of Protestants in Ireland. The court evidently fears all virtuous and good men, for no other reason than their resistance against unjust violence, or their wish to preach and pray, since it is undeniable that 'the nature of everything is to destroy all that is contrary to itself and its principle' (191 MS, p. 188). A good king is to be feared abroad, a bad king at home.

The peroration in the last chapter of the *Court maxims* drives home the central point. In human society, the difference between good and evil matches that between God and the devil. But monarchy is not to be ruled out completely: 'I dare not say all monarchy is absolutely unlawful, for monarchy in the largest sense, as signifying a government where one man has a pre-eminence above others, may be distinguished into many sorts' (197 MS, p. 193).

The historical record, however, is not very promising. Whether we check the Bible, or worldly histories, we see nations like the Jewish or the English err in lightheartedly wishing for themselves a king, and thereby become responsible for the king's subsequent crimes. Whereas in a legal monarchy, in contrast to a despotical one, the well-being of those governed is aimed at, the governor's reward will be contingent only upon his virtue, since the laws 'have the force of a pact between the governor and governed' (207 MS, p. 200). Even in an absolute monarchy the ruler has to prove that he excels his subjects in nature and virtue, and that he lacks the vices that afflict them. Noble birth does not provide an exemption. Even in a legal monarchy, the king ought to be 'a man of admirable valour, justice and wisdom' (210 MS, p. 203) in order to be accepted by everyone. If he brings about 'the felicity and perfection of the governed' (210 MS, p. 203) and his soul is enlightened by God, this will be the kind of king praised by Seneca. But where such a man of qualities is absent, there is no one to claim superiority over his fellow men. Since 'the place of king is above all others, therefore none can be a king according to the rules of nature, reason, and justice' (211 MS, p. 203). Whoever usurps this power, Eunomius is made triumphantly to conclude, becomes an enemy of mankind 'and obliges all that are friends to reason and justice to destroy such a monster, who, having the shape of a man, has nothing else of humanity' (211 MS, p. 203).

Although perhaps not a systematic philosopher, Sidney has developed in the *Court maxims* a set of principles that support his republican convictions and prove why monarchy should be seen as the archenemy of human liberty. Heavily imbued with moralism, the *Court maxims* seems to give pride of place to an elite of the mind, to a moral aristocracy. But it must be a moral aristocracy with a vengeance that Sidney here has in mind. In two periods of English history, the aristocracy was the pivot in the political system, and two times it failed. The nobility during Plantagenet rule, as well as the 'godly English' during the Commonwealth, for all their civic virtue failed to save England from the adverse effects of machiavellian politics as practised first by the Tudor monarchs and then by the Protector. It takes two to keep a contract, and civil society is indeed based on a pact between its members, in accordance with reason which God or nature has instituted in men. This tragic element of politics, that morally good men lose out to machiavellian opponents, has in Sidney's view to be countered by a good constitution, or more precisely by good laws: 'such laws as conduce to a civil harmony wherein the several humours, natures, and conditions of men may have such parts and places assigned to them, that none may so abound as to oppress the other to the dissolution of the whole; and none be so wanting as that the part naturally belonging to it should be left imperfect. But everyone, in his own way and degree, may act in order to the public good and the composing of that civil harmony in which our happiness in this world does chiefly consist' (19 MS, p. 23). Laws are conducive to a civil order in which the morally good can thrive. The matter of law is to be found in its compliance with the law of God, the light of nature and reason in man, and the preservation of society. Here Sidney was taking recourse to Grotius in some general sense, but more particularly to the latter's notion of just self-defence whenever the civil laws fell short of this ultimate standard. Sidney's fellow republicans Milton and Vane also based themselves on a religious conception of natural law, as distinct from, for example, the view held by that other republican James Harrington, for whom virtue was a mere function of the common good.

This exalted view of civil law was complemented by Sidney with a constant awareness of the contingent side of politics. Here his inspiration came from classical authors, Tacitus and Livy in particular, who had stressed the mutability of the world in an attempt to integrate it into their political thought. Machiavelli's reflections on the fall of the Roman republic only underlined that influence. Sidney took a sceptical and relativist stance in contemplating how the unchanging validity of natural law was matched time and again by the contingent flow of history. But in contrast with Harrington who admired the mixed constitution and its prime example Venice, Sidney commented only in passing on the advantages of mixing the three Aristotelian forms of government. In his conviction that the republic was by far the best state, he was looking to the Dutch example rather than the Venetian one.

The role of history as a storehouse of examples to provide help in formulating political precepts for the future can hardly be overlooked in the *Court maxims*. Machiavelli had shown the way; not the Machiavelli of *The prince*, however, since Eunomius time and again derided the immorality of reason of state (20 MS, p. 24; 70 MS, p. 84; 77 MS, p. 91), and not even Philalethes took exception to this view (33 MS, p. 40; 70 MS, p. 83). It is Machiavelli's *Discourses* that provided Sidney with his analyses of the structure and downfall of the Roman republic. From this work of Machiavelli he learned that citizens have to defend their country themselves, and he understood that civil war and revolt '(says Machiavelli) are the distempers of a state, [but] the introduction of a tyrant is the death of it' (142 MS, p. 147). Moreover, from this he derived his insistence upon the necessity of a state's expansion, whenever possible (13ff MS, pp. 15ff).

Next to Roman history, biblical history from the Old Testament made him understand the nature and dangers of monarchy, as it provided ample insight into godly inspired rule, like that of Moses, Saul, and David. Here the basic distinctions are present between monarchy as true leadership and legitimate authority on the one hand, and as tyranny liable to rightful tyrannicide on the other. The Church Fathers gave him arguments against the Anglican Church. The history of England, last but not least, taught him that the present situation, with its degenerate nobility boasting empty titles and its monarchs intent on absolute power, had originated only in the sixteenth century. Under the Plantagenets, 'our boisterous, fighting kings', there had been a 'powerful, gallant nobility' that had not indulged in empty court life. The king had joined forces with the nobility in fighting France and therefore had been content with a limited power. In this 'gothic constitution', the three elements of society had been kept in balance by an ideal, hereditary but unprivileged nobility that had protected the king from the people as well as the people from the king (56–7 MS, pp. 67–8). Sidney's image, possibly under the influence of his family background, was a world apart from that of the republican Harrington, who in his *Oceana* had decried this Gothic period of English history as imperfect and unstable.

No doubt Sidney's historical views were very much dictated by the necessities of his own time. But he was not devoid of historical awareness. Unlike Machiavelli, Sidney did not attempt to combat corruption with the machiavellian notion of a return to the original constitution. Although he clearly understood how his ancestors had succeeded in resisting attempts on their freedom, he was aware that they had lived in a rude and simple age, and that new elements had to be introduced in order for the practices in question to be restored (122 MS, pp. 130–1; 140 MS, p. 145). The beginnings of historical awareness are likewise evident in his plea for the separation of church and state in reaction to recent measures of a royalist Parliament to strengthen the position of the Anglican Church. Doubts about the infallibility of the dogmas of the Church made him claim that thenceforth each individual had to ascertain the truth of their elements for himself before accepting them.

Contemporary history was present in the *Court maxims* in the description of the political situation of the European countries since the Thirty Years war. Turkey was presented as a despotism. Spain and Italy were led by their monarchs into a process of precipitate decay. Although critical of France, he nevertheless admired Louis XIV. The nordic kingdoms at least managed to take care of their interests. The republics received his full respect. Sidney admired Venice, although it had been forced to opt for conservation instead of expansion. The Dutch republic was to be preferred, since it was, as Philalethes was sadly to remark, 'through good government and liberty of traffic so rich, powerful, and prosperous that no state in Europe dares singly contest with it' (159 MS, pp. 161–2).

Like Milton's, Sidney's republicanism was foremost a language, not a clearcut programme. The vices of monarchy, or even its inherent viciousness as Sidney has it in the peroration of the *Court maxims*, cannot be checked by the institutional balances of a perfect constitution, but faith should be placed in the christian platonic ideal of virtue, and the liberty provided by laws. This freedom could and ought to be defended in consonance with the principles of justice against its usurpation by any individual, especially a king, whose striving for power is aimed at oppressing and subduing all others. A king in particular would always see his interest, and that of other kings, to lie in curtailing the natural rights of life, liberty, and estate – and Sidney has it in the word order familiar from Locke (*Second treatise on government* (1689), § 123). Indeed, Sidney's republicanism draws strongly on this one principle of political morality: the rise to eminence presupposes eminent moral qualities which are difficult to acquire, therefore the monarchical pretension will naturally lead to artificial distinctions of moral eminence, which inevitably leads to oppression (29 MS, pp. 34–5). Just like the shortsightedness of a people that chooses itself a king, hubris precedes the fall of a monarchy. The Dutch republicans Johan and Pieter de la Court, much *en vogue* during the years that Sidney composed his *Court maxims*, argued from a comparable but slightly different perspective. Their analysis of monarchical failure drew heavily on the claim that the institutional circumstances of the court prevented the education of a virtuous king, as well as promoting his subsequent moral corruption. Pieter de la Court's king, no longer factually responsible for the nation's policy, was therefore unable to restrain the private interests of the courtiers from exploiting and impoverishing the people. For Pieter de la Court, vicious monarchy produces vicious kings, while

Sidney argues the other way round in claiming that vicious kings produce vicious monarchies. Both republican theories maintain that man has a penchant for vice, and that only a good political order can contain sinful man within the bounds dictated by the public good.

But Pieter de la Court typically stresses that good political institutions permit private interests to be pursued so as to promote the public interest at the same time. Sidney, however, demands a specific, disinterested civic virtue on the part of the country's rulers in order to secure a political order in which ordinary citizens can peacefully enjoy their life, liberty, and estate.

Arguing from this logical impossibility of a virtuous king, republicanism à la Pieter and Johan de la Court then pointed to institutional arrangements that provided for the education of virtuous citizens better than monarchies could. Republicanism, for Sidney, instead depends on real moral excellence. This moral excellence or civic virtue is easily imperilled by a king's promotion of idolatry and artificial inequality, which by employing the petty self-interest of ordinary man corrupts the nation.

But there is more to Sidney's republicanism. At times it may seem hard to get at the core of the *Court maxims*. This is not due to a lack of explicitness on Sidney's part. Sidney's world view presents itself in the strong contrasts of a manichaean perspective. In an endless sequence, opposite pairs of moral qualifications are pressed upon the reader: vice and virtue, God and devil, truth and treason, protection and destruction, and so forth. One is tempted to say with Sidney that the 'evil spirit once raised, seldom rests' (121 MS, p. 130). This black and white, this either/or, is productive of a heavily loaded moral vocabulary of politics which separates those who have seen the light from those who have not. Philalethes definitely is not one of the godly. His understanding of politics is a naive and complacent one. He accepts the wisdom of the day, including machiavellian and hobbesian *obiter dicta*. In a few passages an identification is suggested of the historical Philalethes Sidney may have had in mind (3 MS, p. 3; 7 MS, p. 9). There reference is made to the 'remembrance' of true christian values and to Philalethes's 'ghostly father' who, however, taught him wrong principles as well, most notably that kings were made after the image of the monarch in heaven. One might surmise that this ghostly father is the same Henry Hammond who was 'advanced to one of the richest bishoprics in England', being appointed archdeacon of Chichester in 1643. Hammond used Tertullian in his *Of resisting the lawful magistrate under colour of religion* (1644) to endorse his reading of Paul's conception of political obedience and to demand christian forbearance. He was no doubt involved in Sidney's religious education at Penshurst, but was also the tutor of the young William Temple. If Sidney had a real person in mind while writing the *Court maxims*, it may well have been Sir William Temple, at that time about to obtain his first embassy (1665) for Charles II. Temple had a keen eye for court politics and was well versed in the language of interest. It seems to be precisely Philalethes's lingering scepticism that Sidney wanted to put to use. The best way to attack reason-of-state ideas is by means of more of the same. So this Philalethes–Temple figure permits Sidney to introduce the language of reason of state, as well as to demolish it. Philalethes in the process is urged by Eunomius, who uses Machiavelli against Machiavelli (113 MS, p. 124; 142 MS, p. 147), to part with idolatry and pride, to accept man's equality before God, and to see politics again as a responsible trust on behalf of the people.

Sidney's republic was inspired, like the Christians under the cross, by his conviction that if the godly are persecuted this must imply that the persecutors themselves are evil. Tertullian and Cyprian are his key witnesses, but they are seen in a protestant light. That against a tyrant '[e]very man [is] a soldier' (54 MS, p. 64) was not exactly the opinion of these Church Fathers. Here Sidney took recourse to the Roman lawyers and to Grotius. He did not, however, accept the absolutist implications of Grotius. Nor did he follow Grotius in his criticism of monarchomach thought, but rather enlarged upon the small escape hole Grotius left when he accepted the possibility of the people retaining rights to themselves in the original institution of kingship (195–211 MS, pp. 192–204). He also did not choose to develop a theory of contract, but stressed trust as the fundamental relationship between rulers and ruled. Trust presupposes morality, and morality presupposes laws and justice, since man's depravity is apt to lead him astray.

No single account can bring together Sidney's vision of a well-ordered polity, unless it be that of the pivotal role of virtue. Like Pieter de la Court, Sidney was not totally committed to the virtue of 'classical republicanism'. In the somewhat separate discussions of the chapters on foreign politics, Sidney can be seen to introduce yet another shared element, that of commerce. He criticizes the petty self-interest of the commercial classes of the city of London, who do not understand that trade unites, and that it is the central motive force of sound international policy. Sidney admires the Dutch whose 'delight in liberty and prosperity ... has kept them unanimous in defence against all enemies' (173–4 MS, p. 173). And elsewhere Sidney advocates the absence of social distinction in the Republic, to the effect that the majesty of power has to be earned by good government. However, as with the earlier aspects of his thought, Sidney again refrains from arriving at straightforward conclusions. He notes the strength of this commercial republic, but avoids drawing general conclusions.

In the end, his tract is a vehement moral appeal to understand the more distant effects of self-interest and to act upon the insights obtained. Everyone, whatever his part in society, ought to pursue his own affairs with a view to the public good. In particular, those who have risen above common men should maintain this public spirit, without which the entire order will decay and disintegrate. Narrow self-interest will turn against itself in the end, just as Eunomius had shown Philalethes to be the case with reason of state. This morality is that of republicanism. If it is classical, it is so because of its sources. For Sidney, Cicero's fight against the corruption of the Roman republic, Tertullian's struggle with the Roman emperors, and the decay of the Gothic constitution exemplify the same moral challenge as that of the failed Commonwealth and his own fight against Charles II. Sidney is evasive on problems of modernity. He is aware that the answers and vocabularies of the kindred predecessors he draws upon are highly relevant to his fight against the evil language of interest and necessity, but, by at the same time disregarding the growing importance of 'interest' for modern republics, he seems also to miss the point of modern reason of state. This does not invalidate Sidney's achievement. By drawing upon these very different traditions of anti-tyrannical political thought, Sidney provides a forceful republicanism, many aspects of which are relevant today.

Principal events in Sidney's life

1623   Birth of Algernon Sidney, probably on 14/15 January.

1625   Succession of Charles I.

1636   Sidney lives for six years in France with his father, the second earl of Leicester, who is ambassador from the English court.

1641   His father is appointed lord lieutenant of Ireland.

1643   Sidney returns to England after military service in Ireland.

1644   Fights on the side of Parliament against the royal army in the battle of Marston Moor and is severely wounded.

1645   Sidney is made governor of Chichester.

1646   Takes his seat in the Long Parliament.

1648   Sidney is appointed to the governorship of Dover.

1649   Execution of Charles I. Abolition of monarchy and the House of Lords in England.

1652   Sidney occupies a leading position in Parliament. He favours the war against the United Provinces and works out proposals for a regulation of the situation in Ireland.

1653   Cromwell's army breaks up the Rump Parliament. Sidney is threatened with removal by force.

1653–9 Temporary retirement from politics. Writes *Of love*.

1658   Oliver Cromwell dies.

1659   Sidney resumes his seat in the restored Rump Parliament. Senior member of the embassy abroad to mediate peace between the kings of Sweden and Denmark.

1660   Charles II restored to the throne. Sidney refuses to condemn his own actions under the Commonwealth or to ask for mercy.

1660–3 Exile in Italy. Visits Switzerland, Flanders and Germany. Contacts with other exiles. Attempts on his life.

1664–5 Sidney moves to Holland and writes *Court maxims, discussed and refelled*.

1665 The Dutch grand pensionary Johan de Witt declines Sidney's proposal for an invasion of England and Scotland to turn England into a Commonwealth again.

1666 Louis XIV offers a small sum for a beginning of Sidney's project to invade England with French troops.

1666–77 Sidney resides in Montpellier and Nerac in the South of France. Long visits to Paris. Contacts with French noble families.

1677–8 Returns to England. Financial difficulties cause several months of imprisonment. Initiates legal action against his elder brother to obtain his father's inheritance.

1679 Sidney cooperates with William Penn to secure greater freedom of religion in England. Works with Henry Neville. Stands repeatedly for election in Parliament but without success.

1679–81 Political crisis over attempts by members of the House of Commons to exclude James, the catholic brother of Charles II, from succession to the throne.

1680 Publication of Robert Filmer's *Patriarcha*.

1681 Charles II dissolves Parliament. Sidney writes, together with William Jones, *A just and modest vindication of the proceedings of the two last Parliaments*.

1681–3 Sidney prepares his *Discourses concerning government*, a refutation of Filmer's book.

1683 Leading Whigs plan an armed insurrection and an uprising in Scotland, followed by the assassination of the king. On the discovery of the plot Sidney and many others are arrested (26 June). After a summary trial, in which he defends himself, Sidney is sentenced to death. His execution follows on 7 December.

1698 John Toland publishes Sidney's *Discourses concerning government*.

Bibliographical note

Biography

All previous biographical information has been superseded by the two-volume study of Sidney's life and ideas by J. Scott, *Algernon Sidney and the English republic, 1623–1677* (Cambridge, 1988) and *Algernon Sidney and the Restoration crisis, 1677–1683* (Cambridge, 1991) with full bibliography. A. C. Houston, *Algernon Sidney and the republican heritage in England and America* (Princeton, 1991) gives a documented biography as well. See also J. Carswell, *The porcupine: the life of Algernon Sidney* (London, 1989). There is an excellent essay from his hand on the adventures of the manuscript of the *Court maxims* in J. Carswell, 'Algernon Sidney's "Court maxims": the biographical importance of a transcript', *Historical research. The Bulletin of the Institute of Historical Research*, 62 (1989) 96–103.

Intellectual and political background

The English republican tradition of which Sidney forms a part was extensively discussed for the first time by Z. S. Fink, *The classical republicans. An essay in the recovery of a pattern of thought in seventeenth-century England* (Menusha (Wis.), 1945; 2nd edn Evanston (Ill.), 1962); for its influence in the eighteenth century see C. Robbins, *The eighteenth-century Commonwealthman. Studies in the transmission, development and circumstance of English liberal thought from the restoration of Charles II until the war with the seven colonies* (Cambridge (Mass.), 1959). For the reception of Machiavelli in republican

England see F. Raab, *The English face of Machiavelli. A changing interpretation 1500–1700* (London, 1964). The seminal work on republicanism by J. G. A. Pocock, *The machiavellian moment. Florentine political thought and the Atlantic republican tradition* (Princeton, 1975) concentrates on the ideas of James Harrington and discusses Sidney only briefly. A lucid article on Sidney and his fellow republicans is by B. Worden, 'Classical republicanism and the puritan revolution', in: H. Lloyd-Jones, V. Pearl, and B. Worden eds., *History and imagination. Essays in honour of H. R. Trevor-Roper* (London, 1981) 182–200. See also his 'English republicans', in: J. H. Burns and M. Goldie eds., *The Cambridge history of political thought 1450–1700* (Cambridge, 1991) 443–75. The international impact of Machiavelli will be found in G. Bock, Q. Skinner, and M. Viroli eds., *Machiavelli and republicanism* (Cambridge, 1990). On the theory of interest see Q. Skinner, *The foundations of modern political thought* (2 vols.; Cambridge, 1978) vol. II. For other aspects of contemporary English political thought see G. Schochet, *Patriarchalism in political thought. The authoritarian family and political speculation and attitudes especially in seventeenth-century England* (New York, 1975) and R. Ashcraft, *Revolutionary politics and Locke's Two treatises of government* (Princeton, 1986). For an account of the political events of the Restoration, see, for example, R. Hutton, *The Restoration. A political and religious history of England and Wales 1658–1667* (Oxford, 1985). For Dutch republicanism see E. O. G. Haitsma Mulier, *The myth of Venice and Dutch republican thought in the seventeenth century* (Assen, 1980), H. W. Blom and I. W. Wildenberg eds., *Pieter de la Court en zijn tijd (1618–1685)* (Amsterdam, 1986), and H. W. Blom, *Causality and morality in politics. The rise of naturalism in Dutch seventeenth-century political thought* (Rotterdam, 1995).

Studies of Sidney's thought

The books of J. Scott and A. C. Houston contain profound analyses of Sidney's *Court maxims* and *Discourses*. Houston, however, denies Sidney's adherence to the republican tradition of civic humanism as expounded by J. G. A. Pocock. See also T. West, 'Foreword', in: A. Sidney, *Discourses concerning government* (Indianapolis, 1990) xv–xl, who contends that Sidney was as much a natural rights and contract man as Locke. B. Worden gives a well-balanced view of the man

Sidney, his thought, and his myth in 'The commonwealth kidney of Algernon Sidney', *Journal of British Studies*, 24 (1985) 1–40. On Sidney's use of history for his political views see J. Connif, 'Reason and history in early Whig thought. The case of Algernon Sidney', *Journal of the History of Ideas*, 43 (1982) 397–417. A recent French, predominantly philosophical, interpretation is P. Carrive, *La pensée politique d'Algernon Sidney (1622–1683). La querelle de l'absolutisme* (Paris, 1989).

Biographical notes

AHAB, son and successor of Omri and seventh king of Israel (c. 874–852 BC). His reign was generally peaceful and he successfully withstood the Assyrians. But he stood under the influence of his wife, Jezebel, who built a temple dedicated to Baal and later instigated open opposition to God by slaying the true prophets, tearing down the altars of the Lord and forcing Elijah, the principal prophet of the period, to flee. This, together with Ahab's failure to stand up for the law as exemplified in the fake trial and death of Naboth, provoked Elijah's wrath. He was killed in a battle against Syria, a fate prophesied by Elijah.

ARISTOTLE (384–322 BC), Greek philosopher who left a vast number of works on a great variety of subjects, including ethics and politics. His influence on later western thought was continuous and immense. During the twelfth and thirteenth centuries the whole corpus of his work was translated into Latin. It formed an important basis of medieval christian philosophy and was at the centre of the university curriculum well into early-modern times. Aristotle's ethical and political thought was based on the idea that virtue cannot be practised by the solitary individual. By nature a political animal, only as a citizen can man achieve the good life. Sidney invokes Aristotle's authority to support his claims.

CHARLES I (1600–49), king of Great Britain and Ireland (1625–49). Second son and successor of James I who reigned England for eleven years without calling a parliament (1629–40). During these years he met with increasing opposition. His decision in 1634 to levy ship-money in order to pay for the royal navy aroused widespread resistance by 1638 because he was suspected to have levied this ancient tax not for naval purposes but in order to make himself financially independent of Parliament. In Scotland armed resistance broke out when in 1637 he attempted to enforce upon his northern kingdom the ecclesiastical policy designed by Laud. In order to raise an army against the Scots, Charles summoned first the Short Parliament and then the Long Parliament (1640). The Commons exacted from him acceptance of a variety of bills amounting to a constitutional revolution, but in 1642 civil war broke out over the question of who was to control the militia. Charles and his royalist forces were defeated in 1646 and again in 1648. He was brought to trial in 1649 and, after being charged and found guilty of high treason, he was executed on 30 January.

CHARLES II (1630–85), king of Great Britain and Ireland (1660–85). After the death of his father and the establishment of the Commonwealth in 1649, he was proclaimed king by the Scots. But when his armies were defeated by CROMWELL in 1650 and 1651, he was forced to flee to France and remained in exile until monarchy was restored in England in 1660. Once restored, he acquired much direct power and constitutional rights by the Restoration settlements (1660–2). His requests, however, to extend religious toleration to nonconformists and Roman Catholics – as promised in the declaration he issued from Breda in 1660 – were successfully defied by his leading churchmen. He also remained financially dependent upon Parliament. Charles was not a sober man and like many of his contempories Sidney argued that his reign was marked by a decline of public morals.

CROMWELL, OLIVER (1599–1658), English soldier and statesman. He belonged to the landowning class in East Anglia and supported the Independents among the Puritans. Under his generalship (from 1644) the parliamentarian forces defeated the forces of CHARLES I. After the execution of Charles I and the establishment of the English republic (1649), he became first chairman of the council of state and in that capacity defeated the Irish and the Scottish supporters of CHARLES II. In 1653 he dissolved Parliament and became Lord Protector of England, Ireland, and Scotland (till 1658). While serving in that office, he conducted the first Anglo-Dutch war (1654).

CYPRIAN, ST (c. 200–58), early christian theologian and bishop of Carthage. After his conversion in c. 246 and his election as bishop of Carthage in 248, he fled from the persecution of Roman emperor Decius (249–51), returning in 251. Under the persecution of the emperor Valerian he was first banished, in 257, and then, in 258, put to death. His major theological work, *On the unity of the Catholic Church*, was written in support of pope Cornelius, whose pontificate was complicated by a schism that was partly caused by the self-appointment of the Roman priest Novatian as pope. Cyprian argued that to go into schism is to break that love between believers which is constitutive of the church. He also upheld the principle that a bishop, although obliged to act in harmony for the unity of the church, is responsible to God alone. Sidney, however, invokes the authority of Cyprian to support his claim that bishops are chosen by and responsible to 'the people'.

DAVID, second king of Israel. When the spirit of God had departed from SAUL, David was revealed to SAMUEL as his successor. By divine providence David was also selected to minister to the fallen king. When David in a well-known incident defeated the Philistine giant Goliath, Saul became jealous of him and attempted first secretly and then openly to slay him. David fled, but once Saul was dead he returned to Israel and was proclaimed king. His reign lasted long and was successful. There was much debate in sixteenth- and seventeenth-century political thought over David's motives in not killing Saul when it was in his power to do so and in killing an Amalekite who claimed to have killed Saul in battle. In the pro-monarchic version David had acted out of respect for the lawfully established and sacred king. Another strand, however, attributed his actions respectively to galantry and to the fact that God had ordered the killing of the Amalekites anyway, thus denying that it is intrinsically unlawful to kill a king. Sidney criticized the former and embraced the latter view.

GIDEON, judge and hero of faith who was called to deliver his people while threshing wheat. Trusting in God rather than in a large army, he liberated Israel by defeating the Midianites. After the deliverance he was asked to set up a hereditary monarchy, but he refused. Sidney therefore held him in great esteem, ranking him with MOSES and SAMUEL and with great Roman dictators like Cincinnatus.

GROTIUS, HUGO (1583–1645), Dutch lawyer and scholar. Initially an advocate in The Hague (from 1599), he was encouraged with a premium from grand pensionary Oldenbarnevelt in 1601 to write a history of the Dutch Revolt against Spain. He was appointed attorney-general of the province of Holland in 1607 and in 1613 became involved in the religious and political controversy that tore the Dutch polity apart. This conflict was originally a theological dispute between the Leiden professors Gomarius and Arminius about predestination, but it soon spilled over into political conflict between the province of Holland and the States General over ecclesiastical authority. Grotius took sides with the Remonstrants (as Arminius's defenders were called) but was arrested and sentenced to imprisonment for life when the stadholder, Maurice, ordered the arrest of the opposition in 1618. In 1621, however, he contrived to escape in a chest of books from the castle of Loevestein and fled to Paris. He there published his most famous work *On the law of war and peace* (1625).

JEHU, tenth king of Israel, anointed king by the prophet Elisha to extirpate the dynasty of Omri. The revolt, which was supported by elements of the people, the Rechabites, was short and exceedingly cruel. Jehu then established the fourth dynasty of the northern kingdom of Israel. The story of Jehu's revolt played an important part in the sixteenth- and seventeenth-century controversy over the legitimacy of resistance to a tyrant and over who may actually take up arms against him: private citizens or those who have received divine sanction. It is in this context that Sidney, who seems to have admired Jehu, discusses the story.

JOSHUA, chosen by MOSES as personal attendant during the forty years' wanderings. A capable soldier, he succeeded Moses to the military leadership at the age of seventy and in that capacity led Israel in successful campaigns against the Canaanite confederacies. Tradition has it he died at the age of 110.

MACHIAVELLI, NICCOLO (1469–1527), Florentine statesman and political writer. In 1498 he was made second chancellor and was also appointed secretary to the magistracy, which, under the authority of the governing council, directed foreign affairs and defence of the republic. In this capacity he undertook various diplomatic missions. When the Medici returned as masters of the city in 1512

Machiavelli was dismissed from the chancery. In 1513 he was imprisoned and tortured on the accusation of complicity in a conspiracy against the Medici. After his release in the same year, he retired to his farm near Florence and set himself to write the two books for which he became most famous, *The prince* and the *The discourses on the first ten books of Livy*. Printed Italian editions of these books began circulating in England during the 1580s. English translations followed in 1636 (*The discourses*) and 1640 (*The prince*). Until 1640 Machiavelli was generally rejected as an exponent of immoral politics. During the 1640s and 1650s, however, he was also recognized as a critic of *de facto* rule and as a republican. Sidney used *The prince* to expose the immorality of monarchical politics and it is clear that he drew much inspiration from Machiavelli's republicanism as expressed in *The discourses*.

MOSES, great leader and lawgiver through whom God delivered the Hebrews from Egyptian slavery, founded the religious community known as Israel, and brought them within reach of the land promised to their forefathers. He was moved by God to express Israel's relationship with God in the form of a covenant. The basic stipulations of this covenant, which were transmitted and interpreted by Moses, were the Ten Commandments, in effect moral law as the expression of God's will; and the detailed covenant obligations rooted in this moral law took the form of 'civil' statutes.

NERO, Roman emperor (54–68). He was educated by Seneca and scandalized the senatorial classes by his patronage of the arts and encouragement of musical and dramatic contests. He became notorious for persecuting the Christians under the pretext that they had started the disastrous fire which destroyed half of Rome in 64. After a successful revolt by his army he committed suicide.

PAUL, ST (died c. 60), initially a persecutor of Christians, he was by a miraculous act transformed into Christ's apostle (c. 32). He undertook various evangelical missions in the eastern Mediterranean and Rome, where he was imprisoned several times before he suffered martyrship under NERO. In the sixteenth and seventeenth centuries royalist political writers justified obedience to the existing powers by referring to Paul's famous thirteenth chapter of his epistle to the Romans (13:1). But those who, like Sidney, attempted to justify resistance to kings found support in a passage from the book of Acts (5:29–30) and claimed that one should obey God rather than man.

S A M U E L, last of the judges and first of the prophets. He led Israel to a great victory over the Philistines and subsequently fulfilled the role of judge. In his old age, his leadership was challenged by the tribal elders and the people who clamoured for a king. Samuel at first resisted and warned of the evils of such a government, but he later installed S A U L as king by a divine revelation. This transition from a loose tribal constitution under the judges to the monarchy was much discussed in sixteenth- and seventeenth-century political thought. One strand of interpretation, reflecting a favourable attitude to monarchy, pointed out that Samuel established the kingship according to the will of God as revealed to him. Another strand, however, emphasized that Samuel had misgivings about the kingship, that he annointed Saul as a concession to popular pressure, and that the people had sinned against God in seeking a king. In Sidney's *Court maxims*, Philalethes represents the first view while Eunomius represents the latter, anti-monarchical view.

S A U L, annointed first king of Israel by S A M U E L. His greatest achievement was to defend Israel against many of its enemies, particularly the Philistines. Failing, however, in his religious duties, he caused a break with Samuel and lost the divine sanction necessary for popular support and for his own mental well-being. His subsequent derangement is revealed in his fierce jealousy of D A V I D and in his (unsuccessful) attempts, first secretly and then openly declared, to slay him. Saul was killed in a battle against the Philistines.

S O L O M O N, son and successor of D A V I D and third king of Israel. He preserved the kingdom he had acquired from his father by taking vigorous action against his opponents, by building military fortifications and establishing colonies, and by unifying Israel's administration. He also established close ties with Israel's neighbouring peoples through marital alliances and a complex network of agreements. He initiated a vast building programme including the expansion of Jerusalem. He became legendary for his wealth and his wisdom. His empire was lost after his son Rehoboam succeeded him.

T A C I T U S, P U B L I U S C O R N E L I U S (56/57– after 117), Roman orator, public official, and historian. His works include the *Life of*

Agricola (98), essentially a panegyric of his father-in-law's career, especially his great achievements in Britain; the *Histories*, which cover the period between the Roman emperors Galba and Domitian (69–98); and the *Annals*, which cover the period between the emperors TIBERIUS and NERO (14–68). Both these latter books survive incomplete. Tacitus preferred the republic and although he recognized the necessity of strong, periodic power in Roman government he considered a permanent imperial system as a subversion of Roman tradition and as a corruption of freedom and public morality. Parallel to the rise of the idea of reason of state, there was much interest in Tacitus's works in the later-sixteenth and seventeenth centuries. At least sixty-seven editions of the *Annals* and *Histories* appeared between 1600 and 1649. Like many of his contemporaries Sidney was fascinated by Tacitus's analysis of the art of dissimulation and of legal and political corruption.

TERTULLIAN (c. 160– after 220). Born in Carthage and converted to Christianity before 197, he was the author of many works on theology and church matters. In the *Apology*, which is addressed to the governors of Roman provinces, he appealed for the tolerance of Christians and sought to secure for them protection from attacks by the populace and from illegal procedures when brought up for trial. In *De corona*, he brought up the question of whether it is permissible to serve both God and idolaters.

TIBERIUS (42 BC–37 AD), Roman emperor (14 AD–37). Adopted son and successor of Augustus, his rule was initially marked by moderation. He sought to preserve the imperial boundaries, increased the imperial treasury and strengthened the navy. In 27 he retired to Capri and subsequently ruled through his praetorian commander Sejanus. These years of his reign were marked by terror and have been painted in the darkest colours by TACITUS. He was succeeded by Gaius (Caligula).

VANE, HENRY (the younger) (1613–62), English statesman. Being dissatisfied with the doctrines and ceremonies of the Anglican Church, he set sail to New England in 1635. He was chosen governor of Massachusetts in 1636 but after some controversies he returned to England the following year. In 1640 he entered Parliament and was made one of the treasurers of the navy. With the outbreak of the

Civil War in 1642 he resigned his office and became a prominent member of the parliamentary party. He took the lead in the conclusion of the Solemn League and Covenant in 1643 and helped C R O M W E L L in creating the New Model Army. He took no part in the trial of C H A R L E S I in 1649, but he actively participated in the newly established republic. He was elected a member of every council of state and was involved in the negotiations to unite England and Scotland (1652–3) and in various foreign and colonial affairs. Following a conflict with Cromwell over the latter's decision to dissolve the Rump, he retired and did not return to public affairs till 1658. Though not a regicide, he was executed in 1662 under the restored monarchy of C H A R L E S I I. Sidney was closely associated with him in his policy against the Dutch, a collaboration which was renewed in 1658.

W I L L I A M I I I (1650–1702), prince of Orange, stadholder (1672–1702), king of Great Britain and Ireland (1688–1702). Posthumous son of stadholder William II and Mary Stuart, daughter of C H A R L E S I, he grew up at a court bitterly divided over the course of his education and at a time when his chances of the stadholderate were poor. After the death of William II in 1650 the Provincial States had prevented the appointment of a new stadholder and in 1654 the States of Holland secretly ceded to C R O M W E L L 's demand to exclude the house of Orange from the stadholderate (Act of Seclusion). Following his restoration in 1660, C H A R L E S I I tried to strengthen the Orange party in the Dutch republic through his ambassador Downing. Then, in 1666 accepted as 'child of state', William rose to the stadholderate under the pressure of the French army occupying part of the Dutch republic.

COURT MAXIMS, Discussed and refelled.

The Maxims of the English Monarchy set forth
in Dialogues between Eunomius and Philalethes.

Eunomius, the Commonwealthsman
Philalethes, a moral, honest Courtier and lover of state truth

by Algernon Sidney, Esquire.

First Dialogue

EUNOMIUS: tell me, Philalethes, whither you go in so much haste.

PHILALETHES: I can more easily tell you from whence I come than whither I go; for being wearied with business at court, I do now only seek a few hours' refreshment and do not much care where I find it.

EUNOMIUS: if that be your only design, I may (without the necessity of making an apology) offer to accompany you and, if you please, will lead you into a garden into which I do usually retire when I would avoid company.

PHILALETHES: your company is ever very pleasing unto me, and I have more reason than ordinary now to seek it, since you, perhaps, who are engaged in none of our affairs, look upon them without passion and may be able to explain some things that very much perplex me.

EUNOMIUS: I cannot promise unto my self so much happiness. But if you find any ease in pouring out your cares into a friend's bosom, you may be sure of all the assistance and service that is in my power, and that whatsoever you deliver unto me, shall be most faithful*ly* closed up in secrecy, until you command me to draw it forth.

PHILALETHES: I have ever found in you all the qualities of a perfect friend, and though I have been long enough at court to conform
/2/ myself for the most part to the rules that govern there, | I have yet I know not what obscure remembrance of virtue and piety that makes me esteem persons who are so eminent in both as you are. And

2

though I ordinarily find more pleasure in the conversation of those who seek only to delight themselves and me, than in such scrupulous examiners of things as deny themselves all pleasures and advantages that are not lawful, yet when I have anything in my mind that is important and serious (leaving those lightheads, who, aiming only at vain pleasures or profits, never search into the truth of things, and, being accustomed to make their fortunes by betraying friends,[1] are of very uncertain faith) I seek such as are of a more sober temper, and who, by despising the interests we seek after, cannot be suspected of the vices by which we attain unto them. You are one whose unspotted integrity does assure me of your fidelity; your experience and prudence may be a guide unto me. And in this confidence unto you will I most freely declare all that I have in my heart, desiring you with the same freedom to let me know whether the trouble in which I am does proceed from any defect or weakness in my person, or that it does necessarily accompany the life into which I have cast myself.

To come therefore unto the matter, my difficulties are chiefly these:

First, I cannot comprehend why the people of England, who within these few years did so passionately desire a king, do seem extremely dissatisfied now that one is established,[2] and are hardly by all the art and force that we can employ kept from throwing him from the throne where they had so cheerfully placed him.

Secondly, that the king,[3] having succeeded beyond all he could hope for, does still continue full of doubts, fears, jealousies, and troubles.

Thirdly, that I and many others, having gained riches, power, and honour far above what we expected, do still remain indigent, unsatisfied, and discontented.

EUNOMIUS: I see, friend Philalethes, that you have not so far given /3/ yourself over to the humour of the court as not to retain some remembrance of the education you received under a very pious father, and *that* those seeds of virtue which you had from your birth are not so choked but that you are still desirous to know what is good and true. And nothing does more deserve your consideration than the points you propose, which, certainly together with those

---

[1] MS: 'of friends'.
[2] Monarchy was restored in England with the return of Charles II in 1660.
[3] I.e. Charles II (1630–85), king of England (1660–85).

3

that depend upon them, comprehend the state of our present affairs, together with our miseries and the causes of them. I might unto these answer briefly two ways:

First, it is not at all to be wondered at if those prove discontented who are disappointed of their chiefest hope. And that so well a deserving people as that of England is unwilling to be oppressed and vexed by a prince lately erected by themselves through a generally conceived hope that under him they should enjoy the greatest temporal felicity.

Secondly, he is not happy that has what he desires, but desires what is good and enjoys it. For we very often desire things that are evil and hurtful to ourselves. Nor is there a greater misery than the satisfaction of such ill-conceived desires. The people of England, deceived by the fraud of the courtiers and the priests, grew to that height of madness as to seek servitude rather than liberty, and to restore that king who, with the loss of so much treasure and blood, had been ejected. But this mistake could last no longer than until they found the weight of the yoke with which they were oppressed and the difficulty of throwing it from their necks. And your king judges no better than you. He thought happiness consisted in the enjoyment of a crown, not considering the danger of ill-administering it, nor that the people would remember the oaths and promises by which he did attain unto it, though he did forget them. And their madness is not the least who, rejecting all righteous rules, do by the most wicked ways seek vain honours, hurtful offices, and riches, which they throw away upon their vices and lusts; nothing remaining unto *them*[4] but a raging and unsatiable desire of rising higher and getting more, which is given unto *them* as a punishment of *their* /4/ follies and crimes. |This is said in general. But the exact examination of these points does require a far more accurate discourse.

PHILALETHES: your first answer does more amaze me than all my own doubts. I cannot imagine how you, who have so clear a sight into *this* business, can think these discontents do proceed from disappointments, since to me it does appear that everyone has attained unto what he desires and yet everyone remains discontented. The people desired a king and they have one. The king desired a crown and he is in the possession of it. We desired places, commands,

---

[4] MS: 'you'.

honours, and riches: none of all these things are wanting unto us. And yet we are all as unhappy as if we wanted all *these* things.

Eunomius: if you consider only names, you may think that people, king, and courtiers have what they sought after. But if you examine the nature of things, it will appear that all are in the highest manner disappointed. The people in general desired a king, hoping to see an abolition of taxes *and* the nation established in happiness, riches, strength, security, and glory. It was generally believed that the king, being warned by his father's end,[5] would have been far from entrenching upon the people's privileges. That, having been brought up in the school of affliction, he had there learned temperance in his prosperity. That the experience he had gained when he was abroad[6] would so have armed him against the deceits and flatteries of courtiers that he would yield to nothing but reason and justice. And he was in such manner represented unto all, as a prince so well accomplished by nature, so exercised by sufferings, and called unto the government in the prime strength of his age, *that*[7] all believed he would be the lively pattern of a perfect prince. The old Cavaliers[8] measured the hopes of their reward by the opinions they had of their service. The Presbyterians thought that their present merit in showing themselves so zealous for his establishment would have cancelled the aversion conceived against them for what they had done against his father.[9] The king himself also had adored their idol. And, having as in the presence of God sworn to their Solemn League and Covenant,[10] and afterwards declared at large that he did not comply therein for | any sinister ends, but would continue the cordial friend of those that were friends of that Covenant and be the enemy of those

/5/

---

[5] Charles I (1600–49), king of England (1625–49), was executed on 30 January 1649.
[6] From his defeat in the battle of Worcester in 1651 until his return to England in 1660, Charles II lived in France, Germany, and the Spanish Netherlands.
[7] MS: 'as'.
[8] The word cavalier, meaning horseman, was used for supporters of Charles I in the civil war.
[9] The Presbyterians had sided with Parliament in the civil war against Charles I, although they had opposed the regicide.
[10] The Solemn League and Covenant was an alliance made in 1643 between the English Parliament and the Scots. They pledged to work for a civil and religious union of England, Scotland, and Ireland under a presbyterian–parliamentary system. The future Charles II signed the Covenant in 1650 and 1651, but after the Restoration the Covenant was nullified by the Cavalier parliament as part of a tendency to confirm the authority of the king and of the revived Episcopalian Church.

that were enemies of it so long as he should live, with many like words, they thought he would employ all the power of his crown in accomplishing the ends of it. The Independents and other sects believed the declaration made at Breda[11] and, contenting themselves with liberty of conscience, relied upon the promises made unto them that they should enjoy it.[12] The soldiers thought they should be continued in their employments.[13] The ministers that they should enjoy the living of which they were possessed. Everyone by the new change expected what they wanted or desired.

The king believed the crown had nothing but light and glory in it. He had never worn any and knew not how many thorns were twisted in it. He knew not how many snares would be laid for him by his neighbours, nor how dangerous the discontents of his subjects might prove. He thought the little arts by which he had gained the crown would have continued him in the enjoyment of it, or that men would be ruined for trusting in his promises. The courtiers, who never savoured anything besides getting a little money or an office, knew not how unsatiable a beast ambition is, how inexpleble the desire of money. And when they suffer their thoughts to run upon vicious vanities, they only discover their misery and folly in the emptiness of that enjoyment which they thought would make them happy.

This is enough to show unto you whether they have attained their ends or not. If you find that all this is accomplished, you may very well say they have what they desired and more reasonably wonder to find them discontented with what they desired. If not, it is not at all strange to find they are so.

PHILALETHES: I cannot say that these things were not expected, or that they are not fulfilled. But men should consider that nothing is perfect in this world: enjoyments ever come short of our hopes. But

---

[11] The Declaration of Breda was issued in 1660 by Charles II from Breda for the Convention of Parliament. Intended to reconcile Englishmen to the Restoration, it promised indemnity and pardon to former enemies (apart from those excepted by Parliament), payment of arrears for the army, a land settlement, and religious toleration for all peaceful Christians.

[12] The promise of religious toleration was important for the Independents and other sects, because they rejected a national parochial church structure and favoured independent congregations with an elected minister.

[13] The army, which had dictated English politics for more than a decade, was paid off and completely disbanded in 1661 by the Commons in order to stabilize the realm.

6

when we have a king, which is our principal end, we ought to rest satisfied, though some other things be wanting.

EUNOMIUS: if I did believe that men did propose to themselves as their ultimate end their having of a king, and that riches, | honour, /6/ liberty, and safety were desired only in order thereunto, I should very much condemn those, who, when they had attained him, should complain of any inconvenience that could follow the accomplishment of their wishes. But such folly having never entered into the heart of reasonable creatures, it is not to be imagined that our country-men did desire a king for any other reason than that they were made to believe that this king would take off all their burdens, see justice duly administered, piety promoted, virtue cherished, vice punished, the nation's treasure employed for its own benefit, and the credit, honour, strength, and power thereof increased both at home and abroad. Now, if they find that, instead of all these advantages, they receive as many prejudices; and that, having a king, they want all those things for which they desired him; nothing is more reasonable than that they should repent of their choice *and endeavour to unmake what they have made.*

PHILALETHES: I should incline to think this consonant to reason if it were not repugnant unto those maxims which at court we look upon as certain truths.

EUNOMIUS: I should be glad to know what those maxims are, and if, when they are examined, they prove to be such certain truths, I shall easily acknowledge that to be false which is repugnant unto them. For there is such a uniformity in truths that no one does ever oppose another.

PHILALETHES: those upon which we chiefly ground our belief that the people ought to approve of the government established, cease from murmuring, and submit even to those things that displease them, are:

First, that of all governments monarchy is simply the best.

Secondly, that *monarchs*[14] ought to be absolute in all things, both ecclesiastical and civil, as God's vicegerents and accountable to no earthly power whatsoever. Upon which we conclude that the

---

[14] MS: 'monarchy'.

present discontents do proceed from popular peevishness and some relics of the old leaven that has wrought so many mischiefs in this our age.

EUNOMIUS: if your positions were true, I acknowledge that what you say would naturally follow. But before we come to that, I desire to know what makes you believe that monarchy is simply the best government, and then we will examine which is the best sort of
/7/ monarchy. |

Second Dialogue

First Court Maxim: That monarchy is the best form of government

PHILALETHES: I confess at court we are so employed in our factions and intrigues; in laying snares for our enemies and avoiding those that are laid for us; in finding ways to supplant our competitors, and render those who have power to do us good propitious to us; to get money to supply the vastness of our expenses, and contrive how to spend with pleasure what we have got; that we seldom have leisure to examine the truth of things. But a venerable divine of my acquaintance, my ghostly father, whose learning and merit has advanced him to one of the richest bishoprics in England, assures me of these things as certainly true, and I cannot doubt of what he asserts.

EUNOMIUS: does this reverend prelate only affirm or does he give reasons why you should think these things true?

PHILALETHES: he does not often trouble himself with disputes, but says it is enough for a subject to know that he ought to obey the king and a layman is to believe the clergy. But with me he goes farther and says: By the principles of nature and reason man cannot live well unless joined in society with others. Such societies cannot be maintained but by such rules as we call laws. Such laws cannot be made unless somebody has power of making them. And the agent must be suitable to the act performed by him. And the giving of laws being one individual act, the power of giving them must be annexed to one individual person. Those laws are of no use unless observed; the

9

depravity of man is such that he will never observe them unless obliged by a power that can punish him. This power is placed in him that is supreme and, in exercise of the supreme power, made these laws.

In the infancy of the world every father of a family was a monarch /8/ in his own house. Many families uniting made nations. | And the greatest, most virtuous, prosperous, and therefore imitable nations, rejecting all other forms of government, have chosen that of kings.

But that which gives the most certain siege of truth to this assertion is that as God is a monarch in heaven, he has appointed monarchs to be images of his greatness and power on earth and constituted kings over his elect people Israel, whose example all others ought to follow.

EUNOMIUS: men of that reverend load, who by the vulgar are called divines, do by their pride cover their ignorance when they have asserted things false or truths above their reach. They seem to despise disputes, austerely imposing submission to their doctrines, and endeavouring to make us believe we ought not to examine them but acknowledge all to be true that comes from their mouths. These things would have passed more easily in the last age than now; the late liberty of examining their doctrine, practice, calling, and persons having so uncovered their nakedness that few are so blind as not to see it. Obey the king and believe me, says the bishop. Why not rather, believe the king and obey me, if the king be head of the church as he says he is? I must receive my religion from him, submit to his Act of Uniformity,[15] which is ridiculous if I am not to believe that what he says is true. And if I believe or obey him by the bishop's command, I do first obey the bishop. But this may be deferred to another time. Let us now examine the strength of what is said concerning monarchy.

It is true there is a necessity of society; he that desires solitude (says Aristotle) is a God or a beast.[16] It is also true societies cannot subsist without laws, and laws cannot be made unless somebody have power to make them, and that power must be one. But it is ridiculous to say it must be in one man, for then Venice, Switzerland, the Low

---

[15] The Act of Uniformity passed Parliament in 1662 and was intended to enforce use of the Book of Common Prayer, recently revised by the Convocations.
[16] Aristotle, *Politics*, bk I, 1253a.

Countries, and all others that are or have been a free people, live without laws, because it is not there in the power of one man to make them.

The like may be said of England, France, | Spain, and all civi- /9/ lized nations that have been in the world and lived under kings. In all which the kings have no power of making laws, but parliaments, assemblies of estates, diets, or the like, according to *the*[17] several constitutions that each nation agrees on as most convenient to itself. Those that are devoted unto kings put the title of Supreme Lord on them, and then fallaciously infer all power belongs to him because supreme; not considering he may be *singulis major, universis minor* (as our ancient lawyers say), *first in dignity, but not supreme in power*. But if kings be established for maintenance of society, and societies are constituted because every man is incapable of living well by himself, three things will necessarily be inferred:

First, that they are constituted by men.

Secondly, that the consideration of their own good does induce those men to constitute them.

Thirdly, if it appears that another government does more conduce to their good than that of kings, they may choose some other form of government from which they may expect more happiness. Yet am not I such an enemy to kingly government as not to believe that in some cases, and to some nations, it may be best? I can imagine but two.

One is when a nation is so brutish as to be absolutely incapable of science or governing themselves. Aristotle calls such *servos natura*.[18] Some of Asia and Africa are said to be of this kind. Such have the faces only of men, but as to any political act differ little from beasts.

The other case is, when one man has more virtue, understanding, industry, and valour than a whole nation. Nothing is more reasonable than that the wise and virtuous should govern fools and vicious men. Some ancient kings may have born their crowns on this title. The histories of Peru[19] do show that the family of the Incas came to the government by this means. The first of them, coming amongst a great number of people living without laws, void of all knowledge so much as to provide for their necessary sustenance, or defend

[17] MS: 'their'.
[18] 'slaves by nature'. Aristotle, *Politics*, bk 1, 1254b.
[19] Garcilaso de la Vega, *Royal commentaries of the Incas*, vol. 1, part 1, bk 1.

themselves against sun, wind, or rain; they willingly submitted to him that taught them to build houses, make themselves clothes, sow corn, and the like. So they willingly received laws from him that did /10/ them so much good and by his virtue showed he had | a natural superiority over them. I think none of our kings will pretend to this prerogative. If they keep their crowns no longer than by their excelling in virtue not only every one, but all their subjects together, I fear all of them would descend many degrees below the throne. In either of these two cases, *whether* people generally *are* sots, or one man *has* more virtue than the rest, monarchy is natural. From the same principle it may be inferred that nothing is more irrational and unnatural where a people is able to govern itself, *than* that he that has no prerogative of virtue above other men should exercise dominion over them, much less that he that is inferior to many in virtue should be superior to all in power. The paternal government extends only to a family and so belongs not to the matter of our discourse.

PHILALETHES: but yet I think laws best made where the government is monarchical.

EUNOMIUS: why should not a free nation, full of men who excel in wisdom and experience, rather keep the power in their own hands of governing themselves or one another by turns, than be perpetually governed by one man and his posterity?

PHILALETHES: the greatest nations of the world have rejected other forms and those have flourished most that lived under kings. They ever had greatest success and made greatest conquests abroad, and have been most quiet at home, whereas nations governed by annual magistrates, senates, or assemblies of the people have been perpetually agitated by popular fury, till either despair made them cast themselves into the hands of one man, or, weakened by divisions, they became easy preys to one rising up amongst themselves or to some powerful neighbour.

EUNOMIUS: I wish rather you would show reasons than examples to make good your assertion, or, if you use examples, allege what was done by the best, most learned, valiant, noble-spirited nations, than rely upon the number. If that was best that was practised by the major part of mankind, it would be better to play the fool than act as a wise man, sin than do justly, none doubts. But the number of fools exceeds that of wise men, and the wicked as much exceed the good. But if you value the number of those nations that have lived under monarchs, I will easily overbalance them with the virtue, wisdom, and valour | of those who have abhorred even the name of kings. /11/ While the vicious cowardly Asiatics chose that slavery which suited with their spirits, all those nations which deserve to be imitated were governed by their own laws, according to their several constituted commonwealths. The name of king was not known to the Greeks, Italians, Germans, Gauls, and Spaniards but as the object of their hatred. And that part of Africa which was not barbarous did flourish under the Carthaginian government. But granted that in alleging examples number is to be more valued than merit; the arithmetical proportion to be followed rather than the geometrical; that it is better to imitate the most than the best; yet it deserves to be considered whether that major part of mankind which has lived under kings have done it by choice or by force; it is no argument for its goodness unless it appears they need not do it, unless they thought it good.

PHILALETHES: if you imagine any people governed by kings contrary to their own will, then *such kings were*[20] not constituted by the people, nor in any way accountable to them, which, I think, will prove the power of kings more large than you will allow.

EUNOMIUS: by kings constituted by the people I mean those that have a just legal power. He that without law brings a people under his power, I look on as a *tyrant, thief, public enemy*, against whom every man is a soldier.

PHILALETHES: how can one man make himself master of a nation without their consent?

EUNOMIUS: by force or fraud, or both. There are multitudes of examples both ancient and modern for this.

PHILALETHES: what think you of the right of conquest by which many kings hold their crowns, and particularly ours from William the Conqueror?[21]

EUNOMIUS: I think, first, the validity of that prince's right,

---

[20] MS: 'were such kings'.
[21] William I (1028–87), duke of Normandy (1035–87), king of England (1066–87); invaded England and defeated king Harold near Hastings in 1066.

13

grounded on conquest, depends on the justice of the cause for which he made the war in which he was conqueror. He that unjustly made the war does not justly enjoy the fruits gained by it.

Secondly, it is hard to imagine any man can conquer a nation otherwise than as prince, general, or officer employed by another nation. So the conquest belongs to that nation, not to him that | was the chief person in the enterprise. When Scipio[22] conquered Spain and *a* great part of Africa, he pretended not those provinces belonged to him, but *to* Rome. And Alexander's chief officers shared their conquests under and with Alexander[23] between themselves on his death, not acknowledging any patrimonial right descending on his son. So Ireland belongs not to the king *of* England, but *to* England; Naples and Milan not to the king of Spain, but to Spain; Livonia, Pomerania, and the duchy of Bremen not to the king of Sweden, but to Sweden.

As for William, surnamed the Conqueror, experience shows how little princes deserve the names given them by their flattering servants. A good part of the nobles and commons of England did from the first make him their head and leader. Harold was never king but a pretender to the crown;[24] *after* he *was* slain, both parties agreed to give it his competitor on certain conditions, which, if he broke *them* and governed tyrannically, that could gain him no right of conquest. That would too much honour treachery and perfidy. If he had a right to make the war, he came not in by conquest but right; if no right, he can claim no right by the conquest. What was unjustly got by force may justly by force be taken from him or his successors. If he had a right to make war and conquered in it, he did it not alone but English and Normans helped him. And they were not conquered who with him conquered others, nor deserve their descendants *to*[25] be looked on as a conquered people: England is inhabited by them. He that by William's conquest pretends to the dominion of England, must show that those over whom he will reign by that title

---

[22] Scipio Africanus, Publius Cornelius (234–183 BC); principal general in the war of the Romans against the Carthaginians.

[23] Alexander III the Great (356–323 BC), king of Macedon (336–323 BC). After he became king, he first secured his position in Greece and then conquered Asia Minor, Phoenicia, Palestine, Egypt, and a great part of Africa.

[24] Harold II (c. 1020–66) had in fact held the crown for nine months in 1066 before he was defeated by William I.

[25] MS: 'should'.

are the descendants of those subdued by him. Lastly, whatever right William the first reigned by, that right came not to him that by primogeniture had right to succeed in it as his patrimony. Robert, eldest son of William the first, remained only duke of Normandy; William Rufus was preferred to the crown. He killed nobles and commons, *and* advanced Henry the first *while* Robert *was* still living.[26] The like may be said of all the succeeding kings. So all since William the first can pretend to what they enjoyed only by election (of broken succession to the crown of England). I think this enough as to that point, come we now to consider the conquests made by kings.

PHILALETHES: before you go farther, do you by | kingly and monar- /13/ chical government mean the same thing or not ?

EUNOMIUS: though some kings may rightly be called monarchs, all monarchs cannot rightly be called kings. For every usurper or thief that gains the chief power over a nation is a monarch, but none deserves the name of a king but he that governs by a right legally conferred on him.

PHILALETHES: this is enough to explain your meaning. Let us now return to our former subject.

EUNOMIUS: if you say monarchy is the best government because greatest conquests have been made by monarchs, you must show that the people have been bettered by those conquests; else you only show monarchy is good for the monarchs. That is nothing to our purpose. We seek not what is good for a *man* but for a *nation*.

PHILALETHES: enlargement of dominion and increase of riches and power by conquests are ever beneficial to the nation that attains them.

EUNOMIUS: this is not clear to me, but on the contrary, I think many nations were destroyed by their own conquests, either through want of people or pride and arrogance of their leader, who, being made strong by new subjects, *was*[27] more enabled to oppress those by whom he conquered. If the end of government were the enlargement

---

[26] Robert II (1054–1134), duke of Normandy (1087–1106). William II, byname Rufus (1056–1100), king of England (1087–1100). Henry I (1069–1135), king of England (1100–35) and fourth son of William I.
[27] MS: 'is'.

of dominion, he that enlarges the dominion of a nation may pretend to do good to it. But if government be constituted for *other ends*,[28] that in a society we may live free, happy, and safe, he that makes a conquest is not a benefactor to the nation unless it conduces to those ends. Much less if he draw to himself the benefit of what was acquired by their blood, or turn against them what was gained by them. The several constitutions of government *and* the nature, number, and strength of a people that constitute it, do best show whether conquests be good for it or not.

Rome was so constituted that the condition of citizens and city was bettered by conquests, till the prodigious power it arrived at brought in luxury and pride *and* destroyed discipline and virtue; for then ruin necessarily followed. The constitutions of Sparta were of a different nature. They were admirable for maintaining liberty against foreign invasion or domestic conspiracy, so they continued many hundreds of years in great liberty and glory; but, seeking to enlarge their dominion, their conquests were their destruction. So Venice in our days has nothing to fear more than the enlargement of /14/ its dominions. | The ill-measured desire of gaining the Polesine and the Ghiradadda has brought that noble city to the brink of destruction. And the Swiss, who by their constitution, nature, and situation have nothing to fear from any power on earth, can make no conquest that may be of advantage to them. *Examples of this are infinite, not only in commonwealths, but also in monarchies*.[29] We see Spain weakened, dispeopled, and ruined by its own conquests.

PHILALETHES: in what cases are conquests beneficial?

EUNOMIUS: meat suitable to my complexion, taken in due time and measure, and well-digested, refreshes, strengthens, and nourishes me. In like manner conquests may be advantageous to them that gain them, if suitable to their constitution and tend not to their corruption in discipline and manners; for then they are poison rather than nourishment. And they must be in greatness proportionable to the strength of the state that acquires them. For as he that eats too much of what is good is not nourished but oppressed and stifled, so in states too great conquests do not strengthen but destroy. Seasons

---

[28] MS: 'another end'.
[29] MS: 'And not only commonwealths but monarchies ancient examples are infinite'. This argument refers to Machiavelli, *Discourses*, bk II, ch. 19.

also are to be observed. A discreet man will not take another meal till the former be well digested. Prudent states never desire another conquest till the former be well digested, that is, assimilated unto and incorporated with its own body. Again, as a body oppressed by a disease nourishes not itself but the disease by taking meat to its own ruin, so a nation discomposed by some one man or order of men too much prevailing can never be *bettered by*[30] conquest. All that is gained increases the peccant humour. While nations in such cases by victories seek to increase their power, they find their own destruction. Their sweat, treasure, and blood, intended for their good, is often employed to set up a tyrant, the worst of all enemies. It is also necessary to consider what that I seek is like*ly* to cost me and what need I have of it, for on these two points depends the prudence of our choice. This is as much as is necessary to say of what is politically to be considered in states, relating unto what is naturally good unto them.

Rules of morality also are to be observed in both. It is not enough to see this is good for me, but whether I have a right to it. States are to consider not only whether such conquests may be useful to them but also whether they have a right of war.

PHILALETHES: I find no scruple remaining | concerning this. But you will grant kings have been greater conquerors than commonwealths. /15/

EUNOMIUS: if you examine only the number of victories and extent of countries overcome, the advantage is on the king's side, because there have been more great kings than commonwealths. But if you examine the *difficulties involved*[31] and other important circumstances, you will see commonwealths may better brag of their victories than kings. I think I may prefer the victories obtained by the Romans before all that have been gained by kings since the beginning of the world.

First, their beginnings were less than those of any kings; they gained the victories by their virtue and valour.

Secondly, the nations conquered by them were in valour and discipline incomparably before any that were conquered by kings.

Thirdly, they destroyed many powerful commonwealths, and all

---

[30] MS: 'better for'.   [31] MS: 'difficulty'.

17

the histories in the world cannot show any considerable common-wealth ruined by the power of any king.

The nations over whom the Roman commonwealth triumphed were Italians, Greeks, Carthaginians, Gauls, Germans, and Span-iards, all of them in the height of their fierceness and valour, power-ful in numbers, exercised in war, excelling in military discipline. No one of all these was ever conquered by any king, unless when so weakened by the decline of the Roman empire, to which they were made subject, that, being without arms or discipline, *they were* exhausted and desolated. Rome found more difficulty in subduing a small free people in Italy or Greece, as the Samnites or Aetolians,[32] than in overthrowing all the kings of Asia or Africa. Wars with kings were pastimes to that commonwealth. If they found any difficulty with kings as with Mithridates and Jugurtha,[33] it was exercise of their feet to follow their flights through mountains and deserts, rather than of *their* hands in fighting *them*. And they feared far more their fraud than valour, their poison than swords.

And to show *that* commonwealths better employ their power in war than kings, three modern examples may suffice. The one of the United Provinces, defending themselves against all the power of Spain and increasing in strength and riches during the war.[34] The other of Venice, warring with little loss for twenty years against the

[16] dreadful power of the | Ottoman empire.[35] And the English com-monwealth, which in five years conquered absolutely Scotland and Ireland,[36] and in so many battles broke the Hollanders that they were brought to the utmost weakness.[37] Yet perhaps no commonwealth can be found so imperfect in military constitutions as the first; and in the third, being in its infancy and encompassed with difficulties

---

[32] Rome had struggled with the Samnites for almost seventy years when it finally con-quered them in the third Samnite war in 290 BC. Aetolia was defeated by Rome in 189 BC.

[33] Mithridates, king of Pontus (120–63 BC); formed a permanent threat to Rome's con-trol over client kingdoms in Asia Minor. Jugurtha (160–104 BC), king of Numidia (118–104 BC); enemy of Rome.

[34] The Eighty Years war between Spain and the Netherlands began in 1568 and, with the interruption of the Twelve Years truce (1609–21), lasted until the Peace of Westphalia in 1648.

[35] War between Turkey and Venice broke out in 1645 when Sultan Ibrahim I attacked Crete. The war lasted until 1669 and took at least 100,000 lives.

[36] Cromwell's army defeated the Scots at Worcester in 1651 and it completed the reconquest of Ireland after nearly three years of war in 1652.

[37] The first Dutch war lasted from 1652 until 1654.

which in a little time destroyed it, the actions performed in that time seem rather prodigies than the effects of man's valour and virtue.

The commonwealths of Greece were for the most part destroyed by civil divisions. Athens feared not the power of Philip till in many defeats weakened by the Spartans.[38] Nor was Thebes destroyed by Alexander till its sinews were cut, its captains slain and armies destroyed by the same swords.[39] The Achaean society yielded only to the Romans.[40] Sparta never feared the Macedonian power till domestic tyranny had overthrown its laws and constitutions, destroyed its virtue and valour, the only pillars of its greatness and glory.[41]

Africa could never boast of any great commonwealth but Carthage, which could be subdued by no hand but that of her rival, Rome.[42] All the other famous nations of Italy, Gaul, Spain, and Germany, flourishing in liberty, valour, and power, fell under the same swords, no king having raised one trophy to testify their overthrow. The commonwealths of Italy that arose out of the ashes of the Roman empire never feared foreign force till destroyed by domestic tyrants, as Ezzelino of Padua, Vicenza, and Verona, Francesco Sforza of Milan, the Medici of Florence, and others of small importance.[43] As for the late Commonwealth of England, no man can say the power of a king subdued *it*;[44] we had broken his armies, subdued his whole party in the three nations, but God suffered divisions to arise amongst us for the punishment of our sins, and *so we came to be betrayed*. As to civil dissensions, in all monarchies (but that of Turkey, where these three court maxims take place contrary to all

[38] Philip II, king of Macedon (359–336 BC); defeated Athens and Thebes in the battle at Chaeronea in 338 BC.

[39] Alexander III the Great, Philip II's son and successor, crushed a Theban revolt against Macedon rule in 335 BC.

[40] The Achaean Confederacy or League was founded in 280 BC and consisted mainly of Achaean cities in the Peloponnese which had detached themselves from the rule of Macedon. The Confederacy frequently came into conflict with Rome, and it was completely defeated and dissolved by the Roman general Mummius in 146 BC.

[41] Sparta, ruled by Cleomenes III, was defeated by the Macedonian Antigonus in alliance with the Achaean League in 222 BC.

[42] Rome successfully fought Carthage for dominance in the western Mediterranean during the three so-called Punic wars (264–241; 218–202; 149–146 BC).

[43] Ezzelino III (1194–1259), feudal major (podesta) of Verona (1226–30; 1232–59), of Vicenza (1236–59), and of Padua (1237–56); expanded and consolidated his power over almost all north-east Italy. Sforza, Francesco (1401–66), military leader (condottiere) and duke of Milan (1450–66); founded a dynasty that ruled for nearly a century.

[44] MS: 'ills'.

Christianity: first, as soon as the monarch has a son, all his brothers and nephews are killed so that there be no competitor; secondly, he destroys the nobility and makes that no man can be heir of his father's goods; thirdly, he weakens all conquered provinces to an
[17] impossibility of revolt | – *Atque ubi solitudinem faciunt pacem appellant*[45]) the court factions have been far more pernicious than popular tumults in commonwealths. And those wars which have been made in several places and times by diverse pretenders to the crown have been more furious and mortal than any in commonwealths, besides those that have been made by nobles and people driven to despair by a tyrant. Of this truth England, France, and Flanders give undeniable testimony; each of which has lost more blood in these quarrels than was shed in all the cruel wars of Marius and Sulla, Caesar and Pompey, and all the others that happened in Rome from the expulsion of the kings to the establishment of the caesars.[46] If it be said, these and other nations, after *having grown* wearied with civil dissensions, have sought monarchy as their port for rest, I answer, few or none of them have sought monarchy as their rest, but have fallen or been driven into it as a ship upon a rock. We may as well conclude death better than life because all men doing what they can to preserve life do yet end in death. That free states by divisions fall often into monarchy only shows monarchy to be to a state as death unto life. And as death is *the greatest evil that can befall a person, monarchy is the worst evil that can befall a nation.*

---

[45] 'they made a desolation and they call it peace', Tacitus, *Agricola*, ch. 30.
[46] The period between the expulsion of the kings and the end of the republic with the establishment of Octavian as sole master of Rome covers nearly five centuries (510–31 BC). Sidney here refers to the civil wars and anarchy that disrupted late republican Rome.

Third Dialogue

Second Court Maxim: Monarchy ought to be absolute and hereditary

PHILALETHES: the defects you have mentioned seem rather to proceed from the ill constitution of some monarchies.

EUNOMIUS: what is requisite to the constitution of that you esteem perfect monarchy?

PHILALETHES: that it be absolute and, secondly, hereditary.

EUNOMIUS: what induces you to believe absolute and hereditary monarchy best?

PHILALETHES: there is great difficulty in governing a people. The governor needs all help. Absolute power is necessary that his commands be not contradicted by the peevishness or ignorance of those who understand them not, or would hinder him from doing that that is good. Secondly, reason and experience show that resolutions are more speedy, executions more vigorous, when determined by one man than | when they depend upon such tedious disputes as are *[18]* usual in commonwealths, where many give their opinions. And the most ignorant are often most positive in asserting their opinions. Experience also shows that those resolutions or counsels are steadily and constantly prosecuted which proceed from the prudence of one man and are directed to the interest of him and his family, whereas the counsels of commonwealths change according to the humour of those that happen to be in power.

Thirdly, nothing is more conducive to the good of a state than the incessant care of the governor perpetually intent to procure the good of it, which is most seen in hereditary monarchies, the monarch looking on the state as his patrimony descending to his heirs.

Fourthly, the government of a state requires that greatness of mind that is found only in those that from their infancy are bred up in the expectation of crowns. A nobleness of spirit inherent in their blood, increased by education, banishes out of their minds all those low thoughts which possess them who are born in meaner fortunes.

Fifthly, *there is* no greater encouragement unto gallantry than to act under the eye of a prince who alone is the judge and rewarder of what is done in his service. And we who know our fortune is made if we please only one master do cheerfully run through all dangers and troubles in the hope of gaining his favour who alone has the disposing of riches and honours.

Lastly, as we see, those monarchies have been most glorious that have been most absolute. The best and most learned authors as Plato, Aristotle, and many others, say the most perfect government is when all is in the power of one man, who is above the law, obliged to no law, being himself a living law; as the mind in the man, so he, as the mind or understanding of the body politic, rules all.

EUNOMIUS: why may not all these acts be performed by one body composed of many members as well as by one man?

PHILALETHES: this variety seems to me a certain spring of perpetual confusion. A society so constituted will be like a chaos. *Frigida pugnabunt calidis; humentia siccis;*[47] call it aristocracy, democracy, or what you will, it will in effect be no better than a mere anarchy.

EUNOMIUS: I confess the disorderly fury of a rude multitude may well resemble the dark and barbarous confusion of the chaos. But as God by his word gave order and form to that undigested heap, and by various mixtures produced that variety of forms by which the world is made beautiful and fruitful, he has set a pattern unto us, by
[19] the power of reason, the relics of his image in us, out of that | chaos of a confused multitude to produce a civil society beautiful in

---

[47] 'Cold things will repel hot ones, and humid things dry ones.' According to the theory of the four humours natural decay is the process whereby hot and dry are overcome by cold and humid. Originally in Aristotle, *De genere et corruptione*, 330b 3ff. Commonplace in Renaissance medicine.

perfection of order, regulating by prudent laws the mad and blind fury by which *it was*[48] formerly agitated, and reducing the barren darkness of confusion unto such a state as renders it fruitful in all things conducing to a civil and happy life. Hereby that variety of nature in the individuals is rendered useful to the beauty of the whole, as the variety of elements and humours makes up that temper by which our persons do subsist. He that would have a state composed of one sort of persons only, will appear little wiser than he that would have a body composed of one element, or music of one note.

PHILALETHES: ten men are not to be found but one of them will have more wit, another more courage, than the rest; one will be precipitous and rash, another dull and heavy; one industrious, another lazy; besides many other differences proceeding from their complexions, education, and interest; so that nothing seems more difficult than to bring them to such order as is required for the performance of any act.

EUNOMIUS: this is the work of a prudent lawgiver or political man. If there were not difficulty in it, those endowed with that science they call policy would not deserve the honour which by all wise men is given unto them. That body is well composed as to duration and performance of all acts belonging unto it, which has such a mixture of elements that no one is wanting or too much abounds. And that tune in music is well framed in which the sharpness of one tone is sweetened by the gravity of another; and the perfection of the harmony consists in the due proportion of one unto the other. So in civil societies those deserve praise that make such laws as conduce to a civil harmony wherein the several humours, natures, and conditions of men may have such parts and places assigned *to* them, that none may so abound as to oppress the other to the dissolution of the whole; and none be so wanting as that the part naturally belonging to it should be left imperfect. But everyone, in his own way and degree, may act in order to the public good and the composing of that civil harmony in which our happiness in this world does chiefly consist.

PHILALETHES: before you go any further, I desire to know what you mean by a politic man, for at court we use to call those that have craft enough to compass their ends politic men, but you seem to use the

---

[48] MS: 'they were'.

[20] word in another sense. We also think the government is good if under it we can advance our persons | and fortunes, which, we think, is the end of government. But you speak as if you thought it something else.

EUNOMIUS: I know not any word more abused than that of policy or politic. The mistake will be discovered by the etymology of it. *Polis* signifies a city, and *politeia* is nothing but the art of constituting and governing cities or civil societies. And he that rightly understands and exercises that art is a politic man. These societies are constituted that men in them may live happily. We need seek no other definition of a happy human life in relation to this world than that set down by Aristotle as the end of civil societies, namely, that men may in them enjoy *vita beata secundum virtutem*[49] (Aristotle, *Politics*, bk III). For as there is no happiness without liberty, and no man more a slave than he that is overmastered by vicious passions, there is neither liberty, nor happiness, where there is not virtue.

Man is the noblest of all visible creatures. The noblest acts therefore that can be performed by man towards any creature is to do good to them of his own species. And the good that can be done unto man, diffusible to the greatest part of mankind, is the directing, maintaining, and preserving *of* them in that life which is most virtuous and happy. It will easily appear then, that he who does this of all men deserves the greatest praise, and that the science by which he does it is the best and noblest of all sciences. By this you may see whether the name of policy be fitly given to that wicked malicious craft, exercised with perfidy and cruelty, accompanied with all manner of lust and vice, directly and irreconcilably contrary to virtue and piety, honesty or humanity, which is taught by Machiavelli and others. Or whether Cesare Borgia, Castruccio Castracani, Septimius Severus,[50] and others who by him are commended for excelling in this art, are rightly to be called politic men. And if these deserve it not, how much less ought it to be given to a little courtier whose art is far below all these and, aiming at a little money, office, or title, uses all those mean ways which are suitable unto his end. Let us now

---

[49] 'a happy and honourable life'. Aristotle, *Politics*, bk III, 1281a, b.
[50] Borgia, Cesare (1475–1507), son of the later pope Alexander VI; conquered a large number of Italian cities. Castracani, Castruccio (1281–1328), captain of mercenaries who ruled Lucca (1316 to 1328). Machiavelli wrote his biography. Severus, Lucius Septimius (146–211), Roman emperor (193–211).

proceed to the second reason, grounded on the speedy resolutions, vigorous executions, and steady counsels of monarchs.

PHILALETHES: what say you to those points? [21]

EUNOMIUS: if you mean such resolutions as Ahasuerus took to kill all the Jews and afterwards to save them by the death of their accuser; or such a resolution as Saul took and executed on Abimelech and the other priests and on the whole city, extending his rage to the execution of women and children; or such as Ahab and Jezebel took to kill Naboth; or Nero to kill his mother; or Herod who butchered his wife, his children, the innocents, and all the Sanhedrin;[51] I confess such things are not done in commonwealths. Monarchies only can brag of them. But if, instead of resolutions to do mischief and commit such horrid murders as are rather to be imputed to the devil raging in the heart of a beast than to a man, you mean such general resolutions as are taken prudently and executed with virtue and valour, commonwealths have not been inferior in such to the highest spirited princes.

He that has but a little knowledge of history may easily satisfy himself that after the first Carthaginian war the Romans had reason to fear nothing so much as a second. Yet, receiving some injuries from Hannibal,[52] ambassadors were sent to Carthage to demand satisfaction and to cut off all cavillings. The eldest amongst them told the senate, *Hic vobis bellum et pacem portamus; utrum placet sumite!*,[53] take which you will. The Carthaginians answered: Give which you please. He answered: Then I give you war; which was as readily accepted (Titus Livius, *Initio belli punici secundi*). What could ever be seen more bold, more speedy on both sides unless it were the constancy with which both sides did pursue that war into which they had in this manner entered?

Vibius Virius, sent *as* ambassador with some others from

---

[51] Ahasuerus's chief minister, Haman, was hanged for having instigated the decree to annihilate all Jews living in the empire (Est. 3:8–11, 8:9–10). For Saul, see I Sam. 22:16–19. For Ahab, see I Kings 21:1–14. Nero (37–68), Roman emperor (54–68); had his mother, Agrippina, killed in 54. For Herod, see Matt. 2:15–16.

[52] Hannibal (247–182 BC), the Phoenician general, crossed the river Ebro in violation of the treaty which had been concluded at the end of the first Punic war. He then captured Saguntum (219 BC), a city belonging to allies of Rome, which led to the events Sidney here describes.

[53] 'We bring you here both war and peace; choose which you will'. Livy, *History of Rome*, bk XXI, ch. 18.

Privernum, a poor town but free to ask peace of the Roman senate, was asked by the consul: What peace can we have with you who have so often rebelled? He answered, *Si bonam dederitis et fidam et perpet-uam; si malam, haud diuturnam.*[54] The senate, approving his answer, said, *Viri et liberi vocem auditam. Tales dignos esse, qui Romani fiant,*[55] and presently granted peace as desired and the entire privileges of Roman citizens to the men of the town.

Popillius, a Roman ambassador, finding Ptolemy (rather Antiochus Epiphanes), to whom he was sent, inclined to seek excuses and [22] delays, with a staff he had in his hand (or vinetwig) | made a circle about the king, requiring a positive answer before he went out of it, which he did full of submission.[56]

The world is so full of examples of this kind that I should more prejudice my subject by seeming to think I need such proofs, than advance it by alleging them. And as commonwealths equal or exceed the highest spirited princes in readily taking and speedily executing the most important resolutions, in the constant prosecutions of counsels once taken they do incomparably surpass them. For if there be any steadiness in the counsels of monarchs, it is where the power of kings is limited and a council or some other order of men has some shadow of an aristocracy, which you abhor. But where the king has much power, either by law, fraud, and force, or through reverence to his virtue, *and* the principal affairs are left to his management; all must depend upon his understanding, disposition, or inclinations, and must consequently alter when he dies, according to the humour of his successor, or, which is worse, the humour of his favourites, as is ordinary.

Who is so much a stranger to the affairs of Europe as not to know the great difference between the counsels of the duke of Lerma and the Conde d'Olivares, and how little his were followed by his successor Don Luis de Haro?[57] I hardly know anything in which the

---

54 'If you grant us a good one, you may look to find it faithfully and permanently kept; if a bad one, you must not expect that it will long endure.' Livy, *History of Rome*, bk VIII, ch. 21.

55 'Only those who took no thought for anything save liberty were worthy of becoming Romans.' Ibid.

56 Popillius forced Antiochus, king of Persia, in 168 BC to give up the war against Egypt. Livy, *History of Rome*, bk XLV, ch. 12.

57 Lerma, Francisco, duke of (1553–1625), favourite of king Philip III and first minister of Spain (1598–1618). Olivares, Gaspar, count-duke of (1587–1645), favourite of king Philip IV and first minister of Spain (1621–43). Haro, Luis (1598–1661), favourite of Philip IV and successor of his uncle, Olivares, as chief minister of Spain (1643–61).

proceedings of Cardinal Mazarin agreed with those of his predecessor, Richelieu,[58] unless it were in oppressing the people. And I know not the man that is able to enumerate the mischiefs brought upon England by the frantic furies of the earls of Somerset, Buckingham, Stafford and the archbishop of Canterbury,[59] every one differing from his predecessor.

But if we presume a prince will never be weak; would have no favourites, or choose good ones, or know how to govern them when chosen, of which no syllable is true; who will give security that they who are great and good shall live until their children are of ability equal to them? Was Richard II of England like*ly* to finish what was begun by the Black Prince or Edward III?[60] Was Henry VI[61] able to follow the steps of his father? Or Louis XIII of France able to bear the burden of such a design as was contrived by Henry IV?[62] Could the queen Christina of Sweden at five years old bring to perfection what the famous Gustavus[63] had so far advanced? | Or this young /23/ king,[64] who bears the same crown, now in his infancy pursue his valiant father's undertakings? All these things depend on the person of a man and must therefore necessarily be perpetually wavering and uncertain, according to the life of him that gives the impulse unto them. But in commonwealths it is not men but laws, maxims, interests, and constitutions that govern: men die or change, but these remain unalterable. A senate or assembly, I deny not, may be capable

---

[58] Mazarin, Jules, cardinal (1602–61) and first minister of France (1642–61) after Richelieu's death. Richelieu, Armand Jean Duplessis, cardinal (1585–1642) and first minister of France (1624–42).

[59] Laud, William (1573–1645), religious adviser of king Charles I and archbishop of Canterbury (1633–45); enforced a form of service in strict accordance with the Book of Common Prayer and persecuted Puritan and other religious dissenters, which resulted in his trial and execution by the House of Commons.

[60] Richard II (1367–1400), king of England (1377–99), son of the Black Prince and grandson of his predecessor, Edward III. Edward, byname the Black Prince (1330–76), eldest son of Edward III; was famous for his military exploits, especially his defeat of a French army at Poitiers in 1356. Edward III (1312–77), king of England (1327–77); led England into the Hundred Years war with France.

[61] Henry VI (1421–71), king of England (1422–61; 1470–71), son and successor of Henry V.

[62] Louis XIII (1601–43), king of France (1610–43), son of Henry IV (1553–1610), king of Navarre (1572–89) and the first Bourbon king of France (1589–1610).

[63] Christina (1626–89), queen of Sweden (1632–54), daughter of Gustav II Adolf (1594–1632), king of Sweden (1611–32).

[64] Charles XI (1655–97), king of Sweden (1660–97). As he was only four years old when he succeeded his father Charles X Gustavus to the throne in 1660, the government was entrusted to a regency for twelve years.

of some passions and be deceived. But their passions are not so easily moved when composed of many men of the greatest experience and choicest parts, nor are they so easily deceived as one man, who, perhaps, has small parts, little experience, and is informed by none but those who endeavour to deceive him.

PHILALETHES: but what think you of hereditary monarchy?

EUNOMIUS: you think on this account kings will take more care of the people under them. But I doubt whether that care be worth what the people must pay for it, according to the terms you propose.

PHILALETHES: what mean you by that?

EUNOMIUS: that if kings will not take care of their subjects unless they have an absolute dominion over them, as a patrimony descending to their heirs, such people are slaves and villains, not free men, and, I think, better have no king than at so dear a rate; I mean the sale and loss of liberty. But to come a little nearer to the point, I think there is no evil in absolute monarchy which is not increased by rendering it hereditary.

PHILALETHES: what induces you to that belief?

EUNOMIUS: my reasons are:

First, if ever an absolute power was by any civilized nation freely granted to any man, it was for some present exigence, and *his* great experience and esteem of his virtue, as the *aisymnetes* in Greece, the dictators at Rome, and the judges amongst the Jews;[65] of the continuance of which in their posterity there was no hope.

Secondly, good and wise men will neither seek nor accept such power for themselves or *their* posterity, as the examples of Moses, Samuel, *and* Gideon witness. And ill or weak men are not to be trusted with it.

Thirdly, hereditary right in the king creates a hereditary hatred between him and his people, which is as destructive to the king as to the people.

[65] The *aisymnetes* was an umpire or ruler in the Ionic part of Asia Minor, as on Lesbos. At Rome, the dictatorship was an ad hoc magistracy, admitted to the Roman constitution to allow supreme military and judicial authority to be entrusted temporarily to one individual in times of grave crisis. The judges were leaders invested with temporary and supreme judicial and military power in ancient Israel in the period between the death of Joshua and the establishment of the kings.

PHILALETHES: can you make it appear that these things are true?

EUNOMIUS: I think so, and when I have given my reasons I will leave /24/
you to judge of their validity. The first assertion consists of two
parts, namely, the reason why civilized nations give such power over
themselves, and, secondly, what induces them to make choice of
such a person.

As to matter of fact conveyed to us by history, we know of no
absolute power given to any man by our European nations except the
two above mentioned.[66] Agathocles's, Dionysius's[67] or Caesar's coming to such a power by violence and murders is nothing to our purpose, but what absolute power freely and so legally granted. The
aisymnetes were before the times that are exactly described unto us.
The Roman affairs, being better known to us, there is not a child
who will not tell you why they made dictators. Their subjects revolt,
they name a dictator. The Gauls burn Rome, they name a dictator.
Hannibal after the death of consuls, praetors, and *the* slaughter of
several armies is master of the greatest part of Italy, it is time to name
a dictator. And the election of Quinctius Cincinnatus, Furius Camillus, Fabius Maximus,[68] and others shows that they ever fixed upon
the person in whose virtue they ever had the greatest confidence.
And nothing can be more extravagant and unreasonable than to continue the power granted to a man for such an occasion longer than
the occasion lasts, or continue that to the son without virtue which
was given to the father for his virtue.

Sons are often in all things most unlike such fathers. Lucius
Brutus's[69] sons were traitors to their country, which he had restored
to liberty, and friends to the Tarquins, whom he had expelled. The

---

[66] I.e. Greece and Rome.
[67] Agathocles (361–289 BC), tyrant (317 BC) and then king (305 BC) of Syracuse.
Dionysius I (c. 430–367 BC), sole master of Syracuse (405 BC).
[68] Cincinnatus, Lucius Quinctius (born c. 519 BC); appointed as dictator in 458 BC,
when a Roman army was blockaded by the Italian tribe of the Aequi on mount
Algidus. Camillus, Furius Maximus, Roman statesman and general; appointed as
dictator in c. 396 BC and again in c. 390 BC when the Gauls had captured Rome.
Fabius, Maximus Verrucosus Quintus (c. 275–203 BC), Roman general and consul;
appointed as dictator in 221 and again in 217 BC (during the second Punic war) after
Hannibal had crossed the Alps and, while defeating several great Roman armies,
moved to the south in order to capture Rome.
[69] Brutus, Lucius Junius. According to Roman tradition, he ousted the Etruscan king
Lucius Tarquinius from Rome in 509 BC and founded the Roman republic. He had
his own sons killed when they joined a conspiracy to restore the Tarquins.

descendants of Socrates were blockish and stupid. Alcibiades's race *was* little better than mad. Cicero's son had little wit. Cato of Utica left an heir who was accused of effeminacy and want of courage.[70] Moses's sons appear not to have excelled other men. Nothing is reported of those of good Eli but their lewdness and wickedness, and the ruin they brought on their father, family, and nation.[71] No man [25] can be confident their sons will | inherit their fathers' virtues, when it appears Ishmael was an idolater, Esau a reprobate, Reuben incestuous, Rehoboam unwise, and even the sons of Samuel covetous and unjust.[72] And if the sons inherit not their fathers' virtues, what can be more extravagant than to give them the power wherewith their fathers were entrusted?

PHILALETHES: though this is very contrary to the practice and opinion of the court, I am more surprised with what you say in the next place: that good and wise men neither for themselves nor posterity seek or accept[73] such powers. For we believe wise and good men are men of great spirits, and therefore desirous of power and of transmitting it to their posterity if they think such power good. For he that loves his children will desire what is good for them, else he deserves not the name of a man.

EUNOMIUS: this will not seem strange if you consider who is a wise or good man, and what greatness of mind such men have. Wise and good in a scriptural sense are the same thing, so *are* the wicked man and the fool, else the psalmist would not have said: The fool, but the wicked man has said in his heart there is no God;[74] for the

---

[70] Cato (of Utica), Marcus Porcius (95–46 BC), Roman statesman; supported senatorial government and the republican cause against power seekers, especially Julius Caesar. He left two sons, Marcus Porcius Cato and Lucius Porcius Cato.

[71] According to I Sam. 2:12–17, 22, Eli failed to curb the scandalous behaviour of his sons.

[72] Ishmael, son of Abraham and his Egyptian handmaid; according to Gen. 16:12, 'He shall be a wild man; his hand shall be against every man, and every man's hand against him'. Esau, firstborn of Isaac and Rebehaz; the New Testament letter to the Hebrews (12:16) points to him as an example of an immoral and irreligious man. Reuben, son of Jacob; lay with Bilhah, his father's concubine, and therefore lost his firstborn privileges (Gen. 35:22). Rehoboam, son of Solomon and Naamah the Ammonitess; first ruler of the southern kingdom of Judah, whose folly caused the dissolution of the united kingdom of David and of his son and successor Solomon (Eccl. 47:23). Samuel's sons, Joel and Abiah, were unsuited for kingship because they had grown up as corrupt judges (I Sam. 8:1–3).

[73] MS: 'accept of such'.　　[74] Ps. 14:1.

denying of God is certainly the height of wickedness. This wise man, instead of your light court maxims, obeys the Scriptures, which say: Seek not thow great things for thy self, seek them not (Jer. 45:5). Gideon was of this mind, who said: Neither I nor my sons shall reign over you.[75] And his son Jotham verified his saying in the parable of the trees,[76] of which I infer:

First, that none who has any great virtue will take upon him to reign. This is showed by the cedar, vine, and olive trees, whereas the bramble advances himself when he is not called.

The second thing observable in that parable is the reason why they refused. The vine would not lose its good wine, nor the olive its fatness. This convinces me that he who has any virtue if he begin*s* to reign, loses it. This is also verified by Abimelech. He had all the qualities requisite for one that would make himself a king. He was ambitious to desire power, bold to attempt the gaining it, inhumanly perfidious, cruel and impious in removing all that stood | between /26/ him and the crown and to secure himself in the enjoyment of it. The fire went out of the bramble and consumed the cedars of Lebanon, but it also returned upon the bramble and destroyed it.[77] Considering then the temper of men who refuse power and of him that desired it, you may see that in a Scripture sense he is not the wise or good man that desired it.

If you examine who is a wise or good man in a philosophical sense, some will tell you he is[78] a king, but his kingdom is only over himself and in himself. *Rex est qui *metuit* nihil, Rex est qui *cupiet*[79] nihil. Hoc regnum sibi quisque dat.*[80] But this man is not a king in the

---

[75] Judg. 8:23–4.

[76] Jotham disputed the wisdom of the citizens of Shechem, who had made Abimelech king, by telling them this parable. Once upon a time the trees came to anoint a king, but most trees refused to hold sway over other trees because they did not want to leave their rich oil, their good fruit or their new wine. 'Then all the trees said to the thorn-bush: Will you then be king over us? And the thorn said to the trees: If you really mean to anoint me as your king, then come under the protection of my shadow; if not, fire shall come out of the thorn and burn up the cedars of Lebanon' (Judg. 8:23–4).

[77] After the citizens of Shechem had transferred their allegiance from Abimelech ('the bramble') to Gaal, Abimelech took one of their cities and killed all inhabitants. He then attacked the nearby town of Thebes, but as he tried to set fire to it he was fatally wounded when a woman threw a millstone on his head (Judg. 9:8–15).

[78] MS: 'only is'.   [79] MS: 'cupiet ... metuit'.

[80] 'A king is he who has no fear, a king is he who shall naught desire. Such a kingdom on himself each man bestows.' Seneca, *Thyestes*, 388–90.

courtiers' phrase, nor would his palace be much frequented by such persons as courts are usually full of. Others will tell you he is a wise man who knows what is really good, practises what he knows, spends his life in contemplation that he may know more. This man also will make an ill tyrant. Others say a wise man has all in himself, desires nothing without himself; and that the desire of riches, honour, or power proceeds only from inward defects and imperfections which can never befall a wise man. This also agrees little with *your* court maxims. I deny not *that*[81] a wise, virtuous man may moderately desire amongst his equals the public good, but *he* will not exalt himself above his brethren. But those who have most desired great power over others have been the most detestable of all mankind. The name of tyrant comprehends all that is evil, and the greatest glory has been given to those who hindered *them*[82] from attaining what they sought, or threw them from the possession of it by death or banishment. This may keep you from wondering at my saying that good and wise men sought not after sovereign power, or, if they did accept it, would not desire the same to be continued to their posterity. For though such power may be good for a wise man when well managed, yet if it descends on a child *or a* weak or vicious man, that which had been good to him, to his child, or any unqualified successor would be evil. A wise man has all the reason to take care that any he loves may not have a burden incumbent on them which would oppress and destroy them. *Quicquid recipitur recipitur ad modum reci-*
[27] *pientis;*[83] whatever is not suitable to the receiver, can never be good | or useful to him. Nor can any man make good use of power to the benefit of himself or others that live under him, unless he has strength of mind and virtue proportionable to it. A Turkish emperor, hearing of great acts performed by Skanderbeg,[84] desired and had his sword, but found it no better than others. That noble prince replied he had sent the sword but not the arm which used it. The instability of high fortunes and difficulties of performing what belongs to them, *and the* allurements to vice through the corruption that accompanies them from flatteries and the like, make wise men afraid of such slippery places whence the descent is destruction,

---

[81] MS: 'but'. [82] MS: 'him'.
[83] 'Whatever is received is received on the conditions of the receiver.'
[84] Skanderbeg, byname of Kastrioti, Gjergj (1405–68); under his leadership Albania successfully withstood several Turkish invasions.

much more to place their children in the like of whose virtue or strength they have little or no experience. If sovereign power then be hard to manage by them that have greatest abilities, and allurements to vice which accompany it so great that it is hard to find any virtue so solid as to resist the temptation, how can we imagine it can safely be trusted in the hands of those who can be suspected *of*[85] either malice or weakness?

I shall now, if you please, endeavour to elucidate my third position.

PHILALETHES: I expect with great impatience to hear what you can say on that subject.

EUNOMIUS: hereditary power begets hereditary hatred. It has its root in injustice and its operation contrary to human nature. Man is by nature a rational creature. Everything, therefore, that is irrational, is contrary to man's nature. Hatred is the passion that arises from the discovery of the contrariety. We therefore naturally and rationally hate that that is contrary to nature and reason: virtue is the dictate of reason. We rightly esteem and love those as good and wise men who are endowed with virtue and, living in a virtuous principle, conform themselves to the rules of reason and nature. On the other side, we despise, detest, and abhor those who, degenerating from the rational nature they were created in, do either brutishly neglect the dictates of reason or furiously and impiously violate them. The more enormous that violation is and the greater the injury we receive by it, the greater is our hatred against him that is the author of it.

Justice is that virtue which ought to be the perpetual director of all our actions in the world and the rule of commerce. The fundamental | maxim of it *is*[86] to give that which is equal unto equals. It /28/ is a furious violation of this rule to set up one family that is naturally or rationally not different from others in such dominion over others as to arrogate unto themselves the privilege of being unaccountable to any man. So that all their armies for most part go unpunished, though it be the desolations of cities and provinces sacrificed to their lusts. This, as it is the greatest injustice and injury to them that suffer under it, must necessarily be the root of the sharpest and most implacable hatred.

[85] MS: 'for'.   [86] MS: 'are'.

33

PHILALETHES: justice is the dictate of reason. Nothing that is rational can be unjust. As equality is just among equals, it is unjust to reward equally those who in themselves are unequal. Justice ever observes proportion; in some things the arithmetical, which gives one to one, two to two; in other the geometrical is more to be regarded in giving the most worthy portion to him that is most worthy. Kings, therefore, that excel us in birth may merit privileges above those we enjoy.

Secondly, I look on this prerogative enjoyed by kings as granted for the good of the people to watch over them for their good. And none ought to envy the advantages due to them for so great a merit, but ought to reverence and love them. The devotion, therefore, of subjects to their kings has arrived to the degree of adoration.

EUNOMIUS: it is true what is rational can never be unjust, and as true that what is unjust can never be rational; he that pretends preference before another must show he has the advantage in that very thing which is in question. Cyrus mistook when he decided the controversy between two soldiers disputing for two coats, a great and a little one, by giving the great coat to the great man and compelling the little to take the little one. His tutors reproved him for it, says Xenophon *in* *De institutione Cyri*, telling him he was unjust to regard not what was fit for everyone to have, but what of right belonged to him.[87] So in matters of power and government it is not so much to be considered what place such a man may fitly execute, but what of right belongs to him. He that pretends a power over me must show how I have left the liberty God and nature gives me. That is the power over myself, for I am naturally equal to him in freedom. If this
[29] were not of force, kings | would seldom have advantage over their subjects, though Cyrus's judgement had been just that the great-bodied man ought to have the great coat, and he in government to have the highest place who is fittest for it.

All inequality is natural or artificial; that preference which can be challenged by a natural inequality is reasonable, if the nature of it suits with the thing in question, and the proportion will bear. A wise man has naturally that advantage over a fool that his counsel ought to be harkened to more than the other. He that excels in fidelity, valour,

---

[87] Xenophon, *Education of Cyrus*, bk 1, ch. 3. In fact, the dispute was between two boys.

experience, and all military virtues has a juster pretence to the command of an army than one who has none of these qualities. It would be ridiculous for one to pretend to the government of a province or command of a regiment because he is a good poet or a good orator. For though a good poet or orator has a natural advantage over him that is not so fit, *he has this advantage* only in poetry or oratory, not in those things which require different qualities and *have*[88] nothing at all *in* common with them. Artificial inequality may also give a just preference when that inequality is grounded upon principles of nature and consonant unto them, still observing the due proportion.

Magistracy is artificial, for no man is born praetor, consul, or dictator. He who for his fitness to execute such a charge is advanced to it, has, whilst in it, a just right over him that is in no respect fit for it, or that, however fit, does not at that time enjoy it. But those artificial inequalities which are repugnant and contrary to nature are in all respects to be detested and abhorred. Those laws which should ordain that wives should command their husbands, fathers be subject to their children, and wise men be governed by fools are of this nature. And generally all those which assign unto any man or number of men works of which they are incapable, powers that they cannot manage, or rights over those who naturally ought to be preferred before them.

There is a simple inequality and an inequality *quo ad hanc*, in some one thing and to some end. To know what inequality gives preference to any man in point of government, we must see what the ends of government are and what qualities are required in those that govern conducing to those ends.

Aristotle well resembles the constitution of a | body politic to a /30/ body natural, that is, a society of men to one man.[89] Both direct their actions to some end. Both desire to preserve themselves and enjoy that that is respectively good for both. Wisdom is the power in man of judging what is good or evil, of knowing the ways of attaining good and directing all its actions to the attaining *of* it. Wisdom is seated in the mind and understanding, which has a natural excellency to that end above all the other faculties in man. And that person is out of frame that is not guided by it. The like may be said of

---

[88] MS: 'has'.

[89] For example, Aristotle, *Politics*, bk VII, 1324a.

35

civil societies. Wisdom only knows the end to which they are directed and how to find and use the means of attaining to it. This shows that in all societies he or they that are wisest ought naturally to govern. Which notion he drives so far (following the example of his master Plato) as to affirm, if there were a man in a commonwealth that had more wisdom, virtue, and valour than all the rest, he ought to be a perpetual king; and that they are unjust that will not submit to him.[90] If any can show a man that has that excellency of wisdom, virtue, and valour above all others, and assures us the same shall for ever be transmitted to his posterity, *I will acknowledge him to be my king and desire the same privilege may be annexed to his posterity.*

We all breathe the same air, are composed of the same materials, have the same birth, and though they or their flatterers sometimes say they are Gods, they shall die like men. They are naturally no more than men and can justly therefore pretend to no more than others. Their descendants also are as weak and imperfect as ours. He then that sets up one above those that are naturally equal to him, breaks the laws of nature, gives an artificial preferment where there is none natural. And he that annexes it to his family, as is usual, without distinction of age or sex, does commit the detestable and extravagant injustice *of making weak and evil men rulers of those who are wise, virtuous, and good; submits the wisdom of the aged to the weakness and folly of children.* And that sex which, according to the rules of nature, ought to command, is made to receive laws from that which is natu-

[31] rally | unable to govern a private family and is born to be subject unto another, to the utter ruin, violation, and overturning of all laws of nature and reason. He that pretends to a power that enables him to do evil and remains unpunished, *to me seems like a thief or murderer who pretends exemption from the penalties of the law because his father and other ancestors were accustomed to commit the like.* He that will justify a power derived by succession must show he makes that use of it for which it was first granted, and that he is equally able to manage *it* as he to whom it was granted. For if he employ that power to the people's hurt which was granted for their good, he wants the advantages of body, mind, or experience that the first had to whom it was granted, and so the grant of itself is void. This may show you

[90] Aristotle, *Politics*, bk IV, 1288a.

36

whether it is possible *that* a thing so unreasonable, so unnatural as this can be good for the people or not.

But for your more full satisfaction I will proceed a little farther in answer to your last objection, and endeavour to show you that there is such an antipathy between a virtuous generous people and an absolute monarch, especially if hereditary, that from thence must necessarily grow a perpetual hatred. I know nothing is spoken of so much as the good of the people. Nothing was ever so foul and mischievous that *it* might not be represented under some fair colour. We should not be much troubled with tyrants if they used force only, but their most powerful weapon is fraud. We find more that have made themselves tyrants by fraud than by force, or if both fraud and force were used, fraud was the principal.

Finis. Reliqua desiderantur.

Fourth Dialogue

Third Court Maxim: That absolute and hereditary monarchy where the government is wholly left to the will and all power trusted only in the hands of the monarch is most conformable to and warrantable from the Scripture

PHILALETHES: my business is dispatched for this day and I desire to employ the leisure in the continuation of our last discourse.

/32/ EUNOMIUS: I am willing to continue if | you please to retire into some place where we may be free from noise and interruption.

PHILALETHES: the shadow of these trees will be as good a defence to us against the heat as the solitariness of the place against the importunity of company. So I will resume the discourse where we left and the doubt that remained with me. From a political and moral consideration of government, you may remember, we passed unto a religious *one*. For though I could not well answer your arguments in the way they were proposed, I was not convinced by them, because I think it expedient in the case rather to examine what God has commanded than what we, according to our imperfect reasonings, may fancy to be good for ourselves. Whatever God commands is just and good.

EUNOMIUS: but what makes you believe that in civil things God has not left us a liberty of choosing and constituting such a government as according to the time and nature of the place and people we find most convenient?

38

PHILALETHES: God teaches us by example as well as precept. And it cannot be doubted but the government of a monarch set up by him first in the person of Moses, then several judges, and afterwards of Saul and David is best, because suitable to his will.[91] And that will of his then declared ought to be a perpetual law to succeeding ages. God is one and established one to bear his image on earth whom he honours with the name of his anointed, forbidding any to touch him, commanding all to obey him, and that not for wrath but conscience sake, unto whom also Christ himself gave tribute and was obedient to the time of his death. The free administration of that power in Saul, David, and others shows it had no other rule but the will of him that exercised it. This *is* confirmed by the words of Samuel: This shall be the manner of your king. He will take your sons to be his horseman, drive and run before his chariots. He will appoint them to ear his ground and reap his harvest. He will take your daughters to be his cooks and bakers. He will take your fields, vineyards, and oliveyards, even the best of them, and give them to his servants, etcetera. And you shall cry unto me because of *the*[92] king you shall have chosen,[93] and I | will not hear you, says the Lord (I Samuel 8, 10-18). /33/ And when David had committed that horrid adultery and murder in the matter of Uriah, he said: against thee only have I sinned; which shows he was accountable to no other (Ps. 51).[94]

EUNOMIUS: do you speak this of yourself on serious consideration of these passages or receive them on trust from others?

PHILALETHES: I confess at court we little trouble ourselves with the intricacies of the Bible. If any amongst us were known to read it he would be looked upon as a fanatic, to the utter ruin of his fortune. Our principal study is romances, playbooks, or poets. If we apply ourselves to anything more serious, we read Machiavelli[95] and other books of that kind, which we find more useful to us than all that is contained in the Bible. If therefore we make use of it to justify our actions or maxims, we are beholding to those who are better versed in such matters, learned and grave men; we know no better way than to believe them. But if I knew a better way I would take it.

---

[91] Moses: Exod. 3–4; Judges: Num. 11:16–30; Saul: I Sam. 10:1, 17–27; David: I Sam. 16:12–3.
[92] MS: 'your'.   [93] MS: '... chosen you, and ...'.   [94] Ps. 51:4.
[95] Editorial hand has deleted 'Machiavelli', indicating it to be replaced by 'Hobbes'.

EUNOMIUS: if these learned men can show you that you are not to be saved by any other faith than in them, and that, conforming your life to them, you shall not be damned but they for you, I shall much command your modest submission. If not, I think you ought to seek farther. And, if I mistake not, the sequel of this discourse will discover what use they make of Scripture; and then you may come to see whether you may safely rely on them or not. Another occasion may give us more leisure to discourse upon this point. I will now return to the passages alleged by you, beginning with the first. Pray tell me why do you think Moses was a king?

PHILALETHES: it is said he was king in Jeshurun.[96] He acted as a king, gave laws and executed them with so absolute a power that with one word of his he caused twenty-three thousand of the people to be slain.

EUNOMIUS: Jeshurun signifies the just. Moses is said to have been as a king amongst the just, says the Chaldee paraphrase. And this, I think, will not serve to your purpose. He gave not any law to that people, but transmitted to them what he received from God, and in killing the idolatrous he acted no more as a king than Samuel did /34/ when he slew Agag, that king Saul had spared, or than Elijah who | slew the priests and prophets of Baal without any regal power.[97]

But that it may clearly appear Moses was no king; he himself tells them what kind of king they should constitute if they should desire one when they came to Canaan, the land of their rest. And if Moses as a type of Christ's kingly power and spiritual kingdom had been a king, what is that to our kings? And if one endowed by God with such high and extraordinary gifts be fit to exercise an absolute power, what is that to them that have no such gifts? According to Plato's rules, Moses deserved to be a king, for he eminently excelled all others in wisdom and virtue. He was as a God amongst men, the messenger or mediator between God and them. His illumination by the spirit of God rendered him a living law; he knew how to direct them to goodness and truth by communication he had with him that is good and true. What is this to those that have no gifts either political, moral, or divine above the vulgar? Moses pretended not to the government by a prerogative of birth, but for the assurance of God's

[96] Biblical name for the people of Israel.
[97] Samuel: I Sam. 15:33; Elijah: I Kings 18:40.

presence with him, demonstrated by miracles. And God said he had made him as a god to Pharaoh.[98]

God ever gave gifts suitable to the work he employed any man in. Prudent masters, princes, or others never command their servants to do anything, but they furnish them with power and means fit for the accomplishing of it: he that appoints the end appoints also the means conducing to that end.[99] It is therefore a maxim in law *that* he that appoints not the means does not appoint the end. How impious then is the folly of those that pretend princes are ordained by God for such a great work as the governing *of* great nations as his vicegerents with supreme power in all things ecclesiastical and civil, who often have not spirits *above the meanest slaves?* If all nations were to be servants to princes who are often slaves to their own or favourites' passions, lusts, and vices, I should think the curse of Canaan were come upon them, *a servant of servants shall thou be.*[100] But whatever Moses was, it is certain his sons did not inherit his power. His servant Joshua succeeded him, being filled with a spirit of wisdom from God fit for this work.[101] Who can be equal to him that is raised above us by the spirit of his maker? How fit is such a one to govern us? Not to obey him were impious pride. And no less impious folly to obey them that have no such advantages over us. What is it but as a worshipping for God that which is not God? I think it a greater crime to reverence as Christ's vicegerent him that is not so, than not to obey Moses who truly was so. | It is not easily decided whether he /35/ who is born equal to us and pretends to dominion over us, or we who set up one to exercise dominion over us whom God has made equal to us, do sin most. The one resembles the pride of Lucifer, the other the sottish idolatry of those that made the calf and then fell down and worshipped it.[102] Nor is this humility, there is pride also in it. Corrupted man often shows the highest pride in that which looks like

---

[98] Exod. 3:10–12.

[99] Sidney probably draws on Grotius, *On the law of war and peace*, bk II, ch. 7, sec. 4, 'There is a saying of Aristotle: Who gives the form, gives what is necessary to the form.'

[100] Gen. 9:25.   [101] Num. 27:18–23.

[102] The golden calf, the embodiment of idolatry in the Old Testament, appears first as the one made by Aaron in response to the request of the Israelites for a god to lead them as they awaited the delayed return of Moses from Mount Sinai. Exod. 32:1–4. The second calf was made during the reign of king Jeroboam I of Israel, who wanted to prevent the people from worshipping in the temple of Jerusalem. I Kings 12:27–31.

the lowest baseness, or rather, both pride and baseness are in the same sin. He that is so base as to worship a stone is so proud as to think he can make a god of a stone.

Judges were raised by God only on extraordinary occasions and necessities *raised* dictators at Rome. Nor did Joshua exercise regal power but divided the lands according to the most perfect agrarian law.[103] The judgement of many things was referred to the General Assembly by the people and to the particular congregations of several cities. The administration of the government was left to the seventy chosen for their age and merit.[104] The Senate was composed of these as an aristocracy mixed with a democracy. Their judges, as dictators in extraordinary cases, were raised, qualified, and commissioned by God himself; the whole government remained in the elders and *the* people, not in Joshua or his descendants. There was nothing of monarchy. No man that ever read the Bible can think the succeeding judges kings. Gideon said: neither I nor my sons will reign over you.[105] Samuel was no king, for then the Israelites would not have said to him: give us a king. God did appoint that government which was best for them, consisting in some sort of all the three kinds of government, with this difference that what savoured of aristocracy and democracy was permanent, *while* that which resembled monarchy was only occasional, when necessity required. The two first had relation to constant nourishment, the last was only a medicine.

PHILALETHES: but why did God after*wards* appoint kings in Israel?

EUNOMIUS: the reason is evident. To all their sins they have added this, says the Lord, that they have asked a king. They have not rejected thee but me, says God to Samuel: Nevertheless harken to them and appoint them a king. But when they cry to me to deliver them from their king I will not hear them.[106] The prophet Samuel knew it to be a grievous judgement when God in wrath answered those prayers or desires of the people which were conceived with sin, sent up with folly, and persisted in with obstinate madness. This
/36/ shows that those kings | were appointed by God not as good for the people but as judgements to chastise their folly, being of the same

---

[103] Joshua 13:1–19:51.   [104] I.e. the Sanhedrin.   [105] Judg. 8:23–4.
[106] I Sam. 8:7–8, 18–19.

42

nature as plagues and fiery serpents sent to destroy them. And it no more proves we should set up kings over us by that example than that we should endeavour to bring fiery serpents or any *of the* other plagues amongst us, that were inflicted on that stiffnecked people for their sins.

PHILALETHES: I dare not say we are obliged to establish kings where they never were, but I think we must suffer them where they are, though they be evil, and bear patiently the punishment of our sin. It may not be resisted because he that bears it is sacred and it is absolute.

EUNOMIUS: if men be obliged to set up a monarch in imitation of God's being a monarch over the universe, as you formerly argued, show a man that has created a nation and I will not envy him the dominion over it. Till such a man be found, *I look on those nations who voluntarily set up a king guilty of the same folly and sin as the Israelites were in asking *for* one*. And though the yoke such kings put on us be a punishment for our sins, I know not but we may endeavour to free ourselves from that punishment as well as from pain, sickness, imprisonment, or any plague God inflicts upon us. Taking physics to free me from the disease God has laid on me is not resisting of providence. Wherefore has God in his providence given me means to recover my health if I may not use them? So for defending or recovering my liberty I tempt providence if I use not such means as long as I have life. But you say the persons of kings are sacred as God's anointed vicegerents. Have all kings as kings that sacred character upon them, or some only?

PHILALETHES: I have ever understood that it belongs to them all.

EUNOMIUS: then Moses, Joshua, and Samuel were the wickedest men that ever lived. For Moses and Joshua slew thirty-one kings, that is, in the phrase of our divines, murdered thirty-one of God's anointeds. Joshua hanged five of them at one time before the Lord.[107] The tyrant Polycrates[108] is said to have dreamt he was raised above the earth and that Jupiter bathed and foamed him, Apollo anointed him. Not long after, he was crucified, raised above the earth on the cross, the wind and rain foamed and bathed him, and the sun, called Apollo, melted his fat, and so anointed him with his own grease.

[107] Joshua 10:26.   [108] Polycrates, tyrant of Samos (532–522 BC).

Though all tyrants have not this unction, it is not because they do
/37/ not deserve it, | *but God reserves tophet that is prepared for them*, a
punishment more proportioned to their merit. But from our divines
we must learn to change our thoughts and language of ancient or
modern princes that have been thought and called tyrants, and,
instead of the epithets usually given them, say *sacred Agathocles,
Dionysius, Tiberius, Domitian, Diocletian, and others, holy Caligula,
Heliogabalus*.[109] St Paul then was not called out of his name when
said to be a pestilent fellow and seducer of the people.[110] And *holy
Nero* did very justly take away that troublesome head of his that,
instead of teaching people to worship Nero in the body, as he commanded, preached nothing but a worshipping of Christ in the spirit,
which he abhorred and forbade. And again, holiness and happiness
are inseparable companions. If monarchy and monarchs be sacred,
then that that is opposite to both must be profane. If I therefore
were a papist and invoked saints instead of Peter and Paul, I do say,
sancte Herod, sancte Tiberius, ora pro me. In my opinion the bishops
who lately altered the Common Prayer Book,[111] instead of the goodly
fellowship of the apostles praise thee; the noble army of martyrs
magnify thee; the holy church throughout all the world does
acknowledge thee; should have said, the goodly and sacred fellowship of tyrants praise thee; the glorious army of thieves, murderers,
and blasphemers that uphold them magnify thee; the holy assembly
of proud and cruel bishops, corrupt lawyers, false witnesses, and
mercenary judges who persecute and endeavour to destroy thy
church and people throughout the world, adorning the gates and
towers of the city with the mangled limbs of your choicest servants,
to gratify the lusts and uphold the interest of their two masters, the
king and the devil, do acknowledge thee.

But upon this there do arise two questions.

First, whether those kings that have been thrown out of their
power, hanged, crucified, cut in pieces, cast into jakes, and the like,

---

[109] Tiberius (42 BC–AD 37), Roman emperor (14–37). Domitian, Caesar Augustus (51–
96), Roman emperor (81–96). Diocletian, Gaius Valerius (245–316), Roman
emperor (285–305). Caligula (12–41), Roman emperor (37–41). Heliogabalus (204–
22), Roman emperor (218–22).

[110] Acts 21:28–9.

[111] Anglican liturgical book, first authorized for use in the Church of England in 1549,
and radically revised in 1552, with subsequent minor revisions in 1554, 1604, and
1662.

did lose their sanctity in losing their power; or whether that character was indelible in them. And *whether* the kings destroyed by Joshua, or others afterwards, as Jugurtha, Caligula, Nero, Heliogabalus, and Vitellius,[112] did die saints.

Secondly, whether they were holy that endeavoured to set up this holy government though anathematized for perishing in the attempt. If the intention be to be taken for the act, Gaius Marius, Catilina,[113] and Cesare Borgia, with many others, are to be esteemed saints.

PHILALETHES: by what you have said I suspect I was too forward in comprehending all monarchs | under the title sacred.   /38/

EUNOMIUS: there is no hurt in retracting a mistake. But let us see to what monarchs the title of sacred does belong.

PHILALETHES: perhaps only to those of the true church, as the Jews were and we are.

EUNOMIUS: what belongs to a man as a man belongs to every man, what belongs not to every man belongs not to a man as a man but must be attributed to something else; so, whatever belongs to one as a monarch, belongs to every monarch. And what does not belong to everyone, belongs to none as a monarch, but as something else. If all monarchs are not sacred and anointed of God, then if any monarch is sacred and anointed it is from something distinct from monarchy. You restrain the privilege to jewish and christian monarchs, *yet* Christ paid tribute to a heathen monarch, Saint Paul enjoins obedience to heathens, the christian fathers do the like, so that, if from their words you think the sacred character of God's anointed is upon any monarch, it must extend to all. *And* if it be impious and absurd to extend it to all, it can be applied to none but with the same impiety and absurdity.

But what christian monarchs have this great privilege? The bare name of a christian confers it not; many go under the name of Christians that are as fierce, bitter, dangerous enemies to God's people that are indeed true Christians and to Christ himself as any professed haters of his name.

[112] Vitellius (15–69), Roman emperor (69).
[113] Marius, Gaius (157–86 BC); Roman general and politician who captured Rome in 87 BC. Catilina; Roman patrician who, after being defeated for consulship of 63 and 62 BC, laid plans for a revolution and became an enemy of the state. He was defeated and killed in 62 BC by the army of consul Antonius.

PHILALETHES: by christian monarchs I mean only the true orthodox Christians.

EUNOMIUS: then those monarchs that favour popery or other errors and idolatry have no title to that privilege. And what if the orthodox christian lives like a heathen, shall he enjoy the privilege?

PHILALETHES: I cannot think it to belong to a hypocrite and idolater.

EUNOMIUS: the dispute then will depend upon the determination who *is to*[114] be orthodox and christian? Papists say none but those in the bosom of the Roman church; that Protestants are worse than Turks or infidels, disobedient to Christ's vicar, schismatics, heretics, etcetera. Ask the Protestant who is the true Christian, he says, papists are most gross idolaters, supporters of antichrist, calling him the false prophet, the beast, the whore of Babylon, and the man of sin, whom the others reverence as head of the church, vicar of Christ, etcetera. There is great difference of opinion also concerning /39/ the piety of | persons. Those that some acknowledge to be great saints, others of the same profession think the worst disciples and instruments the devil has on earth; so that, if none must be reverenced as God's anointed but the monarch that is orthodox in faith and upright in life, I that am to give that reverence am to judge whether he that exacts this from me has a right title to it. And certainly I shall never allow it to one of a *profession contrary to that of myself*.[115] A papist will never allow it to a Protestant, nor a Protestant to a papist, yea, or to a Protestant of a different way from him. And then great impurity of life, breach of faith, injustice, treachery, falseness to his own profession and advancing the professed adversaries of it, *will follow*. These in any man, much more in monarchs, show them to be no true Christians, profess or be called what they will. If I may be so happy to see such thrown down from their thrones, I shall wish happy reigns to those that are free from all such like crimes.

PHILALETHES: I would fain know how you understand some places of Scripture which seem to confirm what I first proposed.

First, that of Samuel, who by the command of God anointed Saul king over Israel, telling them 'this shall be the manner of their king'.[116]

[114]MS: 'it'. [115]MS: 'a contrary profession to myself'. [116]I Sam. 8:11.

Secondly, David, though anointed also, when Saul had fallen from his obedience to God and committed great wickednesses, slew him not when in his power, but forbade Abishai to stretch out his hand against the Lord's anointed.[117]

And lastly, he slew the Amalekite that said he had slain Saul.[118] Hence I infer that those who are the Lord's anointed have absolute power and their persons ought to be inviolable.

Thirdly, the act of our saviour in paying tribute to caesar shows he acknowledged in him the supreme power;[119] and the apostle commands obedience to them for conscience sake.[120]

EUNOMIUS: I will answer these in the order you have proposed them. The relation of this is seen *in* I Samuel 8. Some may wonder why, when the people asked *for* a king, God gave them a tyrant; others think here is set down the right of all kings, so that people that will have a king must have such a one.

First, it is no strange thing that those that sin in asking should be punished in what they receive; or if they ask that which is not just, it is just they should receive what they did not ask. But they had just what they asked. They not only asked *for* a king, but such a king as the nations around about them had. The situation of Palestine shows what nations they were encompassed with whom they desired to follow: | Moab, Ammon, Tyre, etcetera, whose tyrants they had fallen /40/ under and been delivered from by judges. God had separated them from all other nations, was himself their king and lawgiver, placing over them a government that ought to have been an example to all other nations. Under this they might have lived happily. But as they left the true worship of God to follow those nations in their beastly idolatry, they reject*ed* also the civil government of God's own institution, and so the government of God himself also, renouncing the liberty of being subject to him only, to make themselves slaves unto a king. And God had not granted their desires unless he had given them such a king. In mercy he warned them by Samuel what such a king would do, what would be the manner of him: this shall be your misery under him, but if you will have him, you shall; but when

---

[117] Allusion to I Sam. 24:4–7.   [118] II Sam. 14:16.
[119] Allusion to Matt. 22:21–2, where Jesus says to the Pharisees, 'pay caesar what is due to caesar, and pay God what is due to God'.
[120] Acts 5:29–30.

he oppresses you and you cry to me, I will not hear you; you have rejected me, I will reject you.

Aquinas, speaking on this place,[121] I Samuel 8, from hence, says he, have some drawn that execrable and detestable doctrine that it is lawful for kings to do all things here mentioned. And, proceeding farther in examining the original of government there described, he imputes it to the invention of the devil as set up by him amongst his servants, having its root in vice, impiety, and idolatry, in opposition to such just government as was appointed by God himself for the maintaining of justice, virtue, and the true religion. By this you may see the doctrine preached unto you by the bishops is no new thing; the devil first set up tyranny among the wicked nations devoted to his service. The Israelites, seduced often by him and them to idolatry, were by the same means easily drawn to follow their example in setting up the like government, which favoured so much all the vices to which they were prone. In succeeding ages the same wicked spirit raised up his servants to impute unto God that which was contrived by him. And our good priests follow them that they may show themselves conformable in all things to him who is their master.

In the future discourse the principle in which they live shall be so explained as may show why they follow such leaders. But let us learn to avoid such wicked examples as carefully as they learn to imitate them. Tyranny was suitable to idolatry, which incited that nation that frequently fell into the one to desire the other. This is enough to teach us that we should abhor tyranny as its companion idolatry. The Israelites sinned in desiring a king, let us be deterred by it. God foretold the misery that would follow *if* they persisted in their
/41/ wickedness | and guilt, and brought upon themselves the deserved punishment thereof. Let their guilt and punishment deter us, let us take warning though they would not. And if we have no communication with satan, let us have none with those thrones which uphold that which he endeavours to set up against God.

But that it may clearly appear *that* the words of Samuel from God to the people were threatenings of what would be, and not rules of what lawfully might be done, you need only read the tenth chapter, where, after the choosing and anointing of the king, it is said *that* Samuel told the people the manner of the kingdom and wrote it in a book and laid it up before the Lord.[122] Now, though this book

[121] Aquinas, *Summa theologica*, 1ᵃᵉ 11ᵃ, art. 1, obj. 5 and obj. 2, resp.   [122] I Sam. 10:25.

be unknown to us, we have all reason to believe it was conformable to the rules of kingly government set down by Moses, Deut. 17, where it is said: he must be one of thy brethren, he shall not multiple horses nor horsemen, he shall not gather much gold nor silver nor have many wives; and that his heart through pride should not be exalted above his brethren.[123] Let us have such kings and we will not complain; and that we may have none but such, let us have means of punishing them if they be not so and I am content with that government.

But without prejudice to myself or country, I may even wish we had that only which was threatened by Samuel as a punishment to the Israelites. It would be a favour to us; we are fallen into such a condition that whatever is not the extremity of misery may be taken for a degree of felicity.[124] That king would take some of their children to make soldiers for defence of his country, or servants for the rise of his house, and take the tenth of the seed and vineyards, but we find nothing there of the multitude of projectors that swarm about our court, nor of the spies, informers, trepanners, and false witnesses, which render every man's house a snare to him. There is no mention of corrupt, obscene, mad favourites, inventions to delude the subjects, pervert the law, sell justice, corrupt manners, and destroy families.

If we had a Saul we might serve God without fear. He forced none to leave the worship of the true God. But amongst us a praying meeting is looked on as a conspiracy, and the chief in such exercises are haled to prisons, cast into dungeons, and caused to perish with hunger or cold; our governors therein most impudently violating the faith given them that they should not be molested. It is no matter whether a man be an Independent, Presbyterian, or Anabaptist, if he can pray or preach he is a fanatic with them. Our prisons are full of such, our churches empty. Those that run hither to hear teachers worse than themselves do by their behaviour show | they think /42/ themselves rather in playhouses. Saul chose out the valiantest of Israel to his service, showing them favour. Probably he took the wisest also. But how many amongst us have fallen for no other crimes than wisdom, valour, and fidelity to God and their country? Ah noble Vane, how ample a testimony has thou born to his truth, thy condemnation was thy glory, thy death gave thee a famous victory and a never perishing crown.

[123] Deut. 17:15–18.   [124] Margins of MS: '20'.

49

As for David's gentleness in not killing Saul when in his power; it, being a negative thing, does only show I am not always obliged to kill a king when in my power; *and he would not suffer Abishai to kill him, saying he would not kill the Lord's anointed*.[125] There is nothing strange in this. His generous spirit was inwardly moved to see a king great in valour, famous for victories, who had reigned in much glory, brought by the hand of God to lie at his feet whom he persecuted. Who on the like occasion would not find the same emotion? It is also certain he was the Lord's anointed. And the prophet knew the time God had appointed for his end was not yet come, and that his was not the hand by which he should fall. But what is all this to us? David, knowing the counsels of God in the matter, left Saul, the anointed of God, to the fate prepared for him. Therefore, I must not kill a wicked king who vainly and falsely pretends to the title of God's anointed, being only man's creature set up for his lusts and anointed by his order. And as for the Amalakite, it is no wonder David, a strict executor of God's commands, slew one of that race God had appointed for destruction, especially when he, being a private man and an enemy, confessed he had killed the king of Israel, Saul's first notorious guilt having been in sparing them. Is anything more vain than arguments drawn from such false hypotheses?

PHILALETHES: do you then deny that kings are God's anointed vicegerents?

EUNOMIUS: I must deny it till they give testimony that they are so by doing his work: or that God himself declares that the kings of England, France, and Spain, for example, are his anointed.

PHILALETHES: how then understand you that text: touch not mine anointed and do my prophets no harm?[126]

EUNOMIUS: I look on it as a text more abused than any in the whole Bible unless that *hoc est corpus meum*.[127]

PHILALETHES: what do you mean by this?

EUNOMIUS: that the words being capable of various interpretations, those who have most endeavoured to deceive and oppress mankind have sought impunity by applying them to themselves. Under this

[125] I Sam. 26:7–12.   [126] I Chron. 16:22, Ps. 105:15.
[127] 'This is my body', are the words spoken by Christ in I Cor. 10:16.

the Roman priests have arrived to the height of their greatness. *Nolite tangere Christos meos*[128] was applied unto them | and so universally */43/* received for truth that, whatever notable villainies were to be done, the execution of them was committed unto such as were priests; or those that undertook them made themselves priests, *so* that, though taken in the act, the civil magistrate could not punish them. They undertook to execute the conspiracy of the Pazzi[129] at Florence against Lorenzo and Giuliano de Medici, the place for the execution was the church, the contriver of it a bishop, the time while mass was said, the signal the elevation of the sacrament, and the person who was to stab Lorenzo that moment was a priest. Giuliano was slain, Lorenzo escaped, the conspirator pretended impunity by virtue of the sacred orders, but the bishop was hanged and the priest used something worse. Few are found in the kingdom of Naples who will commit murders unless they have the old text *nolite tangere Christos meos* for their security. That country was hereby rendered Eden of sacred thieves and murderers. Masaniello[130] cut off four score of their heads, professing he had not touched one of the Lord's anointed. The wisest governors since then have followed his example herein that not many of them escape by virtue of their character. Not long since, five of them, being apprehended for a murder, the nuncio and other ecclesiastics, spoke loud of their immunities; the dispute was deferred till the delinquents came to town, and when they appeared at the gates every one of them was cut in five pieces, the head and four quarters. The like is often done at Milan. In Piedmont a friar was apprehended for conspiring against the state. The nuncio and the rest, according to their manner, spoke aloud of the Lord's anointed and the dispute was not ended till next morning[131] the friar was seen hanging on a gallow by one foot, naked and strangled. This is the manner that wise people have found to treat those *Christos Domini*.[132] Charles V, emperor, taking a bishop in fight, cut off his head and sent his arms to the pope, who complained that ecclesiastical immunities

[128]'Touch not mine anointed servants, do my prophets no harm.' I Chron. 16:22, Ps. 105:15.
[129]In 1478 the Pazzi family, rivals of the Medici, plotted to have Lorenzo and Giuliano de Medici, who then ruled Florence, assassinated in the cathedral at Easter mass. Giuliano was killed, Lorenzo was wounded.
[130]Tomaso Aniello or Masaniello (1620–47); Neapolitan fisherman who led a popular insurrection in Naples in 1647 against Spanish rule and oppression by the nobles.
[131]MS: 'that'.   [132]'the Lord's Christians'.

were infringed, *whereupon he modestly answered*,[133] *vide an haec sit tunica filii sui*.[134] An Italian gentleman of great worth and governor of a considerable province, having taken two priests from the altar, as Solomon did Joab, where they were fled for refuge, having committed a murder, hanged them at the churchdoor. The ecclesiastics threatened[135] him with excommunication; he answered: fathers do what you please, but you shall never make me believe that I can offer up to God a more grateful sacrifice than the blood of villains and murderers, what character soever they bear or unto what place soever /44/ they retire for refuge. |

PHILALETHES: but these men have no just title to the privilege of God's anointed and so are nothing to our purpose.

EUNOMIUS: if these priests are not God's anointed, it is because they are not true priests, having nothing but the exterior unction, which is invalid. If they had the true spiritual unction they would be as sacred as any upon earth. The like may be said of princes. Though any of them were the anointed of God by their institution, when they fell into impurity they had no more privilege due to their character than Judas, after he had betrayed Christ, could pretend to the privilege of an apostle. Let him be accursed and his bishoprics let another take. But I absolutely deny our kings to be at all the Lord's anointed, not finding that they have any other pretensions to it than the outward daubing of their bodies with oil, which is no more than an invention of the devil to gain that reverence to his servants and so to himself, that is due to the true Christ only and his followers. This title is so far from belonging unto kings that *in* psalm 2 it is said: the kings of the earth and the rulers set themselves together against God and his anointed;[136] which shows that kings were not the anointed but enemies to them, as they have continued ever since. If the outward ceremonies were sufficient, the popish priests and others that have it would also have a right to all the privileges belonging unto it, which, being ridiculously and profanely usurped by them, is despised by all that have understanding, and ought not to be less despised in kings who have no better title to it.

---

[133] MS: 'with this modest answer'.
[134] 'see whether this is the habit of a son of yours'.
[135] Margins of MS: 'F.20'.
[136] Ps. 2:2.

Cranmer,[137] archbishop of Canterbury, is thought to have been author of that invention to make the king head of the church. He brought Henry VIII to see his interest in having it first declared that the clergy of England was independent of any other, having in itself all ecclesiastical power; secondly, that the archbishop could grant all indulgences, dispensations, and the like, which usually were sought from Rome; and lastly, that the king was head of the church. And the Parliament enacted it by three statutes, made, as I remember, in the years 1527, 1528, and 1529.[138] And this holy king in few words gave a good character of himself, confessing that in his whole life he had never pardoned woman in his lust, nor man in his rage. This is he whom we were first obliged to acknowledge supreme in church as well as state. This is the idol of their own making that they have set up. And the succeeding | age, which seems to delight in nothing but /45/ monsters, gives such adoration to the civil head set upon a spiritual body that he is looked on as a fanatic and appointed for destruction, who, owning no head but Christ, refuses to worship the impure idol they have set up.

But desiring you to pardon this little deviation, method does require we should now prosecute and finish the point concerning the inviolability of their persons and their being accountable to none, which implies absolute power. To prove the point of inviolability great use is made of the respect David showed unto Saul. I take *what*[139] I have already said to be sufficient to show this proves nothing at all to our purpose. But for your perfect satisfaction we may sift the matter a little better. But first I desire to know whether the king's person and his authority are divisible or not.

PHILALETHES: I think them altogether indivisible as is declared in the act concerning corporations,[140] that whoever opposes the king's

---

[137]Cranmer, Thomas (1489–1556); was made archbishop of Canterbury by Henry VIII in 1533 during the king's conflict with the papacy, and supported his rejection of the pope's authority in the act of supremacy. This act established the king as supreme head of the church in England and passed through Parliament in 1534.

[138]The supremacy of the king over all things ecclesiastical was established by more than three acts, all of which passed Parliament in 1534.

[139]MS: 'that'.

[140]The Corporation Act passed Parliament in 1661 and was intended to exclude Presbyterians, Roman Catholics, and other dissenters from membership of municipal corporations. All office-holders in boroughs were to renounce the Covenant, swear oaths of allegiance, non-resistance, and supremacy, and receive the sacrament of the Church of England.

authority opposes his person. And that to hold the contrary is a pernicious and wicked tenet.

EUNOMIUS: if this be true David did war against the king's person, *it* being most evident he did it without and against his authority and persisted in it.

PHILALETHES: it appears David fled from Saul but not that he made war against him; you hear of no fight he made.

EUNOMIUS: he made such a war as he had power to make, for first he had six hundred men, which were a great hindrance if he intended only to fly.

Secondly, all those were Saul's subjects whom he withdrew from their obedience to him, though God's anointed, and that not for a cause of public concernment but his own private preservation.

Thirdly, he increased his forces what he could, receiving all that were oppressed with debt and the like, obstructing thereby the course of the law in utter contempt of the royal authority.

Fourthly, he maintained these men by exacting from Saul's subjects necessary provisions, and that so peremptorily and violently that he swore to destroy Nabal and his family for having denied him that which he was not at all obliged to give.

Lastly, he joined himself with the Philistines, the irreconcilable *enemies*[141] of the Israelites, and had been in the Philistines' army against Saul and the armies of Israel, but yet the lords of the Philistines would not trust him. And we find not that God or man ever blamed him for these actions, unless Nabal only, who, standing up [46] stiff for the royal authority, reproved him for rising up against his | master. But Nabal was his name, and folly was with him and has continued ever since with all that like him pay such reverence to the name of king, however swerving from all just and right.

PHILALETHES: but what if the other opinion should be true and one may distinguish between the king's person and his authority, so as to oppose the one and not the other?

EUNOMIUS: I think that it is the truth, but it will not help in this business. The authority which renders the person worthy of respect is of more excellency than the person; that is that king that never dies

---

[141] MS: 'enemy'.

or does wrong, whereas the person dies and commits often the most horrid injuries and impieties that are to be imagined.

PHILALETHES: but, perhaps, David being anointed king, Saul was so no more and therefore might lawfully be opposed.

EUNOMIUS: then it was not a private man that feared to stretch out his hand against the king, but a king that spared a private man. And so as to our purpose it does not much import whether Saul continued king or not.

PHILALETHES:[142] but if you allow not that kings are the anointed of God, whom think you to be the anointed that are not to be touched?

EUNOMIUS: the text explains itself: touch not mine anointed and do my prophets no harm. The same thing is more strongly inculcated under two names: anointed and prophets *are* the same persons. So it is said: the Lord of Hosts[143] has said; the God of Jacob has declared it. The same God is meant in both. So: the fool will not consider; the unwise will not understand it. Fool and unwise are the same person, so anointed and prophet. No precept *was* more necessary to that stiffnecked people who would have begun with slaying Moses, the type of Christ, and did all along slay and stone the prophets and crucify Christ himself, the antetype of Moses, and of many other prophets, David, etcetera; thereby filling up the measure of their guilt.

Let us now if you please pass from the example of David and examine in general whether the persons of kings are inviolable or not. God has several times commanded kings to be slain; therefore, to slay them is not simply evil. God in some cases has approved the slaying of kings; therefore, in some cases to slay kings is not evil. And that which is approved to be good and commanded to be done at one time, is an example to be followed in like cases at another time.

PHILALETHES: I think God has commanded sometimes things simply evil, as when Moses from God commanded the people everyone to slay his brother, and Saul by Samuel to slay Amalek, even to the sucking children. Such things are | justified only by God's immediate /47/ command, who has absolute power of doing with his own creatures what he pleases, but on no occasion are to be imitated by man.

---

[142] Margins of MS: 'P.22'.
[143] Divine title of might and power most commonly found in apocalyptic texts.

EUNOMIUS: brother in Israel was any Israelite, not only son of the same father or mother, or if so only such for idolatry that undoubtedly deserves death were to stone their nearest relations at the magistrates command. And *in* psalm 137 it is said of Babylon: happy shall he be that dashes thy little ones against the stones.[144] It is thought fit children should inherit the rewards of their father's vice or virtue. It cannot then be unreasonable they should bear the penalty of their crimes. So for the major proposition.

Now, for making good the minor that God has commanded kings to be slain; the examples of Moses and Joshua show that they reputed so little those whom you call God's anointed that in destroying 31 kings they do better deserve the name of regicides than any man that ever lived in the world. Now, if their examples reach our case I need go no further for I presume we can find no persons *more deserving our imitation*.

PHILALETHES: I find not that this concerns our case, because Moses and Joshua were not subjects but enemies to those kings and ministers of God. *They* executed justice and vengeance on those wicked nations anointed to be destroyed.

EUNOMIUS: if kings are to be looked upon as God's anointed only by their own subjects, not *by* strangers, they will lose much of the veneration divines endeavour to gain for them.

Secondly, then kings' persons are in some cases violable.

Thirdly, if these were violable because wicked idolaters and tyrants, others guilty of the same or like sins are liable to the same or like punishments.

Fourthly, if Moses and Joshua were ministers of God's vengeance on wicked kings in that age, the like may be done by other saints, and will be done as is prophesied *in* psalm 149.[145] They that may bind kings in chains may also lay the sword to their throat. Ehud, in the courtier's phrase, rebelled against Eglon, king of Moab, and slew him.[146] But the Scripture, differing *somewhat*[147] from their style, says that when the Israelites cried unto the Lord, he raised them up this deliverer. So Barak fought against Jabin. Now Eglon and Jabin held their crowns by right of conquest over Israel which is accounted the surest title for the most absolute power (Judges 5). These were

[144] Ps. 137:9. [145] Ps. 149:6–9. [146] Judg. 3:21–2.
[147] MS: 'something'.

succeeded by Gideon (Judges 8), a man of like temper. He rose up against his tyrannous masters and, thinking it a greater thing to kill a king than to be a king, slew Zebah and Zalmunna and absolutely refused to reign over his own people when they offered the crown to him and his posterity.[148] Abimelech, a young son of Gideon, understood the matter better and sought what his father rejected, a crown. He was a politician worthy | to be studied in our days. He hired vag- /48/ abonds and indigent persons that might depend wholly on his favour, so they might have the liberty of rapine. From what is said to have been done to Eglon, Jabin, Zebah, and Zalmunna, I think it will necessarily follow that if he who unjustly seizes on a crown may justly be thrown from it; he that does unjustly execute what he has justly obtained may also be justly deprived. This unjust execution is either by violating the pact made or assuming to himself a power not granted him by the pact. The first is perfidy, the other usurpation.

PHILALETHES: but happily the kings above mentioned had no lawful titles to their crowns, *and* were not such as by descent did rightly inherit their crowns.

EUNOMIUS: a right by descent will not hold good in the son of him that had no just right to the crown himself. I acknowledge only three original titles to be good:
    First, that of those that are made kings by God's immediate command, as Saul, David, etcetera.
    Secondly, when a man by a free people is freely made king.
    Thirdly, when a kingdom is acquired by victory in a just war, all depending upon the conditions on which a power is given or gained.

PHILALETHES: know you any kings who held their crowns by these titles to have been slain at God's command or dispossessed of their kingdoms?

EUNOMIUS: I will examine two noted examples which, with what has been said of Saul and David, do all belong to the kingdom of Israel and Judah, both of them established upon the firmest of all titles, that is, God's designation or command and the people's desire as to government and election as to the person.

PHILALETHES: before you come to the examples, I desire to know

[148] Judg. 8:21–3.

what ground you have for ascribing any part of the title the kings of Israel and Judah had to the election or consent of the people?

EUNOMIUS: nothing is more plain than that kings were first given Israel upon the people's desire (I Samuel 8), for they sinned in desiring them. And chapter 10: Saul, the person anointed by God, did not reign by virtue of that unction only but by the election of the people, which was performed by lots in the most democratical way imaginable, where every man was an elector and capable of being elected. God directing the lot, it fell on Saul and he was made king.[149] Nor this alone, but (chapter 11) after he had given testimony of his valour in the defeat of the Ammonites, Samuel appoints another assembly of the people in Gilgal, and Saul was there made king by them.[150] He
/49/ being dead, David, notwithstanding | his unction from God, reigned not till the tribe of Judah anointed him in Hebron (II Samuel 2),[151] and (chapter 5) he is anointed king over all Israel by the elders and the people of the other tribes.[152] This power being in some degree by God's peculiar designation under[153] certain conditions hereditary in him till forfeited by maladministration, it was to come to one of his sons. And he, as a prophet by the command of God and assistance of Nathan, a prophet also, did design*ate* and anoint Solomon as the fittest to succeed.[154] He, accompanying tyranny with its ordinary companions, loose life and idolatry, *oppressed the people very sorely and*[155] neglected the rules prescribed unto kings by Moses (Deuteronomy 17) and the law of the kingdom written in a book by Samuel, which without doubt was conformable to that of Moses. So the tribes on his death thought fit to come to a new contract with his son,[156] who, not answering their expectation, they replied: what have we to do with thee, thou son of David. We have no inheritance in thee, or we are not thine inheritance, so thy tents O Israel, look to thy own house David.[157] Not long after they set up Jeroboam, already anointed and design*at*ed king by God.[158]

This Jeroboam is one of the two examples I intend to make use of to prove that no king can be so firmly established by God's designation

---

[149] I Sam. 10:21–4.   [150] I Sam. 11:14–15.   [151] II Sam. 2:5–11.
[152] II Sam. 5:3–5.   [153] Margins of MS: 'F 23'.
[154] The death of David and the accession of Solomon are described in I Kings 1, 2.
[155] In the MS 'oppressed the people very sorely' comes after 'which without doubt was conformable to that of Moses'.
[156] I.e. Rehoboam.   [157] I Kings 12:16.   [158] I Kings 12:20.

and the people's choice but that the subjects may justly withdraw obedience from him and set up to themselves another governor or government if he recede from his duty by governing ill. Rehoboam, also the son and grandchild of two kingly prophets, was made king by God's designation, received by the people and elders, and yet *was* thrown by the commandment of God from the government of the ten tribes because he would not take off the grievances and correct the exorbitancies committed by his father, who, falling from the wisdom God had given him to the folly of being governed by women, from the glorious condition of a prophet to the infamous baseness of an idolater. That his actions might appear all of a piece from a righteous lawful king he became a tyrant, oppressing his subjects with impositions and taxes, glorying more in riches than in justice and sought the life of Jeroboam whom he knew was anointed and design*at*ed by God to punish his impiety and folly, as Saul for the same reasons sought to slay David.[159]

All tyrants have the same ends and proceed almost ever in the same way for the effecting of them. Jeroboam fleas to Egypt till Solomon be dead, finding no strength to resist the king's power.[160] But | /50/ Solomon being dead and his weak son succeeding, before his establishment by the people, he is ready to attend the issue, being returned speedily from Egypt. On Rehoboam's answer the ten tribes reply: what have we to do with thee, son of David? etcetera. Somewhat like that of the speaker of the House of Commons to Edward II on reading the Act of Parliament for his deposing as unworthy of the crown: *Edward Plantagenet I defy thee*, said he, that is, thou art but a private man, I am not inferior to thee.[161] Rehoboam sends Adoram to levy tribute on the people; they stone him; he raises a great power to reduce them by force to his obedience.[162] A prophet from God tells him he shall not fight against his brethren, for that which is done is of his hand.[163] Our divines on this occasion would have called the Israelites rebels; *they would have* preached nothing but fire and sword against them, but God justifies them, *acting against* the house of David, having forfeited the crown by tyranny and its companion idolatry. As to the threatenings to the house of Jeroboam also

[159] Reign of Rehoboam in Judah is recorded in I Kings 14:21–31 and II Chron. 10–13.
[160] I Kings 11:40.
[161] In 1327 William Trussell, spokesman of Parliament, told Edward II that he had been deposed.
[162] I Kings 12:18–21.   [163] I Kings 12:22–4.

for their idolatry and tyranny though Baasha fulfilled the prophesies against them in slaying Nadab[164] etcetera. And though Zimri again did the like in extirpating all the house of Baasha,[165] and Omri in killing Zimri,[166] yet because everyone may have a liberty of doubting whether these acts were good or not because we find no particular command for them, I will pass from them to the example of Jehu (II Kings 10), who, receiving the unction from the prophet and a command to destroy the house of Ahab,[167] slew Jehoram, the fourth king of it, seventy of his brethren, and all the rest of the house; caused his mother to be thrown out of a window and left her to be eaten by dogs. Neither spared *he*[168] Ozias nor his forty-two brethren, who were friends to the house of Ahab, but slew all, showing himself to be the fiercest of all the regicides that are recorded in story.

PHILALETHES: but the words of the Scripture: had Zimri peace who slew his master? Show that though the house of Ahab deserved to be destroyed, he[169] sinned in doing it, as many others have done in the accomplishment of prophecies.

EUNOMIUS: I grant it is not enough an act to be good unless I have a just cause to do it. Baasha, Zimri, and Omri for *all*[170] I know wanted this call. But Jehu had the command of God by the prophets[171] to justify his attempt and the approbation of another prophet /51/ for the | execution, and God calls *vengeance*[172] that zeal which you call fury and rewarded it with the continuance of the crown in his race for generations, notwithstanding the idolatry into which he also fell.[173] The tenderness any man requires in such cases is such disobedience to the commands of God as in Scripture is compared to witchcraft. And he that esteems his own opinion or inclination beyond God's command, deserves the penalties threatened against those that do the work of the Lord negligently, which was experienced in the destruction of Saul and his house for sparing the Amalakites. Jehu did far better: what peace while the whoredoms and witchcrafts of thy mother do remain.[174] Nor are the words cited

---

[164] I Kings 15:27–8.   [165] I Kings 16:11.
[166] Zimri was not killed by Omri, but by the fire he himself had set in the royal palace when he saw that Omri had taken Tirzah, the city he had reigned over for seven days. I Kings 16:15–20.
[167] II Kings 9:6–11, 10:7–14.   [168] MS: 'his'.   [169] I.e. Jehu.
[170] MS: 'ought'.   [171] II Kings 9:6–11.   [172] See II Kings 9:7.
[173] II Kings 10:30–1.
[174] II Kings 9:22. This Jehu replied, when Jehoram asked him, 'is it peace, Jehu?'.

by you the words of God, but the words of a whore and a witch,[175] who by her wickedness had brought those judgements upon Ahab's house.

Another example I find amongst the kings of Judah; Joash is slain by his servants;[176] his son Amaziah to revenge his death slays those servants (II Kings 14).[177] Perhaps he followed his own inclination rather than justice, but a conspiracy was made against Amaziah, which he fearing fled to Lachish and they sent after him and slew him.[178] And though they set up his son Azariah, no man was punished that had been an actor in his death. The reason *for* such various proceedings about the death of these two kings may appear to be that Joash was a good king and governed well all the time of Jehoiada, but afterwards ungratefully slew his son Zechariah for reproving his idolatry and tyranny, for which he deserved death. But his servants, having more regard to private revenge for the death of Zechariah than justice, of their own authority slew him,[179] which gave his son occasion to slay them. But in the death of Amaziah all circumstances were different. He was a good king for a while too, but afterwards turned from the Lord, reigned foolishly, made a war against Jehoash, king of Israel, without any occasion, brought great desolation thereby upon his kingdom, and gave just cause to the people by public counsels to slay him.[180]

PHILALETHES: what use can you make of these three examples Jeroboam, Jehu, and Amaziah?

EUNOMIUS: I think I prove all that I did assert, showing that those kings who enjoyed crowns upon the best and strongest titles that can be imagined were for their crimes by God's command deprived of their kingdoms, and they | and all their posterity destroyed. And [52] those actions performed on his command by men inspired by him are to be perpetual examples unto us. The blood of an idolatrous tyrant was then a grateful sacrifice to God, it will therefore be so forever.

PHILALETHES: in saying what God has done for one age ought to be an example for all that succeed, I think you destroy all that from the beginning you have asserted. For if that be true, God having once

[175] I.e. Jezebel.   [176] II Kings 12:20–1.
[177] Joash: II Kings 12:20–1; Amaziah: II Kings 14:5–6.
[178] II Kings 14:19–20.   [179] II Chron. 24:22–6.   [180] II Kings 14:8–21.

established kings over his people and given them an absolute power, all other nations ought to have the like. And wherever there are kings they ought to be absolute and without all restraint of power from man. And it is most absurd to say that any under such a power should call him to an account, dispose or kill him for ill-administration, till by immediate command from God, as some of those in Israel and India were used.

EUNOMIUS: I reckon not that all God's commands to the Jews are binding or examples we ought to follow, as neither the judicial laws that were appropriated to that people nor the ceremonial law that contained types of what now is accomplished, and so they *are* abrogated. But those commands which concern the duty of man to man or man to God are perpetual. By the law we know murder, adultery, and theft are sins. As for your other scruples of God giving them kings as an example to us to set up kings, it is quite contrary. For God gave them not kings till they sinned in asking them, and we ought not to imitate them in their sin that we be not made like them in their punishment, who, after they had groaned long under a race of idolatrous tyrants, were at last wholly captivated by foreigners *so* that to this day we know not what is become of the ten tribes. And the other two were brought to that misery that their very enemies did pity them.

As to your last point of the absoluteness of those kings, I reckon it a plain mistake. In Deuteronomy (chapter 17) the king is described in address as far from absoluteness as can be imagined. No kings resemble him there described more than those of Sparta, who had the least power of any we know of in the world: their heart was not to be exalted above their brethren, they were not to incline to right hand nor to the left from the ways of God, *so* that he and his sons /53/ may prolong their days in Israel.[181] Which | implies a threatening of the contrary if they receded from this rule prescribed to them, as we find it verified in the persons and posterities of all the prevaricating kings.

The next rule we meet with in Scripture for kings to observe is that given by Samuel (I Sam. 10), who spoke to the people the law of the kingdom, *wrote it*[182] in a book, and laid it up before the Lord.[183]

Now if this was suitable to the words of Moses, the power thereby

---

[181] Deut. 17:16–20.   [182] MS: 'writ'.   [183] I Sam. 10:25.

given to kings was far from being absolute. If that book of Samuel gave him absolute power, either Moses or Samuel were not sent of God to speak those words about the king's power and demeanour. The certain evidence of Samuel walking in the steps of Moses gives us invincible reason to believe they cannot in this important point disagree, the exorbitance of the kings of Israel and Judah notwithstanding. All such laws and cautions seems to show to me that kings are such wild beasts as will break all chains that can be put upon them. The only means, therefore, of enjoying safety and preserving liberty is by destroying them, or having none at all.

But to go a little further in the above-mentioned case of Israel's kings, I shall show that the elders and people when they pleased exercised their due power above that of kings (I Samuel 14). Saul, having made a rash vow to kill him that should taste any meat till evening, renewed his oath, when he knew his son Jonathan had ignorantly offended, swearing he should die. But the people said: as the Lord lives he shall not die; and rescued him.[184] And David esteemed his readmission to the crown after the people had made Absolon king to be a new beginning of his reign. The like may be said of Solomon, Rehoboam, Amaziah, and the rest. And no man can say he has absolute power who is not king till elected by the people, and is no longer king when the same disapprove him. Ahab, that could not take a little vineyard from Naboth nor have it for his money, though he passionately desired it, lay sick on his bed for it and would not eat. This argues him to be far from an absolute power. The other proceedings about it are like those common in courts. The witch and the whore[185] is jealous that the royal power should be restrained, reproaching him for not using it with the rigour belonging to a king, according to the custom of our | days. /54/ There were officers and judges to be found like their masters that knew how to murder an innocent man under pretence of justice. Men of Belial, false witnesses were never wanting for such purposes. The next example is that of Zedekiah (Jeremiah 38), who, when the princes would slay Jeremiah for prophesying against the city, desired he might be put to death. The king answered: he is in your hands, the king is not he that can do any thing against you.[186] And in the same chapter we find, when he desired to preserve the prophet from the princes, he could not do it by his authority but by inventing other pretences.[187]

[184] I Sam. 14:24; 39–46.   [185] I.e. Jezebel.   [186] Jer. 38:15–17.
[187] Jer. 38:23–8.

PHILALETHES: how then had Israel such a king as the nations round about them?

EUNOMIUS:[188] Samuel told them what kind of kings they were, but God in mercy gave them a king of his institution, as an example rather to the other nations, – such a king as Moses had described, and Samuel in a peculiar book of the kingdom –, but warned them this king would so degenerate and break all laws as to render himself like the kings of other nations, as they found for a punishment of their folly. Yet the king's power amongst the Philistines appears not to have been such but that, though he would admit David in the battle against Saul and Israel, the lords of the Philistines refused and admitted him not, and the seven princes in Persia had a part of the government.

As for trials at law, those are instituted for protection of the innocent against the powerful. But in the case of Jehu the delinquents were all of the royal house, the chief of them *was* a tyrant, the son of one who had murdered the prophets and others without law, so deserved not the benefit of the law. Every man was a soldier against him.

And if you look on Israel's kings as examples for hereditary crowns, why admit you female heirs, of which no example is to be found amongst them? While you thus regard the good of a family, not of the nation, the crown may descend to a child, a girl, a fool, or anything for its weakness despicable and for its wickedness detestable, so *that* it be nearest of blood.

Secondly, by this means the government of a free and gallant nation falls into the hand of a stranger or enemy, of which we have in England too woeful experience. The Scottish line,[189] having come in /55/ only | by that way, whose reign beginning with a furious plague, has ever since continued with more furious tragedies. To avoid this evil France has rendered females absolutely incapable of succession. Sweden has been more indulgent to that sex, admitting them as heirs of the crown if they either marry within the country or remain unmarried, perpetually excluding them and their heirs if they marry out of the country. By this means the late king Charles Gustavus had

---

[188] Margins of MS: 'Page 25'.
[189] James VI, a member of the Scottish house of Stuart, ruled over Scotland alone (1566–1603) and then succeeded Elizabeth I to the throne of England as James I (1603–25).

no title to the crown;[190] his sister but by the election of the three estates of the kingdom,[191] declaring in this act by which they elected him that his brother, prince Adolphus, could have no pretence to succeed him.[192] But we, by neglecting these prudent cautions, are fallen from the flourishing state wherein we formerly lived to be one of the most miserable nations at home and one of the most despicable abroad, that is, in all Europe. As monarchy is in itself an irrational, evil government, unless over those who are naturally beasts and slaves, the worst of monarchies is that which is hereditary. The worst of hereditary monarchies is that which descends unto women. And the worst of all those monarchies that are inherited by women is that which is absolute. By this you may see that we, who live under a monarchy that is hereditary, even to women, and absolute, are brought into such a condition as can never possibly fall lower than it is.

[190] Charles X Gustav (1622–60) owed his kingship (1654–60) to his niece Christina (1626–89), queen of Sweden (1632–54), who, at the diet of 1650, induced the nobles and the lower estates to recognize him unconditionally as heir to the Swedish crown.

[191] Charles X's sister, also called Christina, was married to Frederick of Baden-Durlach and could thus not succeed to the throne unless the estates approved of it.

[192] When Charles XI succeeded to the throne in 1660 at the age of four and there was thus need of a regent, the nobles in the 'Addition to the Form of Government' excluded the dead king's brother, Adolf Johan, from the regency and other great offices of state, and entrusted the government to Hedvig Eleonora, the queen mother.

Fifth Dialogue

Fourth Court Maxim: Monarchy is not secure unless the nobility be suppressed, effeminated, and corrupted

PHILALETHES: one of our principal maxims is to bring the nobility very low, never thinking monarchy well secured till they be suppressed, effeminated, and corrupted.

EUNOMIUS: I am much amazed to hear this, for we that live farther from court do believe that monarchy and nobility so strictly hang together that one does not well subsist without the other. And nothing is more unreasonable than that monarchy should endeavour to weaken that order which does principally support *its*[193] greatness.

PHILALETHES: though you seem a good examiner of things, I see you
[56] sometimes take up opinions upon trust | as well as others. You hear us speak much of men of honour and quality, and you believe all those to be noble men that have great titles and blue ribands about their necks. These are for the most part creatures of the court, men of low birth and lower fortunes.

EUNOMIUS: what use can you make of such?

PHILALETHES: very much, for by raising them to the highest places who can pretend to no other merit than extreme obsequiousness to his majesty and absolute devotion to his interest, we show to the

[193]MS: 'their'.

66

ancient nobility and others what course they must take if they will arrive at preferment.

Secondly, by setting them in the highest places we do so far abate the pride and power of the ancient nobility, that we bring them to mix their own blood by marriages with them, and to a mean dependence on those men whom they would *have* scorned to admit to their tables or to offices in their houses before the sun of the court had shone upon them.

EUNOMIUS: why desire you to bring the ancient nobility to such a despicable condition if you intend to keep up monarchy, to which it is thought very useful? And if not, why do you raise men of ordinary spirits and low birth to such dignities as[194] men of noble families are fitter for?

PHILALETHES: a powerful, gallant nobility was very useful in those old-fashioned monarchies which were in most parts of Europe till within these last hundred years. Our boisterous fighting kings of the Plantagenet[195] race were content with a limited power at home; they endeavoured to increase the power of the nation by foreign conquests. For such designs it was necessary to have a nobility great in power and credit, full of virtue and gallantry, and exercised in arms that the people might follow them. The kings themselves were usually first in battles and princes of the blood were educated to valour and industry. This inflamed the nobility to follow the kings and princes of the blood cheerfully through all labours and dangers, seeking nothing more than doing good to their country. But these princes understood not the refined policy of the latter age. They exposed themselves to infinite troubles and dangers for a little glory. They passed more nights in the camp than in their palaces. Their soldiers were crushed with the weight of their | arms. And more princes of /57/ their blood and of the nobility that followed them died by enemies' swords than in their own houses. If any of them did commit any irregularities at home, they were in danger to be questioned, as Edward II and Richard II. Or if any of their servants did anything contrary to law, either to serve them or make their own fortunes, they were not able to protect them from justice, as appears by the Spencers, Tresilian, and others. And if any extraordinary burden

[194] Margins of MS: 'Page 26'.
[195] The house of Plantagenet reigned over England from 1154 until 1399.

was laid upon the people, as monopolies or the like, the nobility were the first that exclaimed, talked of laws, privileges, and such unpleasing words. If grievances were not redressed they were presently in arms, and the people, looking on them as protectors, followed them in all their enterprises.

EUNOMIUS: if these were impolitic princes what are yours?

PHILALETHES: we comprehend all in one. Our king must be absolute. All our other politics are either to make him so, or secure him when he is so. Our king minds not foreign designs unless as relating to his establishment in his absolute authority and power at home. An ancient, powerful, virtuous, warlike nobility is of all things most destructive to this. We know therefore how to suppress such and raise others to places above them whose want of reputation we know how to supply with riches and power. We need not strike the highest ears of corn,[196] we can make others spring out of dung so, as soon to overtop them. Nothing makes the king's power to be so adored as the evidence that in a moment he can raise a favourite from the lowest condition to far above what ancient nobles have arrived unto, or what their ancestors in many ages have purchased by their services or blood. All desire to advance their persons and fortunes. That desire obliges them to take the way conducing thereunto. Our court way to it is easy and pleasant, the way of rising by war is with difficulty and danger. It is true there is something of baseness and meanness in submitting their honour and conscience to their interest, but they care not for that. Hence we draw considerable advantages, as:

First, it is honourable for one of us to see the chief of the nobility depending upon and sueing to us.

Secondly, the base ways they must take if they will also gain /58/ favour at court renders their spirits vile and then they are ours.|

Thirdly, by such shameful practices, in seeking to such persons and for such ends, they lose their reputation. And so, if they should grow discontented, they could do nothing to our prejudice. Nobody will follow them, if disappointed of their court end, in such a private

---

[196] Probably an allusion to the story 'that Periander, when a herald (from Thrasybulus) was sent to ask counsel of him, said nothing, but only to cut off the tallest ears of corn till he had brought the field to a level. The herald did not know the meaning of the action, but came and reported what he had seen to Thrasybulus, who understood that he was to cut off all the principal men in the state.' Aristotle, *Politics*, bk III, 1284a.

and corrupt interest. We give hopes to many of them, but satisfy few in their desires. But by hopes we keep the court full of persons of quality, and everyone endeavours to serve the king to the utmost that he may be advanced, and makes large presents to those ministers who may help them in their pretensions.

Another principal advantage of drawing many of the nobility and gentry to court is that we thereby oblige them to spend their estates, and so come to an absolute dependence on the king as much as any new mean man that comes to court. And those are looked upon as the gallantest men who spend most in house keeping, clothes, liveries, coaches, and profuse gaming. We have also certain ladies who well understand the arts of draining purses; so that I never knew any that fell into their nets, escape ruin, and when ruined, he is ours. If any be so stiff as to continue obstinately in the country, notwithstanding of our invitations of him to court, we find persons fit to vex and oppress them, corrupt his servants, raise factions in his family, call him a fanatic if sober, and make that he has no quietness nor safety in his own house. Few will endure this, but either come to court or show they were slandered when called fanatics, cast themselves into extreme lewdness and debauchery to wipe off the reproach. And the roundheads[197] will never trust those that take either of these ways to clear themselves.

EUNOMIUS: but why may not the ancient nobility be useful to the same end as well as these new upstarts, many of them not being much troubled with such scrupulous thoughts about laws and privileges as their ancestors[198] in the Plantagenet's time may seem to have had?

PHILALETHES: I confess they are pliable enough, but we have rendered them so by these ways. When they had spirits suitable to their birth and their reputations and estates were entire, it had been impossible to bring them to that suppleness which is now very general amongst them. And these means so well succeeding, we shall continue them till our design be brought to such perfection that no man shall have any title to nobility but by the | king's gift. /59/

To sum up all, these new courtiers by their insolence and violence break the spirits of the ancient nobility, trample upon them, and by

---

[197] Roundheads, nickname of the parliamentary party during the English civil war.
[198] Margins of MS: 'page 27'.

their craft enslave and ruin them. By their example they are corrupted in manners and effeminated. And whereas the ancient nobility did ever endeavour to preserve the people's liberties and make
them happy, these new ones endeavour as much to impoverish,
weaken, oppress, and destroy them.

EUNOMIUS: are these services to the king?

PHILALETHES: yes, the highest that can be rendered to him, as shall
be evidenced in the ensuing discourse.

Sixth Dialogue

[199] *Fifth Court Maxim: The happiness of people is as hurtful to kings as the greatness and virtue of the nobility*

PHILALETHES: the nobility, while in reputation and power, have been ready to head the people for redress of grievances; and, being thus removed and abated in their credit,[200] is a great service to the king. Yet, as long as the people continue strong, numerous, and rich, the king can never be happy.

EUNOMIUS: I should rather have thought the riches and happiness of the people conducible to the security of the governors. If rich, they will be content and quiet for fear of confiscations. But if poor and that by means of the governors, they will soon grow to furious resolutions, having little to lose.

PHILALETHES: others have been of your opinion, but I think the contrary truer, for in all times seditions have begun in the richest and most populous cities. All the tumults in the Low Countries began in Antwerp, Ghent, Brussels, and other principal cities.[201] The French league began in Paris.[202] And those troubles which in this age distracted France were all hatched at Paris, Bordeaux, or

---

[199] Editorial hand: 'turn to fol. 4'.
[200] MS: 'he'.
[201] I.e. the Dutch revolt (1568–1648).
[202] From 1562 till 1598, a series of civil wars between Catholics and Huguenots disrupted France.

Rouen.[203] Those of Naples grew within its walls.[204] And all ours grew from the greatness and strength of London.[205] Generally all people grow proud when numerous and rich; they think themselves masters of all. The least injury puts them into a fury. But if poor, weak, miserable, and few they will be humble and obedient. The present sense of their wants hinders them from applying their thoughts beyond anything but getting of bread, and their weakness

/60/ keeps them | quiet, abasing their spirit. Despair of success keeps them from attempting anything. Israel, when sorely oppressed by Pharaoh, *was*[206] obedient to him; they had no time to make seditious meetings. But when rich and at ease they rebelled even against God. The people at best is but an ass fit for burdens, and they use them as they deserve who make them bear the heaviest. The unruly beast must be flattered a little at first, till saddled and bridled, and then you may make them carry what you please.

EUNOMIUS: are these rules followed in other places?

PHILALETHES: most certainly, there is nothing we learned more perfectly when abroad than that the number, strength, and riches of the people of England must be abated, and nothing has been more industriously sought by us.

EUNOMIUS: what examples have you for those practices?

PHILALETHES: as many as I know principalities where the prince intends to be absolute master. The French were brought to endure servitude only by their misery. Though they have abundance of all things required to make a people happy, hardly any live more miserably in Europe. So in Naples the people, notwithstanding many pressures being grown in this age very numerous and rich, those dangerous tumults arose which brought it near to destruction. These being appeased *and* the heads of the ringleaders being taken off, wise men saw the peace yet ill-secured till the number of the people *was*[207]

---

[203] Between 1648 and 1653, a series of civil wars known as the Fronde was rampant in France. Precipitated by the discontent about the imposition of new taxes, the Fronde originated in the judicial oligarchy of the Parlement of Paris, spread upwards to the upper nobility and soon found popular support in the provinces. It attempted to put a constitutional limit on the monarchy by establishing the power of 'parlement' to discuss and modify royal decrees.

[204] The Neapolitans revolted against Spanish rule in 1647.

[205] I.e. the English civil war (1642–8).　　　[206] MS: 'were'.　　　[207] MS: 'were'.

soundly lessened. A person of eminent quality (Castrillio) was heard to say: nothing would tame that people but a plague. And that terrible one which did take out of the city 500,000 persons, happening a short time after this speech, about 1655, gave occasion to many to believe that some infected soldiers were purposely brought out of Sardinia to diffuse it in that city. And since that time no signs of commotion have been *heard*, but all *were* obedient to the king of Spain. The policy used by other princes in Italy is yet a greater evidence of this truth, particularly the house of Medici, whose wisdom is famous over all Europe and deserves to be followed. Machiavelli says that in his time Florence and the valley of *the* Arno were able to put into the field one hundred thirty-five thousand fighting men, which cannot afford now above eight or ten thousand at most.[208] Pisa had *a* long war with Florence and Genoa, was able to put good armies into the field and send better fleets to sea. That city now would be much troubled to maintain 200 foot and 60 horses. Pistoia and Arezzo were powerful cities when | commonwealths, *but are* now almost desolate. Siena /61/ when it fell into the hand of the great duke about 200 years ago had in the city and territory above six hundred and fifty thousand souls, now not 40,000. All this was wrought by the art and industry of the princes. Examples of this kind are infinite, but I allege the choicest which we most intend to imitate.

We reckon our greatest enemies *to be* at home, till brought so low that they cannot hurt. By art first we hope to diminish the power of the people, force must do the rest as to keeping them quiet. The court and principally the new-made nobility are fit for such a work; their delight in vanity and sensuality gives them a furious desire to get money for their pleasures, and they are so profuse in spending that whatever they beg or steal, they are little the fatter. The barren womb or the grave will say it is enough sooner than they. Their insatiable avarice makes them industrious in finding ways of getting money, and the more oppressive such ways are to the people, the better we like it. To effect this work of impoverishing and bringing the people low we find it to be the king's interest to destroy trade. For there is no keeping a people low while that continues which increases their number, riches, and strength.[209]

---

[208] Machiavelli, *History of Florence*, bk II, ch. 15, mentions 30,000 civilians in arms for Florence and 70,000 armed men from the valley in 1298.

[209] Editorial hand in margins: 'Chap.7, 6th Court Maxim or 't was of Chap.6 the 5th Court Maxim'.

Sir Walter Raleigh found that the commonwealth of Carthage did in few years so well recover the loss of the first Punic war with Rome (and of that which immediately followed with their own mercenaries)[210] by means of their great traffic, which alone soon enabled them to send forth far more powerful fleets and armies than those that had been defeated, so that the Romans dreaded the first motion of their arms presaging how nigh they should be brought to destruction that conquered others with ease.[211] But to leave old examples, Antwerp, Ghent, and Bruges are almost desolate by loss of trade, whilst Amsterdam by gaining it flourishes in number of men, riches, and power.[212] By increase of trade it is of a poor town grown in short time the richest and most powerful city in the world. This art is well understood by the Venetians and duke of Florence. The first, according to the custom of a well-governed commonwealth, endeavour to increase trade and people, which succeeds so well as with those helps they have been able for twenty years to war with little loss against all the power of the Ottoman empire. The other,[213] following the maxims of a politic prince, has by destroying trade ruined many he suspected, forced others to change their habitation, and so weakened the spirited commonwealth's men of Florence that he reigns securely.

[62] EUNOMIUS: what means do the court use to destroy trade? |

PHILALETHES: there is no great difficulty in it. No nation has such advantages for trade but that they require the help of those in power, who, if they do not encourage and advance it, they destroy it. If they take not care in their treaties and agreements with other nations to gain advantages for their own merchants others will gain such advantages on them as will certainly ruin them. The Hollanders in all business of war or peace with any nation do principally consider trade. The greatest advantage to their state is the increase of people that they may have the more trade, and of trade that they may have the more people. Both these they endeavour still to procure, which has

---

[210] After the first Punic war (264–241 BC) Carthage had to face a revolt of its own mercenaries, which ended in 237 BC with a victory for Carthage.

[211] Raleigh, *The history of the world*.

[212] The closing of the river Schelde in 1585 had been decisive for the growth of Amsterdam as a merchant city.

[213] I.e. Cosimo de Medici.

advanced them from one of the most contemptible nations in Europe to be formidable to the greatest princes in the world.

As for our merchants, they have little trade left and so little opportunity of exporting our native commodities. The merchant, not exporting manufacture, must fail, and then those that prepare materials for manufacture will suffer. So in a short time we shall without noise see our desired end. The courtiers and lords also are very useful in this business by a multitude of new invented monopolies learnt in their travels in France and Italy. And if they can invent something never heard of before to burden the people their ingenuity is commanded, of which chimney money[214] and many other witty inventions are sufficient testimony. The king will not grant all that is proposed presently lest it should make too great a noise, but such things as most conduce to his main designs of keeping the people low and gaining many to depend upon himself he will set up as fast as he dares. Again, no man can trade so cautiously but he will often meet with disputes in foreign countries and receive injuries that a private man cannot right himself in, but must have recourse to the king or council table. And our courtiers take care justice shall never be done *to* them unless they pay so well for it that they had better have suffered the injury. For the same end custom and excise is raised to get a great deal of money to the king and his servants, and advance the main design of ruining trade. Thus all the money in England brought into the hands of courtiers and gallants is spent by them amongst *fiddlers, players, whores, cooks*, and other instruments of idle and vicious pleasures, who of all people are most sure to us except the episcopal | clergy, and will be enriched by what we get from our enemies, the fanatics. /63/

EUNOMIUS: I should assent to a great deal of this but I find three objections against these courses:

First, the people being impoverished, the king must grow poor too, having nothing but what he has from them.

Secondly, the people thus used may grow angry and try to cast off so heavy a yoke.

Thirdly, the nation thus in short time will be so weak as to be easily conquered by a foreign power.

---

[214]The hearth tax (1662) was a direct tax of a levy imposed upon each hearth or stove in a house. It was intended as a source of permanent royal revenues.

PHILALETHES: the first objection is well considered at court. Our all depends upon it, for our principal business is to get money, and if the saving fails, we are disappointed. But after serious debates it appeared, that as the people's power, number, and riches decrease, the king's power will increase. When the people are low the king will be master of them and all they have, and so far richer than if the people enjoyed the highest prosperity and plenty. If rich and powerful, it is impossible to keep them in awe; the king must depend upon them, be at their discretion, have nothing but what they will freely give him. If he impose illegal burdens, *they will oppose him*, such as Hampden, Sir Arthur Hesilridge, etcetera, will choose, as they did (with hazard and great expense, danger, and trouble), to make a long suit against the king rather than pay each of them forty shillings ship money.[215] Such pernicious examples are to be avoided, for so the king may be opposed by one or two of his subjects, be brought to plead against them as his equals. And having law on their side if suffered to proceed, they may gain their cause to the extreme dishonour of the king and perpetual establishment of the people's liberties and privileges. And though all possible care be taken still to choose such judges as will declare whatever pleases the king to be law, the fear of man may restrain them where conscience towards God does not. For though while they think the king's power well established they will venture to condemn some as traitors for no other crimes but wisdom, valour, integrity, and love to God and their country, yet if they see the people's party grow powerful, their liberties and privileges defended, they would bethink themselves the danger the judges were in who were accused at the beginning of the Long Parliament, and so be
/64/ deterred from giving judgements contrary to law to please the king. |

Nothing is more common to find than those that fear not God, yet fear man. The noise such opposers as Hampden, etcetera might make, would gain them credit in the nation, put the people upon demanding a free parliament, and such as are enemies to the king will be sure to be chosen. And then we shall often hear those hateful words *laws, privileges, redressing of grievances, punishing delinquents, and the like*. So the king's authority will be limited and his servants

---

[215] Ship money was an ancient tax for providing ships to defend the country in time of war. Charles I revived it in 1634 in time of peace and without the consent of Parliament. His action caused great resentment and the repeated revivals of the tax aroused resistance, notably from John Hampden, who refused to pay the twenty shillings and therefore had to defend himself in court.

destroyed. If such leading persons for laws and liberties be imprisoned, the king, to allay growing distempers, will be obliged to release them. And then they have so much the more credit, and will endeavour to revenge the injury of false imprisonment. Or if, to avoid these mischiefs some such little helps be given them to hasten their passage into another world, as is usual in such cases (and were dexterously conveyed to Sir Arthur Hesilridge), they will be looked on as the people's martyrs, and everyone will burn with desire of revenging their death. But when the people are brought to be few, weak, and poor, no such dangers are to be feared, everyone's thoughts will be confined to the seeking of necessaries and by extreme labour to get a pair of *canvas breeches, wooden shoes, coarse bread* for his family, as in France and many other countries, and easily consent that all the rest of his gains may go to the king. Expressions of discontent will be vain, they will find no leaders for redress, and when they are so weak there is no hope of success. Princes are never so rich as when their subjects are poor. The opulency of the king of France proceeds principally from the people's poverty. The duke of Florence was never rich nor secure till the people were brought from vast riches to extreme poverty. Everyone will see that no advantage is to be gotten but by the king's favour. So that they that will not submit to the yoke and adore him, will seek other habitations.

To the second objection, time will secure us from that danger. Time is powerful in all human things, but most in political matters. I and time, said politic Philip II of Spain against two. He that not well observes[216] time, seldom succeeds; he that does, seldom miscarries. If the people were oppressed by violent plunderings or exorbitant impositions to destroy trade and ruin all on a sudden, such a thing might be feared. But we have more subtle and secret arts to consume the people by degrees and not | by the violence of a calen- *[65]* ture. Slow poisons are most secure and secret, such are used by refined courtiers. We know how to take away dangerous persons with little noise and ruin London without burning it. Caligula wished the whole people of Rome but one neck, that he might strike off all their heads at one blow. This was a vain wish. We know ways that can never be discovered till they have taken effect. He that in vain might assault a town openly may master it securely by underground approaches. We use arts ever, force seldom, and not at all till

[216] MS: 'well observes not'.

our work is facilitated by art. We hope to keep the people from discovering the danger till the remedy be impossible. If some few crafty people see the art we use, we so awe them that they dare not speak, or persuade the people they are passionate men, speak*ing* only for their own interests. Or if they proceed to talk on pretence of a plot or something or other, we imprison and dispose of them as we please.

To the third objection, why think you that we have any reason to fear assault from any foreign nation?

EUNOMIUS: for reasons that seem evident to me. Certainly England is worth conquering, and whenever there is a probability of getting it, it will surely be attempted. When the people are strong, numerous, valiant, wise, well disciplined, rich, well content with their present condition, a conquest is difficult. If weak, few, cowardly, without discipline, poor, discontented, they are easily subdued; and this is our condition. You endeavour to corrupt, ruin, and effeminate the nobility which ought to be the leaders of the people for redress of grievances and against foreign enemies. You labour to destroy war, discipline, make the people slaves, weak, poor, few, after which nothing can be added to render them an easy prey to a foreigner, unless the sense of their misery and hate of them that cause it make them look on any invader as a deliverer, and rather submit to him than fight for proud and cruel masters at home.

PHILALETHES: I know not well how to answer these reasons but the danger yet is far off. And France will never suffer us to fall under Spain, nor Spain under France, but protect us ever against it. It is prudence to provide against the greatest and nearest danger, which is at home. We must first secure ourselves on that side and *then* take

[66] care of the rest. |

EUNOMIUS: I think this danger not far off. A great power may soon be destroyed by the carelessness of them that manage it. The vast power of Spain, that within these thirty years made the world tremble, is now like a carcass without blood or spirits, so that everyone expects the dissolution of it. No man can think Spain need fear any power whilst Naples, Milan, Sicily, Sardinia, Flanders, and all the West Indies continue united to it, if the forces thereof were well employed. But want of industry in the king[217] and of ability in his

[217] I.e. Philip IV (reigned 1621–65).

78

favourites, has brought it to that despicable weakness, that well-judging men think it will fall of itself, or become a prey to the first invaders. And if so vast a power can fall so low in so few years, how soon may that of England, that is incomparably less, be laid low through the inventions of those that seek to destroy it, cut the sinews of it, and bring it to an utter impossibility of defending itself.

This is not to be imputed to imagination, for not only great powers may by such means be ruined, but very few have been ruined by any other than by weak, tyrannous princes and their wicked ministers. The effeminacy of Arcadius's court exposed the Eastern empire to be overrun by nations whose names were hardly known before. The perfidy of Rufinus gave an easy entrance for barbarous nations into Thrace, Macedon, and Greece. Stilicho's treachery brought them into Italy and rendered them masters of Rome.[218] King Roderico of Spain turned a legal kingly government into absolute tyranny by bringing the people low. The virtue of his subjects was the first enemy he sought to destroy, which he effected by corrupting and effeminating the nobility; taking away by poison, sword, or false witnesses those that otherwise could not be secured; he disarmed the people, impoverished, weakened them; left off military discipline. The issue was, after a few years' tyranny he and his people were utterly unable to resist a common enemy *and* were easily defeated in the first encounter with the Moors.[219] So the noble kingdom of the Goths that had flourished four hundred years in great power, virtue, valour, etcetera, by the vices of one king and his wicked favourites was utterly overthrown in one small battle. | A multitude of such /67/ examples which I might allege, fortified by reason, persuade me that our danger from a foreigner is not so far off as you imagine. That virtuous Spartan king Theopompus, being reproached by his wife for

---

[218] Just before his death in 395, the Roman emperor Theodosius I appointed Flavius Stilicho (365–408) as regent for his son Honorius, who became emperor of the West, and Flavius Rufinus as regent for his other son, the Eastern Roman emperor Arcadius (c. 377–408). At once the two regents became enemies, but before either Stilicho or Rufinus could attack the other, the Visigoths rebelled and began to devastate Thrace and Macedonia, and Stilicho went with his army to Greece. About to engage the Visigoths there, however, he was ordered by Arcadius, acting on Rufinus's advice, to send a number of his troops to Constantinople. Stilicho obeyed and thus enabled the Visigoths to penetrate into Greece, but the troops sent to Constantinople murdered Rufinus there in 395.

[219] Roderigo (d. 711), the last Visigothic king of Spain, was defeated by Tarik, the Muslim governor of Tangier, in 711.

consenting to the establishment of the ephors to the diminution of regal power, answered: if he left his successors less power than he received from his predecessors, it would be more permanent, because more pleasing to them that lived under it.[220]

The king,[221] out of mere gratitude to the nation that freely called him from banishment and set him up, should content himself with such a limited legal power as might render the people safe and not exposed to ruin from others by recalling him. He should make the people's yoke easy, take off burdens, not invent and lay on many more, increase trade, not destroy it, etcetera.

PHILALETHES: this course may be reasonable, but if the king should truly seek the people's good instead of pleasure, he must have perpetual trouble, be intent on business to preserve the nation against strangers, and see the treasure of it employed in public service, in the maintaining of fleets and armies for its defence and advantage. He must punish fraud in officers, so shall we get little either by begging or stealing. Justice must be administered and then we shall have no bribes. Honours must be given to them that deserve them, so we shall neither have nor sell any. The public interest of the nation must take place, so our pensions from foreign princes must fail us. We that for the most part learn no other art then of bawds, spies, flatterers, thieves, and the like must starve when the king needs more statesmen and soldiers than instruments of his pleasures. If such a government should be renewed, virtue would flourish, and, which is worse, religion would be considered, which would destroy all our delights and interests. Shall we who never thought of religion, unless to jest on it and the professors of it, become such as those we use to scorn and laugh at? Can we conform ourselves to their self-denying discipline who are used to spend more in one night's entertainment of a
/68/ mistress than one of you lay out in a year, | and have more at once on our backs than *you* in your fanatical frugality would *need to* clothe a whole regiment? No. *Glorious monarchy, divine monarchy*, it is to thee we owe all we enjoy or hope for; we are thy creatures, and will always endeavour thy exaltation, breaking all chains that would confine thee, and trampling underfoot all precepts proposed by melancholy men to restrain the absoluteness of thy power. Finis.[222]

---

[220] Theopompus, king of Sparta (785–738 BC). The story is told in Aristotle, *Politics*, bk v, 1313a.
[221] I.e. Charles II.   [222] Margins of MS: 'ends page 18'.

Seventh Dialogue

Sixth Court Maxim: No man is to be employed that will not wholly depend upon the will of the king[223]

PHILALETHES: all things natural and civil, the universe and all individuals in it, subsist by order, which broken, dissolution follows. The physical order in a man is the right disposition of parts and mixture of elements, which *if* a little discomposed he is troubled, if much, he certainly dies. The rational order of man is when the superior part has dominion over the inferior, the mind governs the body, the understanding rules the will and passions. Small transgressions of this order, deviations from reason, we call folly or error, but extreme habitual *transgressions* deserve the name of madness. Nature teaches us that he who is the head of a family is to be obeyed, else the order is broken and the family dissolved. The disobedient son in Moses' law was therefore to be stoned. A family is the union of several men into one body to live together. The two greater assemblies are in armies to make war, or in civil societies to preserve peace. Exact order is required in both: subjection and obedience in the inferior to the superior. This is so punctually observed in military discipline that the least prevarication is death, and no merit can preserve the offender. Manlius Torquatus[224] put his son to death, having

[223] Margins of MS: 'fol. 27'.

[224] Torquatus, Manlius. In the Latin war of 340 BC the consuls, of whom Torquatus was one, forbade single combats with the enemy. When his son nevertheless engaged and killed a Latin champion Torquatus had him executed for disobedience.

contrary to order fought with a valiant Latin that challenged him and slain him. And Papyrius Cursor so stiffly adhered to his resolution of putting Quintus Fabius to death for fighting the Samnites contrary to his order in his absence, that though by an eminent virtue he had gained a great victory, | yet nothing but the authority of the whole people of Rome could save him.[225]

/69/

Nor is it less necessary for preservation of civil societies to observe the same strict order. They subsist by the like means and are destroyed by the same defects and distempers. The superior in them must have dominion over the inferiors as well as in armies, or all is disordered. The mind or understanding must govern the inferior faculties in the societies of men as well as in individual persons, or there is nothing but confusion and madness, leading to destruction. The king is that mind or understanding to which all others must be subject, and no more dispute what he commands than the hand does the executing what the mind directs. He that refuses to obey renounces his loyalty. And they are to obey willingly and without any the least reluctancy also or else are not fit instruments for princes. The most subtle princes Tiberius, Herod, Nero, etcetera, never trusted any man much till by some extraordinary act he had evidenced his regarding no other law but his prince's will. This seems to have been Jehu's aim. He would have no other testimony of the eunuchs' being for him but their throwing their mistress Jezebel out at the window at his command. Nor would he think the inhabitants of Israel faithful to him till they brought him the heads of all their masters, sons they were to have educated.

EUNOMIUS: I attribute to order as much as you do. But my conclusions from thence are somewhat different from yours. I think the rule of my actions to be the law. To this rule if I conform I observe that order which preserves human societies. And by this to preserve order I am obliged to disobey the king if he commands anything contrary to that law. This has been confessed by all princes not impudently wicked. The king, by commanding anything contrary to law, breaks the order he should observe and obliges me to disobey him; that I may not break that order by which alone he is king, and by which the society is preserved. The law errs not, the king may be mad or drunk. Order requires also that we obey God rather than

[225] Livy, *History of Rome*, bk VIII, chs. 31–2.

men.[226] And Christ himself enjoins us not to fear him that can kill the body only, but him that can kill and cast body and soul into hell.[227] As I take it the power of the king does at most extend to the first, only the other belongs to God.

PHILALETHES: the fanatics use to hit us in the | teeth perpetually *[70]* with Saint Paul, knowing his precepts too severe for our lives, and that we are not much acquainted with his writings or others of the same strain. But I have heard for all that that he bids us be subject to the higher powers, which we shall examine hereafter. But at present I desire if you would prove anything to me by authority of authors, you would cite Machiavelli, Tacitus, or others in which I am better versed, and not of your Saint Paul, who is too obscure for me, and treats of matters not at all useful to my designs. Otherwise I shall still conclude it is best for a king to choose servants that will blindly obey him, else his business will never be done, and that it is for me ever to yield a blind obedience to the king's will, otherwise my fortune will never be made.

EUNOMIUS: I will follow your method. But why think you it necessary for princes to have servants that will blindly obey their commands?

PHILALETHES: because it is necessary for them often to command things of great importance which no others would do. How should Charles IX of France, contrary to faith, honour, law, and religion, have found men to commit the tragedy of Saint Bartholomew's eve,[228] unless he had plenty of such persons? And how many princes in our days have by reason of state been obliged to kill their fathers, wives, or children, which they could not have done if such persons could not have been found. As soon as Cromwell came to be a monarch[229] he well understood this Arcanum Imperii,[230] got as many as

---

[226] Acts 5:29–30.   [227] Luke 12:4–5, Matt. 10:28.

[228] In 1572 Charles IX ordered a general massacre of Protestants in Paris and in the provinces.

[229] In 1653 the English army expelled the 'Rump' of the Long Parliament and substituted it by the Protectorate, which consisted of a single-person executive, the Lord Protector, restrained by a council and a (nominated) parliament. Oliver Cromwell, leader of the army, became Lord Protector and moved England closer and closer to the old order, for example by assuming the right in 1657 to name his successor. Dominant figures of the Rump, such as Vane, Hesilridge, and Sidney himself, were excluded from power on the institution of the Protectorate.

[230] 'mystery of state'.

he could of those thorough paced men, who would stick at nothing, calling all others men of hesitating principles, fit for no work. And he cashiered and imprisoned those of this temper.

EUNOMIUS: the strength of your argument seems to be this, that kings cannot maintain themselves unless they command the most wicked things that can be imagined. Nor can they do them unless they have persons who will obey them. Machiavelli indeed has this among other court maxims, that he that will be a prince must renounce honour, justice, truth, charity, religion, and humanity.[231] It seems you carry this notion at your court so much farther as to think those qualities equally necessary in those who will serve princes as in the princes themselves. Which I acknowledge to be so far reasonable as it is necessary for kings to be absolute, which, being a most wicked design and principle, must be carried on by means suitable to it. But /71/ as the same Machiavelli is telling you what he must do | to secure himself if he will be prince, does rather advise him not to be one than commit those execrable impieties which are necessary to his preservation, I think I may conclude for the same reasons that it is better not to be a servant of such a prince that engages me to be as bad as he, than, by being so, to enjoy the rewards of wickedness. I think it behoves all those that have any thought of honour, truth, justice, charity, religion, or humanity to join in the destroying of those princes and their ministers, who for the accomplishing of their wicked designs are obliged to be enemies to them and to renounce all honour, justice, truth, etcetera, as enemies of mankind. Tacitus is plentiful in showing that the first work of the Roman tyrants was to destroy all virtue in the nobility and people, so as to render valour, prudence, etcetera unpardonable crimes. And that so, instead of the virtuous and gallant persons who before had rendered Rome so glorious, the whole power was fallen into the hands of such as Sejanus, Pallaris, Tigellinus, and others who by their lives showed themselves to be the worst of all men except their masters, and by their deaths the most miserable. (That of Tacitus, *Annals* 4) *Tibi summum rerum iudicium di dedere, nobis obsequii gloria relicta est*,[232] are not Tacitus's

---

[231] Reference to *The prince*, ch. 15, where Machiavelli argues that 'a ruler who wishes to maintain his power must be prepared to act immorally when this becomes necessary'.

[232] 'You the gods have made the sovereign arbiter of things, to us has been left the glory of obedience'. Tacitus, *Annals*, bk VI, ch. 8.

words but the words of a condemned man, that hoped thereby to
have mitigated the tyrant's fury and have saved his life. Having
thus followed you in citing those authors you most esteem, I conclude with Peter's words *we should obey God rather than man*,[233]
which agrees well with the command of his master: fear not them
that kill the body. If you courtiers and your bishops allow these say-
ings for true doctrine, it must be confessed kings are not to be obeyed
when they command anything contrary to the command of God, that
is, contrary to justice, piety, charity, or truth, which God commands.
Bitter curses are denounced against Israel for having obeyed the
commands of Omri and walked in the way of the house of Ahab, ful-
filling their wills.

PHILALETHES: neither we nor our divines make the Scripture much
our study. But you will confess the king cannot govern unless he find
servants that will obey him. And that we who serve him cannot make
our fortunes unless we please him. And we are resolved to make our
fortunes, therefore *we* must obey and please him.

EUNOMIUS: it is certain the king cannot govern | if none will obey /72/
him, but if he would govern righteously, according to law and for the
good of the people, he would command nothing but what is just and
good, which would oblige all just and good men to obey him. Instead
of that foundation – I will govern according to my will, and I must be
obeyed, and therefore choose those that will obey – I think this foundation better: I will govern well, and desire not to be obeyed but
when I command what is good and just, and then the best men will
obey me. And instead of resolving, as you do, first to make your fortune and then do all that conduces thereunto, I think *it were better
for you to say*:[234] I will do nothing but what is good and renounce all
advantages that can be hoped by the contrary. The honour and satisfaction of doing that which is good is incomparably above all the
advantages that can ever be gained by iniquity. This is not ill-eluci-
dated by a passage related by Plutarch of Aristippus when turned
courtier. As he passed by the way he saw the poor philosopher
Cleanthes gathering herbs under a hedge, invited him to court, telling him if he would learn to flatter Dionysius he need not gather sallets under hedges. Cleanthes replied: if you could be content to

[233] Acts 5:29–30.
[234] MS: 'you it were better say'.

gather sallets under hedges, you need not flatter Dionysius. And sure it is better for kings to content themselves with moderate power justly exercised than put themselves upon those furious extremities into which their ambition leads them. And that they would be more happy in having servants that would not obey them when they command what is not good, than such as will think everything good that they command. It would be more honourable as well as more safe to follow the example of Trajan, who, delivering back the sword to the prefect of the Praetorian bond, said: if I govern well use this for me, if ill against me';[235] than that of Caligula, Nero, and others that would have such as would obey them in all things, however unjust. And it is far better for servants of princes to follow the example of Papinianus, who chose rather to lie than give an unjust judgement,[236] than that of those who think nothing unjust that is for their interest.

PHILALETHES: before we conclude positively upon the point we must do well to examine some other maxims amongst us.

EUNOMIUS: you will do me a favour to tell me what they are.

PHILALETHES: that concerning bishops to be kept up in the height of /73/ power and riches. |

---

[235]Cassius, *Roman history*, bk LXVIII, ch. 16. Trajan, Marcus Ulpius, Roman emperor (98–117).
[236]The story is told in *Scriptores historiae augusta*, *Caracalla*, ch. 8, 5–6.

Eighth Dialogue

Seventh Court Maxim: Bishops are to be kept up in the height of their power and riches

PHILALETHES: we find it very important to keep up bishops in the height of their power and riches.

EUNOMIUS: what advantage can you propose to yourselves in raising such a sort of people so much above their birth or merit?

PHILALETHES: very much several ways.

First, they, depending wholly on the king, increase his power, preach to the people that they must in all things obey him.

Secondly, a multitude of the loose people of England depend upon them and are thereby made ours.

Thirdly, they are very useful instruments of oppressing the people, impoverishing and vexing them with excommunications, censures, etcetera.

Fourthly, they are useful to keep the people in ignorance, whence they easily fall into lewdness, and then they are ours. There is no danger they should disturb the state or be enemies to us.

Lastly, as they are sworn enemies to all fanatics and such as know how to pray *and* preach or use to read the Bible, they will help much to destroy them.

EUNOMIUS: though I use to contradict you in many things, I agree with you here so far as to confess that as the worst instruments *are most fit for the worst works, it was not easy to find men more fit to advance such ends as you propose than the bishops.* Yet I am far from approving of your counsel, because he is an unwise man that chooses an evil end, though he take the right way of attaining to it; as he that throws himself down a precipice does not avoid the imputation of madness, though it be the way to break his neck, which he desires. And also, I think those men unable to accomplish part of what they expect from them, *for though, through the meanness of their birth, want of merit, falseness of their doctrine, and vanity of their calling, they have nothing *that* can maintain them one day in their greatness but the king's favour,* which persuades them wholly to rely upon him, these

/74/ qualities render them rather burdens than helps to him. | And he does rather draw envy upon himself by protecting their hated heads, than advantage by their preaching up his authority. For as the devil is said to speak true sometimes, but is never believed because he never does it but with intent to deceive, these men are so used to speak untruth that *if* they should sometimes say that what is good, it would never be received as truth. Everyone knows that the principal intention of the bishops and fathers is to set forth the glory of the king as an absolute prince. As matters are handled I see not that the doctrine received from the pulpit is otherwise considered than the like which is often heard in the playhouses.

But, secondly, I cannot deny but the king by the bishops' means does fully attain to the second end which you propose. For parity of manners and interest has so united all those persons who are of lewd callings or *have*[237] otherwise become dissolute, that their friendship will certainly be perpetual. And the bishops, excelling all others in these qualities which suit with their professions, will ever be leaders of the others and unite them to the king and his interest. But I think His Majesty thereby no gainer. There is no great advantage of having people that want sobriety, for such usually want diligence, valour, and conduct also. They are of vast expense and little use. In time of peace there is no need of them, in war they cannot be relied on. They are extremely insolent and burdensome to the country, but little terrible to enemies. And the king, living according to your court maxims, may be sure of all such loose people without burdening himself with upholding the bishops to gain them.

[237] MS: 'are'.

Besides all this, there is a natural and perpetual contrariety between sobriety and lewdness, piety and profaneness. So that, if the king endeavour to join to himself those that are lewd and profane, all sober and godly people will certainly divide themselves from him; who, though fewer in number, their diligence, valour, and prudence may, according to ordinary rules of policy, be thought of far more power than a much greater number of disordered people. And God will not long suffer the rod of the wicked to rest on the lot of the righteous, though for the sins of his people he suffers them for a season to be a scourge to them. Nothing gives me more perfect confidence that this kingdom now set up in such glory will soon fall with shame than that I see its | root and principle is in vice and wicked- /75/ ness, and the exercise suitable to the principle in which it subsists, as it must needs be. (Psalm) God hates all workers of iniquity, and will destroy them that speak lies.[238] Kings and princes of the earth gather together against the Lord and against his anointed (psalm 2).[239] The true inward spiritual unction of those who are made sons of God and to heirs of that kingdom that shall have no end is directly contrary to the profane superstitious daubing commonly used by the bishops unto kings. And these kings of the earth, knowing this contrariety, have gathered themselves together against it, and those that bear it. Their craft is folly, their rage madness, their power vanity, they have made lies their refuge and chosen the prophets that speak them, rather than teachers of truth. Being in honour, they have no understanding, but are as the beasts that perish.

Thirdly, as to your third point, they are fit for the end you propose, but these vexatious censures, frivolous excommunications, with all other tricks and inventions they have of getting money and troubling the people, adds more to the hatred against them and those that uphold them than they do diminish the strength of them they oppress. And nothing is more common in the world than to see men that have suffered quietly a long while lose their patience at last and take sharp vengeance on their oppressors.

PHILALETHES: I think it probable the people may grow angry with the bishops and destroy some of them, but the king will not be thereby prejudiced, but have great advantage in advancing other servants into their vacant places. And if the whole order grow so

---

[238] Ps. 5:5–6.   [239] Ps. 2:2.

odious as not to be endured, the king can gratify the nation in taking them away, and himself in taking all their lands and revenues.

EUNOMIUS: I believe that the hatred growing from the tyranny of the bishops will not be assuaged in their destruction only. Everyone knows who has set them up and maintains them. Their punishment will be no satisfaction for the villainies they have committed. Generous spirits will look on him that employed them, and impute all mischief done by them to him that set them up purposely to do all the ill they did. It is true sometimes the rage of the people is so blind as to

[76] punish the | crimes of princes in the persons of their ministers only. But for the most part they judge better than so, and bring just vengeance on the heads of guilty princes for all the evils done by them in person, or by the wicked servants of their choosing. There is a burden upon kings which they seldom perceive till the weight of it destroys them. They are to answer for all the evils they ought to have prevented or punished. This Pausanius understood so well, that he killed Philip of Macedon in the midst of his guards for slighting his complaint and refusing to do him justice about a great injury he had received from Attalus.[240] Some believe the like considering incited Ravaillac, and armed him with a like resolution against Henry IV of France for like reason.[241] Whoever receives an injury from a bishop ought to impute it to the king, and revenge it on him; which, if considered, His Majesty will not have much reason to rejoice in the mischiefs they commit.

Fourthly, there is much of truth in your fourth reason. Ignorance is the way to lewdness, and they who largely partake of both these qualities will ever be loyal, according to your court phrase, that is, wholly devoted to the king's interest. Nor can I deny but all that depend on the bishop's teaching must be ignorant, for none can teach what he knows not. They who study only cheats and tricks to deceive are never like*ly* to instruct others in what they ought to learn. They endeavour as far they can to destroy all others that can and would teach that which they desire none should learn. But their design is full of vanity. They keep none in ignorance but themselves. God will raise

---

[240] Philip II of Macedon was murdered in 336 BC while walking in procession during the celebration of his daughter's marriage by an assassin named Pausanius, apparently because Philip had failed to punish an insult of Attalus towards Pausanius.

[241] Henry IV (1553–1610), first Bourbon king of France (1589–1610); was murdered by François Ravaillac.

up teachers of the truth more and more under persecutions. And wherever he has sown his spiritual seed, he will cause it to grow and prosper in the hearts of his elect, however those that pretend to watch over it do maliciously endeavour and watch only to destroy it. True believers never more earnestly seek wisdom from God than when they see human springs dried up. The frailty of man is apt to rest on such helps as he can receive from others like himself. But those failing, men cast themselves upon God, and more plainly see him their true helper when disappointed of all other helps in which they trusted. In this time of public calamity who will show us any good? *It* seems to be the voice of mankind. When any appears | endowed /77/ through the grace of God with some good measure of spiritual knowledge, the faithful flock unto him. Everyone may see people flying from the cold, empty cathedrals and episcopal congregations, despising the apish postures, frivolous discourses, and ridiculous bawlings that are all there, and flocking into those contemned corners where they hope to hear the word of God from the mouths of his servants.

The bishops are not the first that have had this design of keeping the people ignorant, nor that have been disappointed. This part of the world lay sunk in the blindness and deadness of popery. The monks were their teachers who, being void of all knowledge except that which serves to babble in schools, bred up the people in most deep and supine ignorance. They knew people would be no longer kept in the vanity of their superstition than they continued in the blindness from whence it sprung. Had they not carefully kept the people in ignorance, who would have believed that the priest's eating a wafer was the sacrifice of the body and blood of Christ, that masses sold for 6 pence a piece could deliver souls out of purgatory or assuage their pains there? And but for ignorance, who could believe that the vast revenues which the monks spent in horses, dogs, and whores and all instruments of gluttony and luxury, were employed according to the intention of the givers in holy and proud uses? All possible means were used to continue people in this ignorant temper. And if the design had universally succeeded, the so-much controverted question whether the prelates' whores were ecclesiastical person*s* would probably have been carried, and without contradiction or restriction all ecclesiastical privileges and immunities had been granted them. But God raised up men to spoil this work and brought in the so-much hated name of reformation.

PHILALETHES: if any turbulent fanatics should endeavour to mislead people from that blind obedience the bishops design to keep them in, we know where to provide them lodgings, whence they will not come to disturb our peace.

EUNOMIUS: you may easily reduce all your ways for the attainment of your end unto two heads upon which your master Machiavelli does so much insist, force and fraud. Fraud is *by* far the most useful means and suitable to the temper of the most powerful amongst you. By fraud you labour to keep the people in ignorance that they [78] may not understand the tricks that are used, and so to weaken the | nation that you may bring it at last to be governed by force. But thanks be to God these things are now understood by many that can discover them to others. And though you poison some of these and assassinate others, the seed is too far spread to be rooted up. We depend not on any one man nor number of men but God. He that has raised up some to be witnesses of justice and truth can give the same spirit unto others. And his promise is so far engaged that we doubt not but that he will do it. Nor is the delay that is caused by our sins any advantage to them. He that suffers our oppressors to run on in guilt, filling up the measure of their iniquity and ripening themselves for destruction, will fit us for mercy. And as was said not long since by a person of approved fidelity to his country, 'if we were as ripe for mercy as our enemies are for vengeance, our desires would soon be accomplished'. But God's time is best. They that depend upon him fall not into impatience for the delay of his coming, nor are frightened at the boasting of his and their enemies. They live in and by faith, they see things that to other eyes are invisible. That spirit that has planted faith in their hearts does perpetually bring forth fruits of hope and joy. They have resigned themselves and all they have, and are into God's hands as willing sacrifices. They know themselves safe under his protection, and that when the time of their suffering is accomplished, deliverance will come. But to leave this discourse grounded in faith, which by you is accounted fanatic, I pass to the consideration of the fifth advantage you mentioned that you receive by the bishops.

No man can deny but that there is a perpetual irreconcilable enmity between them and the fanatics. Though the name of bishop does not justly belong to the lustful, lawn-sleeved parasites of whom we speak, yet, to avoid disputes upon words, I shall give them that title. And though that of fanatics does as little belong unto pure spiritual Christians, I am content to comprehend the best men under it.

PHILALETHES: do you think the name of bishop does not properly belong to those to whom we give it?

EUNOMIUS: *episcopus*, which we translate bishop, in a general sense signifies overseer. Now if you mean overseers of the church and flock of Christ, they deserve it no better than wolves and thieves who carefully observe and watch over the flock to destroy. As for the character they pretend to, that is as vain as their lives are impious. No man can desire any title to it, that is not either interior and | spiritual, or /79/ exterior according to succession, or composed of both. If they assume to themselves the interior spiritual calling and anointing, they would fall under the guilt for which they detest the fanatics, and could not persecute and destroy those who preach, pray, and act *bad*[242] things by the impulse of the spirit of God. If they do pretend to it and give no better testimony of it than is seen in their preaching, praying, and whole course of their lives, all the world will laugh at them. Their pretext to an exterior call is yet more ridiculous, for that must depend on an uninterrupted succession. For if interrupted, it is utterly lost. He that has not the order or character in himself, can never confer it upon another. Or if it be true that they have the uninterrupted succession to which they pretend, it has passed through the most polluted sink of popery and continued in it for about 1,000 years, which is no less than to say the false prophet, the whore of Babylon, the beast, and Antichrist (which name even they give the pope with many others of like nature) has made them ministers and bishops in the church of Christ. If they say the church of Rome is the true church, they are detestable heretics for leaving it, and having caused several Roman priests to be hanged for having the same character for which they so highly prize themselves, that is, either they have no divine character in themselves, or hang those that have it, because they have it. If they say the church of Rome had errors that justified them for leaving it, yet continued a true church, I answer, 'an obscene, spiritual adulteress, living in errors and idolatry, cannot be a true church of Christ'. But if it were a true church, I

[242] MS: 'mal'.

deny our bishops can derive any benefit from them. As Cyprian says
in *De unitate ecclesiae*, a bishop or priest that leaves the church is a
branch torn off from the tree that has no more life in it, *and has* no
right at all from the execution of his office.[243]

Again, such orders and sacred characters, as they call them, could
not be conferred but by the rules and to the ends constituted for
them. Now the office of priesthood in that church has two powers
belonging to it: the one is that of the keys, as they call it, whereby
they pretend to have power to remit or retain sins which is exercised
in confessions. The other is that of sacrificing for the living and the
dead, which is done in saying mass. These are the two powers and all
the power that is pretended to be given to priests. Whoever by his
[80] priesthood has not the power of retaining or remitting sins | and the
exercise of it in receiving confessions, and that of sacrificing for the
living and the dead in saying mass, has nothing conferred upon him
by that action which should make him a priest. Now the protestant
bishops take away one by taking away confession, and the other by
abolishing the mass and denying purgatory, which only could make
it effectual for the benefit of the dead if it were to be celebrated. So
have they destroyed all that could give them the least title or pretence to priesthood and consequently to episcopacy.

PHILALETHES: if you allow them not to be bishops, what do you take
them to be?

EUNOMIUS: teachers of lies, workers of iniquity, persecutors of
saints, and apes of Rome.

But to return from this digression about the validity of their name
and calling, I do confess them to be as fit instruments for the
oppressing of the fanatics as any heathens or papists have ever been
or are. Which, in my opinion, does more than anything show their
vileness and the vanity of their calling. If they had the least valour of
christian charity, they would endeavour to convince those that (as
they say) go astray. And if they had so much as an opinion of truth in
their doctrine or right in their calling, they would show it by reason
or Scripture. Instead of this they use vexatious summons and tyran-
nical censures. And, by rendering themselves slaves to those who
have usurped the civil powers, make use of their swords to oppress

[243] Cyprian, *De catholicae ecclesiae unitate*, par. 5.

94

all that are truly godly. If they were bishops or Christians, they would draw people to their churches by an upright preaching of the word and not force them by fires and imprisonments. If they sought the good of souls they would endeavour to convince, not destroy them. When they hear of any Christians gathered together to hear the word or call upon God, they would join with them, not send constables or soldiers to dissolve them.[244]

PHILALETHES: I see not how church or state can subsist without order, nor how that | order should be preserved unless one rule be /81/ set unto which all should conform themselves. This rule must be set by superiors, obeyed by inferiors. And if there were not a coercive power to keep hotheaded fanatics in awe, there would be no order but all ran into confusion.

EUNOMIUS: no man can too much extol the excellency of order. But as great mischiefs are seldom done in the world but when something of good is pretended, they could never have overthrown order but under colour of establishing it. The power of princes could not be fully established unless they had a power over consciences. And those priests that have nothing to uphold them but the prince's power can never make that propitious to them unless they make themselves useful to it. Hence grew the necessity of acknowledging the power of the civil magistrate in spiritual things, ridiculously setting a temporal head upon a spiritual body. This is the poet's monster reversed. He framed one of which he said *Mulier formose superne desinit in piscem*.[245] But here the body is the beautiful woman, the pure and undefiled spouse of Christ. Unto this body they give the head of a filthy devouring fish or a savage wolf. Hence spiritual men in spiritual things are forced to receive law from worldly and carnal magistrates. Nothing can be imagined more directly opposite to right order than that princes that for the most part are utterly ignorant of spiritual things should impose rules in them to be followed by those to whom God has given the true light of his spirit to see their own way. And having resolved to set up such an interest, they propagate what they call gospel by force and violence, whereas the true gospel

---

[244] MS: 'Here is to begin (says A.S. in the margins) the chapter entitled No religion is to be suffered but what is established by authority of parliament. Court Maxim', inserted by the copyist.

[245] 'Beautifully, the woman ends in the shape of a fish at her head.'

was always propagated by meekness, suffering, and spiritual arms. All fraud, force, and mischief follow the erecting *of* such a corrupt interest in the church. All public*ly* avowed persecution arises hence under the notion of suppressing heretics and seditious persons, to the ruining of the liberty, fortunes, and families of the choicest Christians. Cruelty, fraud, and malice were ever the inseparable companions of superstition. They are of their father, the devil. And his work they will do who was a murderer from the beginning, and [82] seeks yet whom he | may devour, so do they. The kings of the earth that for a long time have gathered together against the Lord and his anointed, have the same master still, Satan, and have not changed their design. And false prophets are never wanting to them that say go and prosper. Does God stand in need of acts of parliament to teach me to worship him? Does he need the worst of men and that in their worst condition? When they have most unmanned themselves, coming drunk from the bishop's feast to the committee that framed the Act of Uniformity? But I see my error, it was necessary they should be such persons for there was no possibility of gaining assent to it from any others.

PHILALETHES: would you have all suffered to be loose and believe what they please, worshipping God after their own humour? They will do so unless a law be set and a power exercised for conforming men thereunto. And to this agree the words of Tertullian, *Contra Praxeas*, as that *heretica durities frangenda est non allicienda.*[246]

EUNOMIUS: one of the greatest and venerable of the English rabbis, commonly called a pillar of the church, endeavoured to abuse me once with that text of Tertullian. And the words sounding fitly for his purpose, I could not discover the deceit till I read the author. And then I found plainly that it could be nothing but ecclesiastical censures and excommunications that he could mean, for breaking the hardness of heretics. Let the bishops abstain from all other weapons against heretics, and we will not complain of their frivolous, profanely abused censures. This was the author's sense, for Christians then had no temporal jurisdiction, nor could therefore inflict any temporal punishments. That he incited not or counselled christian princes to assist the churches who had no temporal jurisdiction in

---

[246] 'heretical intransigence is to be broken, not wooed'. Reference to Tertullian, *Adversus Praxean*, chs. 1–2, or ch. 29, sec. 1.

themselves or invoked their aid; he does plainly show in several places, that he did not think any Christian could be a prince. In his *Apologeticum* he says *sed et Caesares credidissent super Christo, si aut Caesares non essent necessarii saeculo, aut si et Christiani potuissent esse Caesares*,[247] and fully confirms this opinion in many other places. He, observing how men came to be princes, and maintained themselves when so, in his treatise *De corona militis*,[248] viz by fraud, violence, rapine, and cruelty. So it is no wonder that Christians, who in his terms are *nullius hostes omni gloria et dignitatis ardore frigentes*,[249] therefore could never desire those powers that were sought for ends so contrary to theirs, nor exercise that which set itself directly against all that was good. I leave any impartial man to judge whether princes in our days walk in better ways or aim at better ends. | /83/

My second reason why he means not the secular sword is because no man ever wrote who more detested violence on consciences than he, which he shows almost everywhere. In his treatise to Scapula, he says *humani juris et naturalis equitatis est unicuique quod putaverit colere nec alii alterius obest vel prodest religio. Sed nec religionis est religionem cogere*.[250] In his *Apologetic* he adds, *videte enim, ne et hoc ad irreligiositatis elogium concurrat, adimere libertatem religionis et interdicere optionem divinitatis, ut non liceat mihi colere quem velim, sed cogar colere quem nolim. Nemo se ab invito coli volet, ne homo quidem. Atque adeo et Aegyptiis permissa est tam vanae superstitionis potestas avibus et bestiis consecrandis et capite damnandis, qui aliquem huiusmodi deum occiderit*.[251] After the reciting of these passages I think you will no more allege Tertullian for violence upon consciences. So, having

[247] 'Yes, and the caesars also would have believed in Christ, if caesars had not been necessary for the world, or if the Christians, too, would have been caesars.' Tertullian, *Apology*, ch. 21, sec. 24.

[248] Tertullian, *De corona*, ch. 2.

[249] 'Nobody's enemy, cold for all lust for glory and dignity', reference to Tertullian, *Apology*, ch. 38, sec. 2: 'We, however, whom all the flames of glory and dignity leave cold, have no need to combine.'

[250] 'According to human law and natural equity everyone is permitted to choose his own religion; and the religion of one cannot favour or prejudice that of another. For one religion ought not to compel another.' Tertullian, *Ad Scapulam*, ch. 2, where it says *potestatis*, power or authority, instead of *equitatis*, equity.

[251] 'Look to it, whether this also may form part of the accusation of irreligion – to do away with freedom of religion, to forbid a man choice of deity, so that I may not worship whom I would, but am forced to worship whom I would not. No one, not even a man, will wish to receive reluctant worship. Why, the Egyptians are allowed full freedom in their empty superstition, to make gods of birds and beasts, and to condemn to death any who may kill a god of that sort.' Tertullian, *Apology*, ch. 24, secs. 6–7.

taken away the edge of what you cited, I shall proceed to your last objection, desiring you before you conclude violence upon consciences justifiable, to consider:

First, whether it is possible by force or fear to make any man believe anything?

Secondly, whether *it is* acceptable to God that a man worship him when his heart is far from him?

Thirdly, whether those who are not spiritual men are fit to judge of spiritual things?

Fourthly, whether a prudent good man can have such assurance he is in the right as to dare force others to his way?

For the first, if it be true that belief is not the act of the will, it is neither in my power to believe what I please, nor what pleases another man that is stronger than I. He that endeavours to force me to that which is neither in his power nor mine, does necessarily declare himself to be most furiously mad and equally wicked *as he* who, without any hope of good, vexes and destroys innocent persons.

PHILALETHES: be pleased to take the pains to explain and resolve your own questions. If you conclude anything that seems contrary to truth, I will contradict it.

EUNOMIUS: though this method be a little extraordinary, yet to obey you and explain myself, I say, the utmost effect of force is to induce my will to do what is in my power. If the thing be out of my power, the will is in vain induced. Now I cannot but believe everything to be as it appears to my understanding. I believe the three angles of a triangle to be equal to two right angles. Torment may perhaps force me /84/ to say they are equal to three right angles | or but to one, but all the tyrants in the world can never make me believe they are not equal to two. It is from God, not the prince or hangman, that we must learn religion. His spirit discovers truth unto us by the wings of love and faith which he gives. Both grounded on the knowledge of his being good and good to us, we rise unto that spiritual height as makes all worldly things appear dung and dross unto us. The same means may probably bring England, that have kept Italy and Spain to a uniformity in superstition, flat atheism and belief of lies. God wholly looks at the heart, and that wholly departs from him in all their superstitious religion, in obedience to man, which serves only the political ends of princes. God expects the resignation of the spirit to himself. Human impositions may make hypocrites, never Christians. To make men renounce what they think true religion, and embrace what they believe to be false, is the height of atheism and impiety. Italy and Spain have been long kept in their ignorant uniformity. But abundance of people in England see through those mists the bishops cast before their eyes, and discover the deceitfulness of those pretences with which they endeavour to delude them. The nakedness of the prelates and their disciples is discovered. Their cold empty churches show how their persons are despised and hated. And the vanity of their doctrine is made to appear as well as the profane*ness* of their worship. The fury of Francis I and Henry II[252] of France against the reformed brought the whole nation into most horrid troubles, to the utter destruction of that wicked race that caused them and *the* full toleration of the religion they intended to extirpate. Let the Spaniards brag of all the blood shed by the duke of Alva[253] and others in the Low Countries on this account. When *the* duke of Alva went out of Flanders he boasted that beside what he had slain in battle, he had put to death in six years above four score thousand heretics. Grotius, *De rebus belgicis*, judges not whether the present state of the Low Countries be not a good testimony that the seed of truth sown by God cannot be rooted up by man. Have the king and bishops better armies, more treasures and power than Philip II of Spain? Have they captains of more experience, skill, industry, and valour than *the* duke of Alva etcetera? The bishops, imprisoning, banishing, and killing some dissenters, will not bring the people of God to join in their frivolous profane worship, or associate | themselves with the /85/ obscene and impure crews that attend it. You only thereby heap up to yourselves wrath against the day of wrath etcetera. The blood of martyrs has been experienced to be the seed of the church. And we have many sure promises from God himself, that he will most powerfully protect his people, when the devil and his ministers do most furiously rage against them. Your cruelty is a testimony of our election. We know when we suffer for Christ, we shall also reign with

[252] Francis I (1494–1547), king of France (1515–47); Henry II (1519–59), king of France (1547–59).

[253] Alva, third duke of (1507–82). Spanish statesman who in 1567 was sent to the Netherlands by Philip II to crush the Dutch revolt. As governor general (1567–73) he instituted the council of troubles (nicknamed the council of blood), which set aside laws and condemned thousands. See Grotius, *De rebus belgicis: or the annals, and history of the Low-Countrye-Warrs*.

him. It is truly said all businesses have various faces, but you can turn this impious tyranny over consciences no way that does not show its deformity, and show it to be equally foolish and detestable. We are obliged to discover to you the wickedness of your ways and to pray for you, notwithstanding the lewdness of your hearts, as Tertullian and other Christians in his time prayed for the caesars because commanded to love their persecutors and pray for their enemies. If you turn not we know our redeemer lives. And in his appointed time will deliver us from your hands.

But to carry the argument a little farther, if the prince has a just right and power of commanding in matters of religion, I have no right of examining or disobeying his commands. So I am obliged in conscience to be a papist, Jew, Turk, heathen, or to sacrifice to the devil if my prince so command me. That great person then did well, who was a papist at the beginning of Henry VIII in England and when the king renounced the pope's supremacy he with the king adhered to the Roman doctrine, but denied the pope's authority in England. The same person professed himself a Protestant under Edward VI, who of a Protestant became a papist under queen Mary, under queen Elizabeth finding all his former errors became protestant again. Being asked how he preserved himself in all such changes, he said: by being a willow, not an oak. If obedience be absolutely due to kings, this man was not only the wisest but most pious man of that age. And with the same certainty it will follow, they who in ancient or modern times renounced Christ to follow their prince's religion and sacrificed to the devil were most godly persons. And they that suffered death for the testimony of the truth, obstinate heretics, seditious fellows, as Tertullian called Paul.

[86] But you say, | first, it is not all princes that have power of obliging others to their religion, but those only, who are professors of the truth. Secondly, men are obliged only to use passive obedience to their princes. To the first I answer, till the prince can evidence that it is the true doctrine and worship which he requires submission to, he must be content we resist him as far as we can. For pretences not justified are of no force. The Ottoman family and their mufties pretend to truth as well as the Stuarts and their prelates, and both are to be considered alike till one of them proves the truth of his assertions. The objection against this, that some are so obstinate in defence of their opinions that no evidence of truth without force will convince

them, is so frivolous that it deserves no answer. For the constancy of those that suffer, equal to that in the ancient martyrs, is an infallible testimony that they in their hearts believe what they profess. Man's nature is so prone to seek his present convenience and advantage that doubtless the whole nation would soon submit to the religion and worship appointed by the governors if they could bring their consciences to consent. But when the cause of God is in question and I must disobey the king or sin against God, the choice is easy. But that which wholly removes this objection is that faith is the gift of God. None receive it unless he give it. And the disputes of religion are so many and intricate; every sect so furnished to defend their own way; so many arguments used by men of great parts, learning, and understanding every way; that no human understanding can of itself hope to find a way through those straits. The spirit of God only must give us the clew of thread to show us our way through that labyrinth.

The second objection will be as entirely removed. I take it to be a clear, universal, eternal truth that *in injuste vim inferenti vis justa opponenda est.*[254] First, because whoever acts unjustly breaks the common pacts by which human society is established, renders himself a delinquent, and gives him that is offended a right against him. Grotius, though a gentle spirited man, says, whoever endeavours to injure another *jus in se dat infinitum,*[255] though christian charity ought to restrain us from the full exercise of our strict right, as he shows also, unless the greatness of the injury oblige me to it. But I think no body will say any injury is greater than to compel me to a profane worship or banish or kill me for refusing. No injury therefore offered to a man can be more justly repelled than violence offered to the conscience.

Secondly, the same author sets down two principles:

First, *frustra datur jus nisi detur jus illud tenendi.*

Secondly, *frustra conceditur facultas nisi sit jus facultatem exercendi.*[256] Whence I infer | that, no man having a just power over my [87] conscience, whoever offers violence to it, or to me for it, injures me

---

[254] 'against force that is injustly imposed just force has to be opposed'. Reference to *Digests*, bk xliii, ch. 16, sec. 1: *vim vi repellere licet, Cassius scribit.* See Grotius, *On the law of war and peace*, bk i, ch. 2, secs. 1–6.

[255] 'confers upon me an unlimited moral right against him', Grotius, *On the law of war and peace*, bk ii, ch. 1, sec. 10.

[256] 'a right is conferred in vain, if it does not involve the right to defend it'. 'a perfect right is conceded in vain if there were not the right to exercise it'. Reference to Grotius, *On the law of war and peace*, bk iii, ch. 1, sec. 2.

in what is most clear unto me, gives me a right in self-defence of repelling the injury. And Pontius in Livy says well, *justa piaque sunt arma, quibus necessaria, et necessaria, quibus nulla nisi in armis spes est salutis.*[257] Those that by violence are brought to the hard necessity of sinning against God or suffering their families to be ruined and persons perpetually imprisoned, banished, or murdered, may seem enough to justify those who by force seek to repel such violence.

But this point must be carried a little further. Our bishops and royalists say the christian doctrine commands patience and meekness, loving of persecutors, praying for enemies, and confirm this doctrine by the opinion of many ancient christian authors, principally by Tertullian (*Apology*, ch. 37) who says, Christians *vim inferentibus non resistebant cum potuissent*,[258] when their number is so great (ch. 30)[259] that no one nation *is* equal in power to them, and that a few such as they that could cheerfully die were to be feared by the greatest powers of the world, or destroy countries only by departing out of them and so dispeopling them, so numerous were they in all provinces. And Cyprian (Epistula 57) says *Christianos vinci non posse, mori posse et hoc ipso invictos esse quia mori non timent nec repugnare contra repugnantes in occidere innocentibus nec nocentem liceat sed prompte et animas et sanguinem tradere ut cum tanta in seculo seavitia grassetur a malis et saevis velocius recedatur.*[260] Many other passages are alleged by them, but these are most insisted on by Doctor Hammond, Salmasius[261] and others of like temper, so a clear answer to

---

[257] 'those arms were just and pious that were necessary, and necessary when there was no hope of safety by any other way'. Livy, *History of Rome*, bk IX, ch. I.

[258] Christians 'have not resisted those who impose force upon them whenever they could'. Reference to Tertullian, *Apology*, ch. 37.

[259] In fact, ch. 37.

[260] 'that Christians cannot be conquered, but that they would not evade to die – they are invincible precisely because they are not afraid to die, nor will they use violence against violators as the killing of innocent and culpable men alike is not permitted, but they give freely their spirits and blood, in order to recede the sooner from the brutes and the vicious, leaving this world that grows in brutality and vice', Cyprian, *Opera omnia* (ed. Hartel, 1871), Epistula 60, sec. 2, par. 3. The numbering by A.S. is the one customary in the sixteenth and seventeenth centuries.

[261] Hammond, Henry (1605–60); royalist divine, in 1633 was appointed rector of Penshurst by the earl of Leicester. Hammond educated Sir William Temple there, before in 1643 being installed as archdeacon in Chichester. The reference is probably to his *Of resisting the lawful magistrate under colour of religion*, 1644. Salmasius, Claudius (1588–1653); French classicist scholar who in 1649 was commissioned by Charles II to write the *Defensio regia pro Carolo I*. In this book he defended prelacy and absolute monarchy, and attacked the ideas and actions of the English Independents, particularly their execution of Charles I.

them may serve for all the rest. Who would not think these sons of violence were about *to* return from their evil ways and have some taste of humanity when they so zealously preach the perfection of meekness and patience? It made me incline to hope the bishops and their disciples were turned Christians. But I soon found my error; *this*[262] means nothing less.

They preach patience that people may submit to their tyranny, as the thief persuades the traveller to go unarmed that he may safely rob and kill him, or the wolf that would persuade the shepherd's dogs they ought to be gentle and not bite, that he may (without disturbance) destroy the flocks they are to guard. Let them that preach this doctrine first conform to it. If it oblige Christians, let them follow their own rules. But they only persuade others to suffer that they may tyrannize. The Quakers[263] indeed get some credit to this doctrine | of not repelling force with force, because they practise it in patiently suffering all injuries, though mistaken in that doctrine. But these prelates do most impiously endeavour to deceive others. *Quis tulerit Gracchos de seditione quaerentes?*[264] Who will endure that bishops, the greatest incendiaries in the whole world, should now preach the highest meekness? They who said it was better all the streets in England and Scotland should run with blood than the power of the clergy be diminished, say now, it is better England should be dispeopled, the best men in the nation banished and destroyed, than that their lusts should be resisted. If that they say were true, it is but with a design to deceive, as the devil used to do. No impudence is greater than that of those who preach doctrine so contrary to their practice. But that the fraud may more plainly appear, let us examine the authorities they allege. Many pious and learned primitive Christians did preach this patience under violence, but it must be confessed they laid the same obligation not to resist a thief as not to resist a persecuting prince, as is plain in the forecited words of Tertullian and Cyprian, who, giving the reasons why Christians did not resist, says,

[88]

---

[262] MS: 'the'.

[263] Members of a religious movement that originated in the rural north between 1650 and 1653 and was properly called the Society of Friends. Because of its religious and political radicalism the Society came under a state of siege during the Restoration. The Quaker Act (1662) was used by the government to persecute the Quakers, and as a result thousands were imprisoned and hundreds died. The first clear declarations of Quaker pacifism were made during the early 1660s.

[264] 'Who drove the Gracchi aim at rebellion?'

quod male velle, male dicere male facere vetarentur quod est magis occidi quam occidere liceret;[265] to which he adds, *nihil temendum est a christianis.*[266] They had so far renounced the world as to have no interest in it. *Deum non pro consulem timemus Christianus nullius hostis est.*[267] And in his treatise *De corona militis* in most express words he declares all exercise of the sword, or power of those magistracies who were to be employed in capital punishments, to be absolute*ly* unlawful for a Christian to exercise.[268] And Cyprian as in many other things expressly followed him. Let the bishops declare this doctrine to be true and we will lay aside most part of the controversies we have with them. But if they take only the naked words, denying the grounds from whence they are drawn, that may make them of any authority, they that allege them are to be rejected with the utmost scorn and hatred, as corrupters of the doctrine they intend to maintain. But they whose calling is a lie have in all things made lies their refuge. They cover their vices with the gravity of their habits and

[89] beards. | *Curia simulant et bacchanalia vivunt.*[269] Being most savage wolves, they put on lamb's clothing.

But for satisfying those who perhaps may be deluded by them, I will go one step farther and acknowledge many of the primitive Christians to have deemed the legality of all use of arms or capital punishments, which gave occasion to Julian the Apostate[270] to say they were enemies to all human society in disallowing the use of force without which innocency could not be protected, nor society maintained. But men of greater authority in those primitive times, who have ever been followed by all the chief christian churches, affirmed and practised the contrary. At this day we find none to espouse those opinions but our Quakers, some few Anabaptists[271] in

---

[265] 'that to wish evil, to speak evil, to do evil are forbidden, that there is greater liberty to be killed than to kill', Tertullian, *Apology*, chs. 36 and 37.

[266] 'a Christian has nothing to fear'.

[267] 'We do not fear God as our ruler, a Christian is nobody's enemy', Tertullian, *Ad Scapulam*, ch. 2, sec. 6.

[268] Tertullian, *De corona*, ch. 11, sec. 1.

[269] 'They pretend to be as if in curia, but they celebrate bacchanalia.' Reference to Tertullian, *Apology*, ch. 37, sec. 2.

[270] Julian the Apostate (331/2–63), Roman emperor (361–3).

[271] The Anabaptists were a radical movement of the sixteenth-century protestant Reformation. Their most distinctive tenet was adult baptism. They believed that the church, which to them was the community of the redeemed, should be separated from the state, existing only for the punishment of sinners, and they therefore refrained from holding public office.

Holland and Germany, and some of the Socinians[272] in Poland. It is most generally known all christian churches have rejected the opinion of those that thought no use of sword lawful, having made use of it against such princes and their ministers as have governed contrary to law. But if a coercive power may be exercised in spiritual things, shall it be exercised by him that understands them not? Shall a blind man be made judge of colours, or a deaf give his opinion of music? In the last age religion in England was changed five times in less than thirty years. By this means kings are of a mere civil constitution, for mere civil ends, *and* are perpetually therefore to be confined to civil matters. Spiritual men are the best or only judges of spiritual things. This establishes not the bishop's throne, though called spiritual persons. It is the gift of the spirit of God which they deride that makes the spiritual man, gives a spiritual calling, not a usurped title, by favour at a wicked court. The king gives them lawn sleeves, titles of lordship, great palaces, vast revenues, seats in parliament, power of persecuting the fanatics and all such as have the spiritual unction but not the true unction itself. They do in truth imitate those heathen priests in their rage against Christians, as well as by the obscenity of their lives. They followed such of them as sacrificed to Venus, Hera, Bacchus, or Priapus.[273] Their wild howlings in churches, joined with the amazing sound of organs and brass instruments, well represent the bacchanal solemnities. And their cruel thirst after the blood of innocents does in barbarity excel the bloody altars of Diana, Mars, or Pluto,[274] all instigated by the same spirit, | aiming at the *[90]* same end: the destruction of all that worship God in spirit and in truth. This is the spirituality I acknowledge in our mitre-bearing parasites, in enmity and opposition to the spirit of God and all godliness. But if not so, they can never have a pretence to impose their opinions or doctrine on others unless they were infallible. For it is madness to oblige another to think as I do if I may be deceived myself. If the bishop cannot be deceived, he is infallible. We laugh at

---

[272] Religious group that originated in sixteenth-century Italy, derived its name from its founders, Laelius and Faustus Socinus, and flourished principally in Poland. Socinians rejected Christ's divinity and the doctrine of the Trinity.

[273] Venus: Roman goddess who at an early date came to be identified with the Greek goddess of love, Aphrodite. Hera: Greek goddess of marriage and of married women. Bacchus: Latin name for the Greek god Dionysius. Priapus: God of fertility.

[274] Diana: Roman goddess of woodland and wild nature. Mars: Roman god of war. Pluto, Latin form of Plouton, in Greek myth the personification of wealth.

the pretence of infallibility in the bishop of Rome, and shall we allow it in him of Canterbury? If they exalt their wills thus against God, and persecute Christ in his followers, they are as much antichrist as the bishop of Rome. They, like the pagan tyrant, are for casting them into a fiery furnace, or something as bad if they will not worship the idol they have set up, the worship and service book they have invented. And finding no occasion against them but in this relating to their God, as Daniel's case was, they pretend their meetings to pray *to be* seditious, and punish them. They prohibit all worship of God but what they and their king set up in a Common Prayer Book. The fanatics yet meet to call upon God, pray and expound the Scriptures, comfort one another in their afflictions, know the mind of God, and humble themselves before him for their sins. Let kings and princes threaten them, they are not careful to answer them in that matter. If the king command them to worship in his way, they will not do it, knowing it *to* be absurd and profane. If he forbid them to worship God as they know God has commanded them, they desist not from doing it, having his word for their warrant. If God delivers them they give thanks, if he leaves them to suffer they rejoice as thought worthy of bonds or death for his name's sake. Tyrants and priests ever agree together against God and his anointed, as pagan idolaters and Turks do. And the fanatics or true Christians follow the examples also of their forerunners, the prophets, apostles, and all the saints from the beginning of the world; continuing in faith, prayer, and exercise of the gifts God has given them, fearing nothing but sin and being found unworthy of the graces they have received. Here are Augustine's two cities of God and the world, or of God and the devil, still in a uniform, fixed, constant opposition to each other. The powers of earth and hell united, conspire against the elect seed. The one vainly boasts and triumphs in a momentary perishing power, the other is steadfastly fixed upon the rock of [91] Israel, | which never fails those that rely upon it. The perpetual rage of the prince of this world and of all the powers depending on him, under what different titles soever against the people of God, is well set forth in that admirable treatise written by Augustine, *De civitate Dei*.[275] If bishops be not infallible it is a mad thing for them to force men to that worship or doctrine that for ought they know may be

---

[275] Augustine, *City of God*, esp. bks xv ff.

false, and so leave that which may be true. The papists, seeing it absurd that he who might be deceived should oblige others to conform to his faith, resolved, right or wrong, that there should be in their church an infallible power of determining all controversies. Some assert this infallibility to be in the person of the pope, others allow it him only when he is *in cathedra Petri*, in a general council (as if annexed rather to his chair than him). All controversies of the church of Rome may be reduced to one head, the infallibility of the pope. If there be infallibility, their doctrine is true and church true; if no infallibility, none can have the confidence to defend that church or impose its doctrine on others; every man having a rational and natural right of disputing what is uncertain, and of not receiving it till convinced that it's a certain truth. If our prelates follow the steps of Rome in this as many other things, they must prove infallibility in themselves, in the king, in the parliament, or in all together. If in themselves, I desire to know how they come by that infallibility they deny in all others. I should much wrong our reverend doctors if I suspected they pretended to any such authority by virtue of any spiritually infused gifts. This is that they tax for madness in the fanatics who have the spirit of God leading them unto the knowledge of all truths necessary to salvation, not expecting others should believe them farther than they evidence their doctrine to be true by the word of God; nor hope yet to be believed till the same spirit that dictated the word do interpret and plant it in the heart of the hearer. I have proved them before to be no bishops but only in name. But if they were, Cyprian, bishop of Carthage, (in Epistola 50 ad 62^dam) says he was chosen bishop there *a plebe domini*.[276] He says the same[277] of Cornelius, chosen bishop of Rome, reproves Novatian, as I remember, who pretended to be bishop without consent *Dominicae plebis*.[278] Ambrose also confesses himself chosen bishop of Milan | by the peo- /92/ ple.[279] All primitive writers are full of the like testimonies. I infer that as he that institutes is above him that is instituted, the people or church that makes the bishop is above the bishop, *and* therefore[280]

---

[276] 'through God's people'. Cyprian, *Opera*, Epistula 59, sec. 6. The letters referred to in the text are numbered in *Opera* as 2, 4, 53–62, 64.

[277] Cyprian, *Opera*, Epistula 43, 1.

[278] 'of the godly people'. Cornelius, pope (251–3). His pontificate was complicated by a schism that was partly caused by the self-appointment of the Roman priest Novatian as pope.

[279] Ambrose (339–97), first bishop of Milan (374–9).   [280] MS: 'to'.

give laws to him, not to receive laws from him. Both points are confirmed by Cyprian, Epistola 12 *Ad Antonianum* and Epistola 68 *Ad plebem et clerum asturiensem*,[281] that *the* people *is* required at their ordination which else not valid and that they might reject their bishop if he fell from the truth.[282] And in another epistle on that subject, he shows power of excommunication and receiving again excommunicated persons was in the whole church, clergy, and people, exhorting them all not to receive persons excommunicated for great errors or scandalous sins till full proofs of their amendment, *ne darent pacem danti periculosam, accipienti mutilem.*[283]

Thirdly, if ours be true bishops, the Roman bishops from whom they pretend to have had their ordination are true also. But they themselves teach me to have the usurped authority of the Roman bishop, which shows me that I ought as little to esteem them who are but his apes. And, notwithstanding the profound supine ignorance of our bishops, they know that such as have been true bishops have fallen into the most foul heresies and practices.

The next point to be considered is the infallibility of the king, or parliament, or both, with the bishops. They that say the king is head of the church and make men under highest penalties submit to his proclamations or the parliament's acts in matters of religion, do either believe there is an infallible certainty of truth in them, or they are guilty of the most impious, profane abusing of holy things that can be imagined. All kings and parliaments have not this prerogative, because they often differ and are clean contrary to each other. As for prudence, piety, learning, or presence of God, I see nothing extraordinary in this king and parliament beyond all other. So I shall take my liberty to differ from them when I see them apt to fall into the lowest pits of sin and darkness, as well as I, wanting light and therefore subject to the same errors I am. I can easily discern the same spirit acting them in their furious imposing their religion upon oth-
/93/ ers, that in the oppression of saints has | maintained the devil's cause from the beginning of the world. They broadly discover themselves lovers of lies, and every mark of their malice against Christians

[281] 'To the people and the clergy of Asturia', Cyprian, *Opera*, Epistula 67. The letter to his brother Antonianus, in the old numbering 52 instead of 12, is *Opera*, Epistula 55.
[282] Cyprian, *Opera*, Epistula 67, 4.
[283] 'in order not to give a peace dangerous to the giver, nor mutilated for the receiver'. Reference to Cyprian, *Opera*, Epistula 67, 5.

declares them heathens. Those that persecute true Christians, it is all one what they are called, Christians or Mohammedans, Turks or heathens, nor whether it be a crown or a mitre, that covers their impious heads. The devil has changed the course of his policy since the primitive times. He then openly raged against Christians by heathen emperors, but now finds none more able to destroy the people of God than they that pretend to preserve them. When the pagan sword had lost its edge and point, he stirs up more crafty instruments of mischief. He knew none could so well destroy the flock of Christ as those who were set to guard it. He carries them to the top of the temple, shows them the riches and glory of this world, which he offers to give them if they will fall down and worship him, set up a worship and interest in the church, contrary to the command and spirit of God, and he will give them that that shall gratify all their lusts, and answer all their expectations. They swallow the bait and do his work. They have sold themselves for these fine worldly things to do all manner of wickedness to please the lusts of their king and the devil, under the shelter of whose wings they may be upheld in their greatness and pride. But as there is nothing but vanity in their calling, lewdness in their lives, unworthiness in their persons, and wickedness in their ends, we may confidently believe God will not only blast their designs but the tottering monarchy itself, which is so strictly united to their interest, being by them rendered so hateful to God and man, will be involved in their ruin. This we expect in faith, knowing that the redeemer of Israel lives. And many signs persuade us to hope that salvation is near at hand.

PHILALETHES: I have harkened attentively to your discourse, and have little to reply against it. But I desire you further to satisfy me in three points.

First, I find you draw arguments against the bishops both from the authority of ancient authors and human tradition, as also from the Scripture and the immediate constant acting of the spirit of God in his people nowadays. Now it appears to me that the bishops, pretending only to the first, there is no necessity to show they have no great measure of the second. The second is that I find you often cite the fathers, make great use of their authority, whereas I am apt to think you do not much value it. | [94]

Thirdly, I desire to know why you should say the bishops endeavour to destroy the fanatics for reading the Bible, for we do not easily confess that to be the reason for which they are destroyed.

EUNOMIUS: it must needs seem strange that sometimes I speak against the bishops as pretending to spirituality and to be guided by the word and spirit of God, interpreting it[284] at other times as if they renounced all this, wholly relying upon their outward calling and human tradition. But the fraudulent and perverse dealing of the bishops obliges me to take this course. For where they dispute with papists they find prescription, human authority, succession, and outward call is all against them. And that the romanists, having been for many ages in possession of the government of the churches of Europe, whatever advantages could be challenged by all those ways belonging to them, and all the bitter things that in general were said by the ancients against those who left their mother church, might with appearance of truth be applied unto them, who, having been brought up in the Roman church did dissent from it. And they could neither prove the right succession of their ecclesiastic order that they so much brag of from Rome. Nor, if they had rightly received it, could they have denied but that by their receding from them that gave it, they had lost all power and right of executing it, or receiving any benefit by it; being, as Cyprian says, as boughs turn from the stock which have no life at all in them.[285] When they are thus pressed, they say with Tertullian *nullum tempus, nulla praescriptio occurrit veritati.*[286] That the Scriptures contain the only rules to be observed; that the spirit of God which dictated them is their only interpreter; that the same spirit plants faith in us and teaches us all things belonging to salvation; that God out of the mouths of babes and sucklings ordains strength, delighting by the weak things of the world to overthrow the mighty, and by the foolishness of the gospel to overthrow and blast all the wisdom, learning, glory, and power of man; that the holy Scripture needs not the testimony of man, pope or councils, many like passages learnt for the most part from Luther, alleged by him in the treatise about a dispute he was to have had with cardinal Cajetan,[287] true in themselves, but not at all applicable to our

---

[284] MS: '... it cand(?) at ...'.   [285] Cyprian, *De catholicae ecclesiae unitate*, sec. 5.
[286] 'No time, no precept counteracts truth.' Reference to Tertullian, *De verginibus velandis*, ch. 1, par. 1.
[287] Cajetan, Cardinal (Thomas de Vio) (1468/9–1534), one of the major catholic theologians of the Thomist School, who as a papal delegate in Germany was authorized to examine Martin Luther on doctrinal matters in 1528.

bishops. For when the same things are alleged by the | fanatics, who /95/
have much more right unto them, walking by the light of them, our
prelates then turn quite the other way. Nothing is then insisted on
but the obedience we owe to our pastors; they only have the holy
unction, the interpreting the oracles of God belongs only to them;
laymen must submit and believe them that watch over their souls.
All the honours given unto the apostles or the succeeding bishops
belongs to them. Nothing but decrees of councils and canons are
cited; all pretensions of being directed by a private spirit scorned,
those that follow the impulses of God's spirit detested. They show
the weakness of their cause by making use of the puritan arguments
against the papists, and the papist arguments against the puritan to
be such as they that have no arms of their own or means of defending
themselves on either side but under the cloak of one of their enemies.
Which obliged me in the unfolding of their cause to show they could
neither pretend to advantage by the authority which belonged not
unto them, and which they had despised in their predecessors, nor
by the far truer and stronger arguments drawn from the actings of
the spirit, to which the whole course of their lives and doctrine
declares them to be strangers or enemies. And being thus deprived of
the help they hoped to have received on both sides, they remain as
naked as the bird that was covered with the other's feathers, when
everyone had taken his own.

As to the second point, I do not acknowledge myself obliged to
receive as truth all I find in the ancient fathers. But as they were of
piety, learning, and knowledge, respect is to be had to many things
they say. And certainly many excellent things may be learnt out of
their writings. I take these writings to be of two sorts, the one partly
historical, either telling what was the custom, practice, or belief of
the churches in their times, or arguments drawn from those customs,
practices, or belief. The other is merely composed of such things as
they themselves thought or believed. I make great difference
between these two; I yield much to the first, but as for matters of
their opinion I think I am to receive no more than what they prove to
be true, there being hardly one of them that has not left in his writings some notorious error and several opinions clashing one with the
other. | I learnt these cautions in reading of them from Monsieur /96/
Daillé, that excellent and learned preacher of the gospel in

Charenton.[288] Having these opinions, I am induced to cite the fathers because I see the bishops gain great advantage by perverting them. You hear of nothing in their pulpits and writings so often as the great names of Augustine, Jerome, Tertullian, Cyprian, etcetera, making people believe that they walk in their steps, and thereby obliging many to receive lies upon their authority. Others, finding things related as from them to be contrary to the word of God without examining whether they are truly cited and understood or not, absolutely reject the authors to the great damage of the christian church, which might certainly draw great advantage from their writings. I thought both of these inconveniences were to be avoided. And, finding nothing in any of them that could justly serve for the bishops' purpose, I thought not amiss to show how they abused them in many places, and how those whom they take to be their patrons, being rightly understood and applied, destroy all that they endeavour to set up.

As to their third point or scruple, I think nothing more clear than that the fanatics are persecuted principally for reading the Bible, and doing what they learn in it, since they are thereby sought to discover and oppose the frauds of the priests. The only way to maintain their authority is to keep people from perusing the Bible as well as the Romanist, for that discovers the vanity of both their callings and all their fig-leaf pretences. They cannot burn men for reading it as Cardinal Beaton (Buchanan, *De rebus Scoticis*)[289] did in Scotland, making people believe that the old testament was writ*ten* by Luther, the new by Calvin. So have I finished what I have to say of bishops.

[97]   Finis[290] |

---

[288] Sidney's father regularly visited the huguenot church in Charenton, near Paris, where Jean Daillé (1594–1670) – after serving as a tutor in the household of Philippe Duplessis-Mornay – was a minister in the late 1630s.

[289] Buchanan, *History of Scotland*. Beaton, David, cardinal (c. 1494–1546), prominent Scottish Catholic at the court of James V. Appointed a cardinal in 1538 and archbishop of St. Andrews in 1539, he persecuted the Protestants.

[290] The first part of the MS ends here. Although the numbering of the second part of the MS restarts at page one, we have opted for a continuous numbering, as is the case in Scott, *Sidney and the English republic*. The manuscript page numbers of the second part in fact are minus ninety-six the numbers in this edition.

Ninth Dialogue

Eighth Court Maxim: The corruption of lawyers is useful to the king

PHILALETHES: in our last conference we discoursed of bishops, of the right of judging and punishing heretics and blasphemers, and of prescribing rules in matters of religion. Let us now consider what use is to be made of lawyers depending on the court.

EUNOMIUS: you will much oblige me to let me know whom you comprehend under the name of lawyers, how you bring them to a dependence on the court, and what advantage is expected by them.

PHILALETHES: the name is given by some only to pleaders. But we give it in general to all that live by the practice of it, together with all attorneys or offices of court, who have a united interest as one body. And little industry is required to bring them to depend on the king.

Secondly, the way has been made long since, and they that enter upon the profession must follow it. There were anciently two great faults in our law. One, that being framed by men that loved their liberty and country, it much favoured the subject and restrained the power of kings within narrow limits. The other, that our ancestors through a virtuous simplicity had made those laws so plain and easy, that when the king stood in need of a judgment in favour of prerogative, or to take away a suspected head, it either could not be gained at all, or so as the judges, | by plainly perverting the sense of the law, *[98]* were in danger of punishment. Many evils proceeded from the same cause. For this plainness of the law lessened the number of suits and rendered the determination of them so speedy and certain that the number of lawyers was not great, the gain small, and they were of little power in the nation or use to the king. If any of them did arise to considerable credit, it was gained by virtue, integrity, prudence, learning, and loyalty to their country, which obliged them to uphold the subject's rights and cross the king's designs. Now, as the wisdom of man is seen in nothing more than in gaining several advantages by one and the same act, our kings in this alone deserve to be esteemed as teachers and masters of all others. They have found a way, by dexterously proposing businesses to the Parliament under several pretences, through the power and subtlety of their creatures in Parliament, to obtain a multitude of statutes by which the whole body of the law is brought into such a confusion that no man fully understands it. The ablest men rather give opinions than certain judgments. All questions in law are subject to *a* variety of interpretations, and the number of suits is infinitely multiplied. All of them prove *tedious*[291] and expensive, many are never to be determined. Lawyers and their dependants are grown exceeding numerous. Everyone sees that all things in law are questionable; those questions for the most part are full of inextricable difficulties. By this means men are often involved in snares, no man is free from danger. The

[99] whole nation is hereby brought into *such* a dependence upon the | lawyers and courtiers, that by the craft of the one or power of the other they may be preserved. And neither of these is to be rendered propitious otherwise than by money. If any be so simple as to rely on the justice of his cause, he is soon taught to see his error by the miscarriage of it. And others, seeing his ruin, are warned not to run into the same folly. Thus the treasure of the nation with a full stream flows into their bosoms and ours. They know the king is the author and preserver of this their felicity, and must therefore as lawyers endeavour to maintain the government that upholds their profession. The most eminent amongst them to gain favour and preferment are brought into an entire and immediate dependence on the person of the king from whom only they can expect it.

Thirdly, the advantages the king receives from hence are so plain, that any ordinary understanding may discover them in part; but so many and great, that it is hardly possible for any fully to express or

---

[291] Due to the binding of the MS, this word is not entirely legible.

enumerate them. But in short the king, by being master of the lawyers, is grown master of the law. And consequently of the lives and
fortunes of all the subjects, who have no defence for either, but from
the law. The Scotch Solomon,[292] who, having a padlock on his
sword, applied himself wholly to kingcraft, used to say: let me create
bishops and judges, and I will have what law and gospel I please.
Whatsoever the king now desires to do is found to be legal.[293] If any
man be suspected he is easily made a traitor. When judges, pleaders
and all officers are the king's creatures, it is easy to find pliable
jury-men and useful witnesses. If the pretended delinquent be not
very crafty, he will be sure to be ensnared. | If he proposes anything /100/
for his justification that is not easily answered, or cannot be determined without danger, the court never wants a pretence to overrule
the plea. Such course also is taken for instructing the jury, that no
verdict hardly is brought in that is not agreeable to the king's ends.
By these means the most active heads of the disaffected party are easily removed and the spirits of the whole nation broken. Everyone
sees there is no safety but in the king's favour. So His Majesty's
throne is safely established, lawyers increase in riches, and we enjoy
our so much envied felicity.

EUNOMIUS: you extend the name lawyer beyond what most eminent
in the profession can like of. But I should not complain, though you
also comprehended as spies, trepanners, false witnesses, counterfeit-
ers, hands or seals, knights of the post, perjured jury-men, and those
that corrupt them; and generally all those who either live by the
calamity of others as well as the others mentioned by you, as deserve
to be esteemed of the same body because they have a united interest.
And as those by you mentioned are by that interest brought to
depend upon the king, and are esteemed good, loyal, well affected
subjects, but cannot often serve His Majesty so effectively *as* they
would without the help of the others, they, being joined with the
others in the same interest, must necessarily depend upon the king,
be sure of him, and for being so deserve his favour. If this be true we
ought not to wonder at the strength and number of the royal party.
All those who are lewd in manners, or by their callings *are* right for

---

[292] I.e. James I of England (reigned 1603–25).
[293] Probably an allusion to Justinian, *Digest*, bk 1, ch. 4: 'what pleases the prince has the
force of law'.

the king by their union of interest with the bishops and all knavish, [101] false, treacherous, | and perfidious persons, become loyal subjects by means of the lawyers. All which joined together are so numerous, that the rest of the nation seems few in comparison of them. This must needs have a fair appearance, but I doubt whether it can rationally give hopes of a permanent felicity.

PHILALETHES: why, what can a prince fear, who is in possession of the whole power, and, besides foreign allies, has so strong a party in the nation to maintain it?

EUNOMIUS: he ought to fear God, man, and the principles of his government, enemies unto both. God seeks the happiness and perfection of his creatures, has given laws to mankind which show the way to that happiness and perfection. He that walks in this way and draws others to it does a work beneficial unto man and acceptable unto God. Whoever does the contrary becomes an enemy to man and incurs the wrath of God for his disobedience. Such ought to fear, unless they have power above both, so as to be able to defend themselves against God and good men.

But, it may be objected, the world is so divided, that the king finds many who find it beneficial to them to join in the same interest with him. So it may seem no man's actions or principles can have a direct contrariety to the interest of mankind. This is true, but all this diversity proceeds from contrariety of principles, and those principles from contrary roots. All that is just, good, and true begins and ends in God; that which is contrary must be by the impulse of the devil, whose devices and designs are against God, and those that [102] depend on him. This obliges all who | act wickedly under that evil one to use all manner of evil ways, means, and instruments for the accomplishment of their evil ends. Man is not able to stand in his own strength. If he leave his dependence on God, he must become the servant of the devil. The root of Saul's first sin was pride and presumption in himself; the first fruit that sprang from it was disobedience to the command of God. Then, finding himself under the wrath of God, he slays the priests, with a multitude of other innocent persons. Amongst other wicked ministers he joined unto himself Doeg the Edomite, enemy to God's people.[294] The spirit of God

---

[294] I Sam. 22:6–23.

departs from him, good men are looked on as his enemies, God answers him not by dream, Urim or prophets, and not being able to subsist of himself, he falls under the power of the evil one, by whose impulse he was wholly governed. In the former part of his reign, when he walked in the ways of God, he was directed by Samuel, served by David, fought the Lord's battles, gained famous victories for his people, slew the witches, and had no enemies but the men of Belial. When he fell from God into the devil's hands, the whole frame of things was changed. God answered him not. Samuel departed from Abimelech. David and all good men, even his son Jonathan, were looked on as his enemies. The enemies of God were his servants, Nabal and other men of Belial his friends. In his distress he goes to the devil for counsel, brings a great slaughter upon Israel, flies before his enemies, and desperately falls upon his own sword. Ahab walked in the same path. False witnesses and corrupt judges were | necessary helps to him in shedding righteous blood. A witch /103/ was his counsellor, and false prophets ever encouraged him. Julian the Apostate was a diligent disciple of the same master. When he *has* renounced christianity as inconsistent with the tyranny he resolved to exercise, he places the greatest powers in the most wicked hands, shows favour and gives the highest preferments to the most subtle inventors of new frauds to subvert and persecute the church of God. And, applying himself to the worship of the devil, the upholder of his throne, he used all the most detestable arts that he has taught unto his servants who ask counsel from him. Andronicus[295] the Greek emperor is an eminent example of the same kind, who, though retaining the name of a Christian, was as notorious for following the counsels of witches, astrologers, soothsayers, and the whole rabble of satan's servants, as for his execrable tyranny and wicked frauds, for the subverting of innocent persons under pretence of law, through the perfidiousness and corruption of those who ought to have administered justice. The cruel and filthy Tiberius Caesar, whilst he sat meditating mischief on the rocks of Capri, encompassed with a crew of Chaldean magicians and witches, seemed to think the swords of his guard had lost their edge with frequent slaughters. But the tongues of accusers and false witnesses would never be wearied. Whilst he had the judges at his command, he was master of the law,

---

[295] Andronicus of Constantinople, vicarius Thraciarum (365–6).

and put a colour of justice upon the most wicked murders and detestable rapine. But the tragical ends of all these and a multitude of others related in the histories of all nations, show how the devil [104] deceives his followers. | When he has brought the hatred of God and man upon his servants, he cannot preserve them from the punishment deserved by their crimes.

PHILALETHES: I must confess some princes have succeeded ill in these courses. But that may be ascribed only to their want of prudence, diligence, or courage. They either did not understand the ways of securing themselves, or neglected to use them through a confidence that they were not necessary. Or perhaps they gave themselves wholly over to sensual *and* trivial pleasures, and would not apply their thoughts to things of greater concernment. Others of them have perished for want of *spirit* vigorously to employ their power in destroying their enemies and preserving themselves. Or *if* there were no defect in their persons, they have been overthrown by some vast power far above theirs. When there is none of these visible causes, their ruin is to be imputed to the infinite variety of human accidents, which is such as allows no steady assurance unto any man in any condition. All sorts of persons are equally exposed to all sorts of evils. Or if there be a difference, those who according to your rules have been the best men, have been most miserable. Those you most extol, have ever lived in affliction, been exposed to all manner of crosses and often died shamefully and miserably; whilst those we esteem, have flourished in the highest splendour and prosperity. We hear of no man who enjoyed *a* longer and more uninterrupted [105] felicity than Augustus Caesar.[296] And certainly never man | attained to any with more cruelty, violence, and fraud. It is generally seen the foundations of thrones are best cemented with blood, and those stand most firm that are fullest of it. No king can be safe that is not feared. He will never be feared that has but one way of doing hurt. If suspected persons could be removed only by the sword, they who hate us might also use it to our ruin. We care not much for all the discontented speeches and complaints with which the fanatics fill all men's ears. But we so well remember the temper of their swords, that we avoid all disputes that are determined that way. The subtlety of lawyers is far more useful to the king than the violence of soldiers.

---

[296] Augustus (63 BC–AD 14), the first of the Roman emperors (27 BC–AD 14).

By their means suspected persons are ensnared one by one, and destroyed without noise or danger. Yea, sometimes upon such pretences, as we gain honour by their deaths as men careful to maintain peace, do justice, and preserve the nation from those evils which might have been brought upon it by their dangerous practices. By this means all men's lives and estates depend upon the will of the king. Against spies, informers, false witnesses, and fitly chosen judges there is no other defence than such a conformity as may gain favour. The whole nation sees this and trembles; their fear is our security. So they may be kept in fear, we despise their hatred. He that fears hatred understands not the arts of reigning. Kingdoms are preserved by fear. All men desire to be free unless it be those who have advantages by making others slaves; and, if not deterred by danger, they will endeavour to attain | what they desire. Our business is /106/ so to fix the yoke that none shall dare to attempt the breaking of it. Men are apt to undertake great things when there is hope of succeeding, but that being taken away, none but madmen will attempt anything against the government. The dexterity of the lawyers has taught us a policy whereby we know how to keep them in awe, who fear no other arms than what they provide for us. They tremble at one of our barons who used to go into battles with such cheerful and serene countenances as showed the terrible constancy of their hearts. This terror which is generally spread over the whole nation is not more beneficial to the king than to his ministers. He is an unskilful courtier who knows not how to make them pay dear for their safety who know they must owe it to their favour from whom they can expect none but what they buy. But that which puts the matter quite out of question is that these useful servants desire nothing out of the king's purse. They are contented with what they can get from their clients. And when any of them is preferred to be a judge or other great officer, they scruple not to give such liberal acknowledgments as are no small helps to our wants. I know it may be said that by this means all things become venal; that justice cannot be expected from corrupt lawyers and mercenary judges; that the nation will be destroyed, God offended, and the like. For all which we are little solicitous. If the | judges might not sell justice, they would not buy /107/ their places. If all these things were not venal, we could not live by the sale of them. If judges were not corrupt, they would neither bend the law to the king's interest, nor value our solicitations when we desire to pleasure a friend, oppress an enemy, or squeeze a rich man. They would not favour us in our suits that come before them, if they did not know that they have often need of us to uphold both their profession and their persons. By this means the king would lose his principal strength and advantage; and we that depend on him should be left poor, despicable, and obliged to live according to law. We obviate all these evils by that venality which you dislike. They, buying their places, execute them so as to reimburse themselves, whereby they must depend upon the king and have need of us. We, growing thus necessary unto them, have an absolute power over them. Men that have suits are obliged to come to us. It is not less necessary to have a courtier to solicit than a lawyer to plead. Thus we become masters of the law in private cases, as the king in those of public concernment. Nothing could be more irrational than for the king or his ministers to dislike this temper so beneficial to them. The prejudice befalling the nation little troubles us. We may often judge of those who have suits at law as queen Catherine de Medici[297] did of both factions in the civil war of France between the Protestants and them of the League. Whenever she heard of a fight between them, in which many were slain, she rejoiced, not much caring which had the victory, | but, summing up the number of those that fell on both sides (as for example, one party lost a thousand, the other two thousand), she would say: God be thanked, we are delivered from three thousand enemies. In like manner we seldom have reason to make a difference between the plaintiff and defendant. If the lawyers can ruin both, they often take from two enemies the power of hurting us.

[108]

The arguments you draw from religion sway not with us. For it is a most settled maxim in policy *a prince should have religion in his mouth, but none in his heart.*[298] It were impossible for a prince to govern gallantly, as he ought, if he listened to Bible counsel. He could not enrich himself or *his* servants, advance his friends, ensnare and oppress his enemies if he consulted the Scriptures. All political proceedings would be obstructed with scruples of conscience. If he know not how to leap over all those *blows*, he must necessarily

---

[297] Catherine de Medici (1519–89), queen consort of Henry II of France (reigned 1547–59), and subsequently regent of France (1560–74), often portrayed as a ruthless machiavellian because of her extremely realistic politics in maintaining the house of Valois.
[298] Reference to Machiavelli, *The prince*, ch. 18.

perish. When the fanatics governed it was good for us to speak of mercy, gentleness, and justice. We and our friends who are concealed amongst them gained security to and credit to themselves by such discourses. The nation was brought to believe that if the king came in he would govern by these rules. The impolitic fanatics were brought by this means to spare those who destroyed them. We are warned by their errors, and assured we shall never be ruined by following Scripture rules. Private men may study those books if they will, and learn to live quietly and obey their master. Some of them do so fill their melancholy heads with notions of heaven and eternity that they less easily attempt anything for a temporal end, | so trouble /109/ us little. But a prince must be exceedingly unwise that ever troubles his mind with these matters. We live in a world where art and force, which you call fraud and violence, have ever prevailed. We must use the ways wherein others prosper. If God governed it he would give the pre-eminence to moral and christian virtues. But the experience we have of the contrary, persuades us that there is no God at all, or that he cares not for us or regards *not* our prayers or curses. In this principle we live the life of men, that is, enjoy a short pleasant being in this world; leaving those to muse on another life and please themselves with expectations of happiness in it, who have not wit enough to understand the advantages of this. Thus we secure the king's throne, enjoy the next places under him, and please ourselves with seeing those heads set upon towers and gates, which were formerly filled with the fine airy notions they had learnt from Moses and Paul.

EUNOMIUS: you have said very much in a short time. And though I do no farther assent unto any part of your discourse than to acknowledge it to be a true description of what is at present practised, I will not contradict any part of it, but, proceeding more fully to show from what principle such actions do proceed, reserve a liberty of more narrowly examining at another time, from grounds of reason and Scripture, what issue is to be expected from such practices. Experience shows that those who continue in the same way go to the same place. And it is equally evident that those who agree in a continued series of actions aim at the same end, live in the same principle, and are | /110/ acted by the same spirit. If then it be *made to* appear what sort of princes or governors have forced people to submit to them, who, that they might be feared, have made the laws of their countries numerous and intricate to ensnare men, what sort of men have brought in all manner of corruption, subverted justice, favoured wicked judges, spies, informers, and false witnesses that they might be feared, and when their end was in desiring to be feared, whose servants they were, whose work they did, and what spirit directed them, we may easily guess who is their guide who now walk in the same paths. Commonwealths or civil societies are constituted for the attaining of justice, that everyone living in them may enjoy that which justly belongs to him and suffer nothing from others but what he has justly deserved. The links of these societies are the respective laws. These laws are either compacts made by men, or are given by God, who has a true sovereign power about all. All laws made by men ought to tend to the preservation of those societies in doing justice to all the individuals thereof. Every man thereby is to see that he shall suffer what he would not, if he do what he ought not. If his just penalty be death, his blood is upon his own head. Hence I infer:

First, those laws only do answer the end for which they were made, that take care no man shall be deprived of what justly belongs unto him, unless he forfeit *it* by some act prejudicial to the society.

Secondly, laws being made to punish offences tending to a dissolution of the civil society, the penalties thereof are justly inflicted [111] when proportioned to deter those that are viciously inclined from | like offences. No man can be deterred from anything but by knowing his danger, and he cannot know his danger, threatened by law, unless he understand that law for the transgression of which he shall be punished. No man can walk according to a rule that is unknown to him, nor be deterred from offending unless he know when he offends. The justice therefore of all laws does necessarily and essentially depend on the plainness and clearness of them, that every man may understand them if he will, or justly bear the penalty of his neglect if he will not when he might. Otherwise offences are not prevented that are prejudicial to the society, and consequently the society is not thereby preserved.

The essence of the law consists solely in the justice of it: if it be not just, it is no law. The justice of it depends upon the end: if it conduces not to a good end, it cannot be just. Laws are made for the right regulating and preservation of societies, and to obviate offences tending to the disturbance thereof. Those acts or decrees which tend not thereunto have no justice in them, nor in any respect deserve the name or power of laws. Instead of landmarks to warn and prevent dangers, they become snares to catch and destroy men unawares. The utmost deviation that can be from this rule in making laws is when through the multiplicity and intricacy of them they are rendered unintelligible. The lawyers tell us *the law is written reason,* and that whatever they find in their books is just. But that is Westminster Hall prate, hardly worth an answer. If the law were written reason, it would be universally and eternally the same, as reason is; ever just and good, as reason is; ever suitable to his law who is justice itself. If this were true of the law, every wise man would be a good lawyer. He that is a good lawyer in England would be so in France | and Spain /112/ also. As reason is the same on this side *of* the sea and beyond it, that law which they call written reason would be also the same. For the understanding of this law we should not need to study Littleton and Coke,[299] but Plato and other great masters of human reason. But above all the Scripture, which, being the dictate of God's own spirit, is the efflux or manifestation of the eternal word, which is the reason and wisdom of the father. I need not say such study would little advance a suit in Westminster Hall. The craft of a little, paltry attorney will be of more use in those courts than the wisdom of Seneca, Aristotle, Moses, and Paul. All mandates of those in supreme or legislative power must be reasonable and just, or are no laws. Otherwise the edict made by Nebuchadnezzar for worshipping the statue he had set up;[300] that of Caligula for setting up his own image to be adored in the temple of the Jews and all others; that of that no man should pray to any God for *such* a time, save to him only; that, anciently among the Romans, mentioned by Tertullian,[301] that no God should be worshipped but by the authority of the senate; and generally all those made in several parts of the world to hinder the propagation of the gospel and put those to death that would not obey them and those of the inquisition, and the like now in force in many countries, punishing with axes, halters, and fire all that recede from the filthiness of Roman idolatry; must also be reverenced and obeyed

---

[299] Littleton, John (1422–81); jurist and holder of various judicial offices. Coke, Edward (1552–1634); English politician and the most influential legal writer of the early seventeenth century. His *Reports* and *Institutes* commented on many aspects of the common law and English constitutional history, and defended limitation of the king's power by English custom.
[300] II Chron. 36:7, II Kings 24:13.
[301] Tertullian, *Apology,* ch. 5.

as written reason, full of justice, righteousness, and truth. The same must be confessed of that law made in Scotland in the time of Eve- [113] nus, whereby the king had | a liberty of using the wives and daughters of noblemen at his pleasure, and they, as a recompense for their loyalty in granting His Majesty so large a prerogative, gained unto themselves the like privilege and command over the wives and daughters of the commons. Though we do not know, perhaps, that any of such barbarous enormity as these has been made in England, it is affirmed by those that are learned in the law that many abbey tenures and others of like nature in England were so instituted by law, that whoever did not prostitute his wife the first night to the abbot, or furnish so many maids every year to satisfy the lusts of the monks, did forfeit their tenements, or incur other punishments specified in the respective obligations of their tenures. But if no man can be so impudent to affirm such laws to be rational and just, it is certain something else is required to make a law besides the authority of the lawgivers.

PHILALETHES: do you conceive the justice and essence of the law to be the same?

EUNOMIUS: I will not trouble you with niceties; too much subtlety rather conceals truth and perplexes the mind of him that seeks it, than gives satisfaction in the discovery thereof. I shall therefore make no other distinction between the justice and essence of any law, than such as is necessary for the understanding of anything in nature. All things consist of matter and form; where there is no matter there can be no form. The matter of which any plant, animal, or other creature is composed, is not the creature, but that without which it could be no creature. The form is that which gives it its distinct being, making it what it is. In like manner justice is so far the matter of the law, that where it is not there is no law. The form or distinct being of it, in which consists its power and efficacy, is from the seal or stamp it [114] receives from him or them who have the | legislative power, whereby that which was ever just is manifested to be so and declared as a rule to be observed by those of the society; the obedience to which is to be rewarded, and the contrary to be punished.

PHILALETHES: what do you conceive is required to the justice and essence of a law, besides the authority of him or them that make it?

EUNOMIUS: three things are requisite:

First, that it be consonant to the law of God, the great sovereign Lord and creator of mankind, whose authority is above all. He that opposes him incurs the guilt of undeniable wickedness and injustice. An act in opposition to him cannot be obliging to any other, and therefore can be no law, if repugnant to his law.

Secondly, it must agree with the light of nature and reason in man. This is full of truth, as having its beginning in God. The authority thereof is revered by all that deserve the name of men. What man or number of men soever enact anything contrary to this light, do most unjustly oppose all the rest of mankind, who are above them or him, and God, who is above all. Such laws are void and null also for the reason above alleged.

Thirdly, no law can be just which destroys or impairs the ends for which laws are made. If they are made to preserve societies, societies established for obtaining of justice, justice sought because good and helpful to mankind; what law soever is made prejudicial to those of that society, perverting justice, destroys the end for which it ought to be established, is therefore in the highest degree unjust and utterly invalid.

PHILALETHES: I am not yet fully convinced but that those decrees which are in themselves unjust, and therefore ought not to have been made, are to be obeyed as | laws when made; least if power be /115/ granted to private persons of judging whether that which the magistrate declares to be law be according to the rules of justice or not, all law should be overthrown.

EUNOMIUS: if the decrees be unjust, they must necessarily be invalid. For they are made only for the attaining of justice. No act of injustice can be imagined of a deeper dye than for the creature thus to oppose the law of the creator. For one or a few men to enact anything contrary to the light by which all mankind should be governed, as for him or them who have received power to preserve societies, administer justice, and procure the good of those that gave it to them; to turn all against their masters and benefactors, setting up some invention of their own, for maintaining of a private interest above and against the dictates of reason, written in the heart of every man, and this upon pretence that their authority may not be disputed; such acts certainly are invalid.

This will appear more evidently if we consider these three particulars. First, the definition of the law agreed on by all *lex est sanctio justa, jubens honesta, prohibens contraria*;[302] that, therefore, which is not just, is no law.

Secondly, *salus populi est suprema lex*.[303] The safety of the people depends upon the administration of justice; justice cannot be administered by a decree that is not just; therefore, such a one cannot be a law.

Thirdly, all such acts must be invalid because the doer of them forbids the authority or power he was entrusted with, according to the forecited words of Grotius; *quia eatenus non habet imperium*.[304]

These steadfast truths cannot be overthrown by any evil conse-
[116] quences whatsoever, much less by any | imagination of an inconvenience that might follow. No evil consequence can be rightly drawn from that which is true and good. Whoever therefore pretends to overthrow what is found to be true upon pretence of evil consequences, does only discover the vanity of his own imaginations, fancying to himself that which will never be.

PHILALETHES: but what if those laws which were rightly made be perversely administered? Think you that thereby they lose their validity?

EUNOMIUS: he were contentious, who should so nice*ly* criticize upon the administration as to deny the validity of the law for every error committed in the administration thereof. We ought not to be too quick-sighted in other men's faults. We have our own. Much is to be imputed to human frailty. We ought not to blame every mote we see in our brother's eye. But if the ill-administration be such as proceeds not from ignorance but malice; is not a transient but permanent evil; not in some small circumstances, but such as destroy the end for which the law was made; so that the people, who sought justice thereby, falls under oppression; the trust is broke, all acts done upon pretence of powers given are void, and those that exercise them become enemies and traitors to their masters that entrusted them.

---

[302] 'the law is a righteous stipulation, prescribing what is virtuous, forbidding the contrary'. Reference to Cicero, *De legibus*, bk 1, par. 19.
[303] 'the welfare of the people is the supreme law'.
[304] 'for the reason that his authority does not extend so far', Grotius, *On the law of war and peace*, bk 1, ch. 4, sec. 13.

PHILALETHES: what do you take to be the greatest evil in the institution or administration of laws?

EUNOMIUS: the greatest evil in the institution is when that is enacted by man which is contrary | to the law of God, to the light of nature in /117/ man, and the ends for which societies are established, that is, the obtaining of justice.

The greatest evil in the administration is, when the law, made conformable to these ends, is by corruption turned against them. This will be best explained by examples. The law of God given to Israel was certainly the best and most perfect in its institution, as to the true ends for which all laws ought to be made. Those, therefore, which are most conformable unto that are the best, next unto that which is best of all. And those which differ most from it, or are most contrary to it, are the worst. Magistrates ought so to exercise their power, as that under them we may live in all godliness and honesty, says the apostle.[305] The like is said by all philosophers who deserve to be harkened to. Aristotle says the end of civil society is *vita beata secundum virtutem*,[306] Socrates and Plato say the perfection of action and contemplation,[307] others,[308] the attaining of justice in order to *arrive at* that perfection in action and contemplation; which must needs be much hindered by injuries and molestations, unless speedy and easy remedy can be had. We may truly say that all rational men without the law, and all inspired men under the old law and new, have agreed in showing this to be the end of government. Whatever decree therefore is contrary to the law of God and light of nature, is consequently unjust and evil, and so cannot be a law.

The next point to be considered in the law itself is, that the law given by God relating to civil government was in all points the most short, | easy, and plain of any that is known unto man. Those facts /118/ were punished which by the light of nature were known to be crimes. Punishments were proportionable to the offences. The whole tended to make the nation happy. No part favoured in the least degree, nor the interest of one or a few men promoted to the prejudice of the nation. God the giver often respected not persons. Those parts of it which determined propriety were so clear and simple that there could be no long, intricate, or expensive disputes upon any title unto

---

[305] Paul in Rom. 13.   [306] See n. 49 above.   [307] Plato, *Republic*, 497a.
[308] E.g. Cicero, *On duties*, bk 1, secs. 157–8.

goods moveable or immoveable. Such judges were appointed for determining all controversies arising among the people, who were most knowing, upright, *and* that had neither interest to incline them to pervert judgment, nor power to preserve themselves from punishment if they did prevaricate. The utmost contrariety unto this that man can imagine, is when the law is made various, flexible, uncertain, infinite, unintelligible; when things are punished as crimes which are themselves eminent virtues; when grievous punishments are inflicted for slight offences; when the interest of one or a few is set up in opposition to that of the nation; and lastly when it favours vice and wickedness, tending to corrupt and oppress the nation, that is, to make it vile, naught, sottish, and miserable in soul and body.

As to the administration, it may be rightly said that law is imperfect, which does not take care that it may be rightly administered, hindering or punishing corrupt practices. As the imperfection of the law is the cause of the mal-administration; the mal-administration /119/ does | as well increase the perversity of the law, as evidence it. Both these evils, as proceeding from the same root, are to be mended by the same pattern. God shows us the way in both that his law might be as pure in its administration as perfect in its institution. He appointed a leader unto his people,[309] excellent in wisdom and holiness, seventy chosen men to be his assistants,[310] gives of his spirit to them and to Joshua his successor. The other qualifications required in them are expressed in Exodus (18:27). They were to be able men, such as fear God, men of truth, hating covetousness. These were to be rulers of thousands, hundreds, fifties, and tens. And, lest a king should come in and overthrow this whole fabric of justice, you have seen what shackles were prepared for him. Deut. 17. In this model the chief interpretation of the law was given to the seventy, that is, *the great Sanhedrin*, who were least to be suspected of such corruption as should lead them to unjust practices, or to give unrighteous judgment. He foresaw how apt man is, if drawn by a powerful interest, to fall into wickedness, and did therefore, as far as did consist with the nature of man, choose the best means to obviate all manner of corruption. The number of seventy chosen for their excellency in learning, wisdom, piety, and all virtues were not likely to be easily

[309] I.e. Moses.
[310] Moses appointed seventy men on the advice of Jethro, his father-in-law. Exod. 18:18–27.

corrupted. The like care was taken to allot unto inferior magistrates
that which was proportionable to their abilities. The success proved
suitable to the wisdom of the institution. Nothing was able to overthrow that government but a universal defection of the nation to
idolatry, which drew them at length to that mad and wicked desire of
setting up a king, like unto the | Gentiles. In all the strange revolu- /120/
tions of that people we see not many marks of the Sanhedrin fall
from administering justice according to the law. Even when the great
catastrophe approached wherein the government was to be overthrown, the people led captive, Jerusalem destroyed, they continued
so sincere, that Herod, not being able with all his wealth, subtlety,
and power to corrupt them, slew them. The like rectitude seems to
have continued in the elders and chosen persons of every city or
tribe. They were also kept in awe by the personal punishments they
were subject unto, as in the case of Susanna,[311] if they prevaricated.
All this considered, it cannot be imagined how better provision could
be made for maintaining of justice, unless God had sent angels to
administer the law, which he had given by them to that people
(Psalm 68:17, Acts 7:53). This holy, just, and perfect law thus
administered, discovers the imperfection, injustice, and wickedness
of other decrees called laws, as a straight line laid by a crooked *one*
discovers it to be so. That which lies in most direct opposition to this
is when, besides the marks of perversity above specified, a law which
consists of various and heterogeneous parts, as statutes, customs, and
precedents, or judged cases, comprehends an infinite number of particular laws, many of them thwarting one another, and not a few contrary to the letter and intent of the ancient purist constitutions,
which ought to have been taken as foundations upon which all others
should have been built. These evils are much increased when one
part is written, another | unwritten. And when both the written laws, /121/
and discourses upon them and upon the unwritten, are not only in an
unknown language, but a barbarous gibberish, never spoken by any
people, understood only by those of the profession who invented it,

---

[311] The story of Susanna and the elders is an apocryphical addition to the canonical
text of the Book of Daniel, not included in the protestant or jewish Bible canon.
The righteous, god-fearing, and beautiful Susanna, wife of Joachim, rejected two
elders who lusted after her. They then accused her of adultery and she was condemned to death. Daniel, however, refused to accept the verdict, interrogated the
two elders separately, and discovered discrepancies in their story, thereby showing
that they had given false witness. He had them executed instead.

that the law upon which our fortunes, liberties, and lives do depend might continue a mystery to all others; this gives them a free exercise of all manner of frauds to pleasure the king or enrich themselves. The law itself is made a snare, and we, who should be protected, are destroyed by it. These mischiefs arise from the prevalence of a party, favouring the private interest of one or a few men to the prejudice of the commonwealth, and this causes a perpetual contest between such as would increase the usurped power, and those who defend the nation's rights, as has been in England in these last ages, between the rights of the nation and the prerogative of kings. If the corrupt party have great riches and power, if they advance so far as to gain the disposal of employments, honours, and rewards, it is very hard to restrain the lusts of those that favour it. Some will be corrupted, some frightened, and many destroyed by them. If the first institution admit them to a part in the legislative power, they will make themselves masters of the whole. Then those laws which favour liberty will either be abrogated or frustrated and enervated by some additions, explanations, or new statutes. This evil spirit once raised, seldom rests till it has established a perverse interest in those that govern against that of the nation. It is then no longer considered what is good in itself or for the people, but what is good for him or them that rule. Such actions as are really good are termed crimes and punished if they thwart that interest. The slightest errors are often

/122/ punished with the most bitter and violent cruelty.|

PHILALETHES: if you find these defects in our law, you must needs think it corrupt, whereas it is said, none equal it in goodness.

EUNOMIUS: I believe it was anciently good enough, perhaps better than that under which many of our neighbouring nations do live. But that which you brag of as the mark of the prudence of our late kings or *of their* servants' industry and loyalty is the cause of all our misery. That which should be clear, open, and plain is become a heap of confusion. The common law is so entangled with statutes and cases often unjustly judged, that no man can be said to understand it. They found the craft of the lawyers useful unto them, and the lawyers found as great advantage by the power of kings. They therefore helped forward the great work of turning a legitimate monarchy into tyranny, and by the monarchs were upheld in their perverse practice. This agreement has been the overthrow of liberty and the nation.

Many things in our law do show the intention of our ancestors to
have been good. They sought the best ways that were known in a
rude and simple age to maintain their liberties, all *of* which is
totally frustrated by the power of kings and the malice and fraud of
the lawyers, their servants. It was an easy matter for them who knew
which were the principal bulwarks set by the law to defend our liberties to overthrow them. Such as could not be taken by force might be
undermined by fraud. You have well showed that this work, which
has been long in hand, is now so completed, that we have nothing left
that we can call our own. We may be every day questioned for our
liberties, estates, or lives, and the determination of these questions
lies in the breasts of our great enemies and such as depend upon
them. The law that should be our defence is a snare. This labyrinth
is full of such twistings and windings that it is | impossible without /123/
favour to find the way through it. The intricacies are so various that
those who are cunning in it make it speak what they please. They
never fail to find something in their books to put a fair colour upon
the most wicked and unjust acts that can be committed or imagined
for their own gain, or to please their masters. These faults in the law
introduce all manners of corruption into the administration of it.
They who corrupted the law for corrupt ends will certainly make a
corrupt use of its corruption. The effect of this is that the king does
what he pleases, and the courtiers and lawyers get what they please.
That which you mention as the happiness of the king and those
depending upon him is the destruction of all the rest of the nation.
From hence proceeds an infinity of long, chargeable, and often never
to be determined suits. No man is able to comprehend the extent of
this law upon which his life, liberty, and estate depends; everyone
must have recourse to those who can make the best guess at it. The
kings find the advantage they have hereby gained and pursue it to
our ruin. They have assumed the power of naming judges, and put
such into all places of judicature who have sold themselves to do all
manner of wickedness to please them. This is contrary to the practice
of the most civilized nations, where those who have once been advocates or mercenary pleaders are never advanced to be judges. But
they choose none but such as by the practice of the law have learned
the art of canting and deceiving. By this means bar and bench
are[312] filled with a corrupt crew of mercenary persons. They who

[312]MS: 'is'.

regarded their fees more than truth, when they were pleaders, will value bribes more than justice when they come to be judges. These, together with the rabble depending upon them, and joined in one interest as brethren in iniquity, do combine together to involve the nation in perpetual disturbance, whereby they gain treasure to themselves, and leave those who sought justice, as far from attaining it, after long attendance, as from recovering the money spent upon them. All this being directly contrary to justice and the law of God, /124/ must be evil in the same decree that the other is good, | that is, in the highest that can be imagined, or above our imagination.

When the law is good, it directs how it should be rightly administered. The observation of such rules we call just government. This good government still refines and betters the law. The melioration of the law strengthens that which is good in the government, and still adds something better than what was before. Where things are in this right order, there is a perpetual advance in all that is good, until such nation attains unto the political perfection of liberty, security, and happiness, which were the ends for which government was constituted. As the rectitude of the will is wrought by the illumination of the understanding, that understanding advances in the discovery and knowledge of truth through the rectitude of the will.

In like manner, perverseness in the will proceeds from error, and darkness in the understanding increases it and is increased by it, until he that walks in those ways of death falls into that extremity of falseness in doctrine and wickedness of life which comprehends all the evil that can be in a man. The effects of those evils that creep into governments are so like unto these, that if there be a great defect in the law, it leaves an easy entrance for corruption in the administration, as the will which is not guided by a right understanding is easily overcome with the allurement of vice or deceits of the devil. Again, if there be corruption in him or them who administer the law, he or they will corrupt the laws, as the depraved will darkens and corrupts the understanding. This corruption of the law perpetually adds to the evil of the administration. Thus, then two plagues, if suffered to continue, *are* still increasing one another, till the body that was strong, healthy, and beautiful becomes a carcass full of ulcers and pacrid sores. This in physics is called κακα ἕξις or *malus habitus,* which must be followed by death and dissolution; in politics it is /125/ called ἀταξία, | contrary to the εὐταξία mentioned by Moses

Maimonides.[313] A people that falls into it is in the lowest degree of misery. All order is overthrown. They who ought to be shepherds become wolves. That mischief which the law should prevent, it establishes.

PHILALETHES: if these evils do thus increase one another, when either of them enter, the disease seems to be incurable. Wherefore, when we observe a government to be fallen into that condition that we dislike it, we ought to content ourselves, since there is no remedy.

EUNOMIUS: Nothing less. The perversity of the will may be corrected by the illumination of the understanding, but if the will do continue perverse, it will corrupt the understanding. For perfection of knowledge and extreme perverseness of will did never long continue in the same person. In like manner the rectitude of the law may correct the perverseness of the administration. The integrity of the administrator may amend some defects of the law. But if either continue extremely evil, the other will be infected. Men's ends are judged best by their actions. By comparing the practices and ends of the ancients with those in our days, we may judge of these that concern us. They are of two sorts. The one of righteous princes, lawgivers, or magistrates; the other of unrighteous. The first were truly good shepherds. They were ready to lay down their lives for their sheep. They were fathers of their countries, who did in all things seek the good of the people under them. They governed not for their own pleasure, but the good of them they governed. Of this sort was Moses. He desired to die that the people might be preserved. Joshua, David, and others amongst the Israelites imitated him. There were some amongst the Gentiles who walked in the like paths, though with unequal steps. | Lycurgus[314] suffered a voluntary and perpetual *[126]* exile, that the people, who swore to observe the good laws given by him till he returned, might never be discharged from that obligation. Solomon instituted a government in which he had a very small part. Trajan desired the sword, which he gave the prefect of the praetorians, *and* might be *used* against himself if he governed ill.

[313] Maimonides, *The guide of the perplexed*, bk III, ch. 10, referring to Aristotle, *Physics*, 255b24. See on ataxia (dissoluteness) and eutaxia (discipline) in character Aristotle, *On virtues and vices*, 1250b11 and 1251a22, and in politics Aristotle, *Politics*, bk V, ch. 2 (1302b28) and bk VI, ch. 5 (1321b7). See also Thucydides, *Peloponnesian wars*, bk II, ch. 92 and bk VI, ch. 72.
[314] Lycurgus, mythical legislator of Sparta.

Antoninus Pius[315] in the book he writ *De seipso ad seipsum* seems to
have had no other end, than to show that the chief and necessary
duty of a governor is to divest himself of those interests and passions
which sway with men intent on their private interests, so as to apply
himself wholly to promote the public welfare; that being his principal good, true felicity, satisfaction and glory, far above all other
advantages or pleasures that were possible to be attained. These and
all others that have had *a* like sense of their duty, if they have prescribed laws or amended those that were defective, or redressed
those that were corrupted, having the people's good for their end,
have ever sought to make them pure, just, plain, clear, such as punished nothing but crimes, and those justly, that is, proportionably.
Subordinate ministers of justice were punished with greatest sever-
ity, if they falsified their trust, and by evil administration perverted
the law. The skins of corrupt judges were thought the best orna-
ments of the tribune where they had committed their crimes. Spies,
informers, trepanners, and the like were by these looked upon as the
worst of all creatures, to be destroyed rather than wild beasts or serpents. Amongst Trajan's virtues, which were very eminent (except
his hatred to the Christians, because he comprehended not their doctrine), Pliny finds none more worthy to be praised and set forth in all
the glory of his wit and eloquence (in his panegyric of him) than the
[127] care he took | to destroy delators or informers.[316] And Macrinus,[317]
leaving all other state crimes, without any inquisition diligently
sought out all the informers and servants who had accused their masters, and put them to death. Vespasian and Titus caused such execrable villains to be driven through the amphitheatres and beaten with
scourges and clubs to deter all from bringing in accusations.[318] Domitian for a while followed the example of his father and brother,
appointing the same punishment to accusers as to common robbers
and murderers. But afterwards falling into the utmost degree of
wickedness and tyranny, he grew so far to favour these instruments
of mischief, that all places were filled with them. No man was safe.

315 Antoninus, Titus Aurelius Fulvius Boionius, Roman emperor (138–61), nicknamed
the pious for his veneration of the memory of emperor Hadrian.
316 Pliny, *Panegyric*, ch. 34. Delators were fiscal auditors and prosecutors in public
offences. They had a negative reputation in so far as operating from private interest,
for which, however, they could be punished by exile.
317 Macrinus, Opellius, Roman emperor (217–18).
318 Pliny, *Panegyric*, ch. 35.

Informers feared an informer. Many lawyers, finding that wicked tongues could gain more by accusing than pleading, left their former calling to betake themselves to the other. When the soldiers, who had been ministers of cruelty under Commodus,[319] grew to detest that monster, their master, who only was worse than they, and desired to make a propitiation for their crimes, his death showed it was possible for hands polluted with innocent blood to do an act of justice in delivering the world from its oppressor. But the greatest advantage the people of Rome could hope for from the advancement of the virtuous Pertinax[320] was the destruction of those informers and perverters of law, who in the time of his wicked predecessor had filled the palace and senate. They knew the safety of innocent persons could only be secured by the destruction of those beasts of prey. Whilst therefore they congratulated his exaltation, they cried out, as with one voice, *delatoribus fastim delatores ad leonem.*[321] If he had intended to govern wickedly, this had been no less than to desire him to kill his best subjects and most useful servants. But he, being of another mind, hanged and crucified them as the people desired. He set those free who | had been by their means imprisoned, and revenged the /128/ death of many who had been oppressed by them. Princes of contrary inclinations and designs have ever taken contrary ways. Their business was not to provide for the people's good, but their own pleasure and security, exalting themselves in their pride and the satisfying of their lusts. These were not shepherds that took care of the flock, but butchers that sought how much they could make of it, or thieves and wolves that endeavoured to destroy, fattening and enriching themselves by it. An infinite multitude of ways have been invented for the attaining of this end, but those which relate unto our present discourse are chiefly three:

First, by variations, explications, and additions they have so turned the point of the law that what was intended for the public good was brought to aim chiefly at their private good.

Secondly, by intricacy and multiplicity they have rendered it full of snares.

---

[319] Commodus, Lucius Aelius Aurelius, Roman emperor (180–92). Although a son of Marcus Aurelius, he was one of the most cruel emperors in Roman history. At last murdered by his soldiers, he was succeeded as emperor by Pertinax.

[320] Pertinax, Petrus Helvius, Roman emperor (193).

[321] 'by means of informers the informers are lawfully thrown to the lions', Cassius, *Roman history*, bk LXXIV, chs. 5–11.

Thirdly, by rendering the administrators of it corrupt and wholly depending upon them, and by favouring a multitude of informers, spies, and other rascals, *they* have brought all manner of corruption into the administration of it. Hereby the government which might have been tolerable, became detestable. Subtle contrivances were devised for their preservation, but almost ever ended in their own destruction; the providence of God bringing to naught wicked counsels of men. The most eminent examples for this are of most force. These truths therefore shall be chiefly evidenced by those of Rome, which exceeded all in worldly glory, and of Israel, which, as the chosen people of God, who was their lawgiver and king, enjoyed a prerogative above all that was worldly.

[129]   When Rome lived in the fullness of liberty, the scope | of the law was to preserve every particular man in the enjoyment of his liberty and property, and to beat down any presumptuous head that should arrogate to itself a power above others. It was then treason to act or attempt anything against the public welfare. He who affected dominion was the traitor, whom everyone might lawfully kill. All great powers were divided, and often shifted from one hand into another to curb the rashness of those who had aspiring thoughts and render the execution of them dangerous and difficult. By this means there were ever many citizens at the same time who had enjoyed or might reasonably aspire unto the highest dignities. When this happy state had continued many hundreds of years, the fatal period came, which God seemed to have set to the highest worldly greatness and felicity: man could not pass it. The Roman virtue was the effect of their good laws and discipline. The world could not resist just and wise laws, exact discipline, and admirable virtue. Less glory might have been more permanent. The vastness, strength, and greatness that commonwealth had attained to, resembled that athletic complexion or habit mentioned by Hippocrates:[322] when it comes to the highest pitch of strength, health, and activity that a human body is capable of, it must be diminished by letting blood, or purging, or it will break within itself. Their valour had conquered their foreign enemies. Rival Carthage lay ignobly hid in its own ruin. The proudest kings had died under the weight of their chains, or by submission received life as their gift and a testimony of their generous mercy. Many of the most

---

[322] Hippocrates of Kos, Greek physician and natural scientist (460–370 BC).

powerful and warlike cities were buried in ashes. This success followed with a prodigious affluence of riches, introduced ambition and avarice, raising some citizens above the power of the law. Then | did /130/ that victorious people turn its conquering hand into its own bowels, and fell by its own sword. That unequalled commonwealth which had sat like a queen ruling the nations, fell under the feet of one of her wicked sons. His impious successor destroyed all that excelled in valour, virtue, prudence, experience, or reputation. This alone changed the state of the universe. The power of the empire, which was no less than the government of the world, fell out of the hands of the Cornelii, Fabii, Claudii, Valerii[323] to be managed by Sejanus, Tigellinus,[324] Hareis, or others like unto them: for the most part manumitted slaves, raised from the meanest fortunes for exceeding all others in enormity of vices. The senate that had been composed of men eminent in nobility, great in valour, admired in virtue, famous for victories, and, as its high honour, had Cato for their head and leader, was now full of unworthy wretches, depending wholly upon the will of a Caligula, Nero, Vitellius, or other such like monsters. The people, that had had the spoils of all the richest provinces, now wanted bread, whilst the revenues of the whole world were spent upon the prodigious lusts of their cruel masters and their accursed favourites. The power of the nation was so lost by this, that in few years the conquered provinces recovered hopes of liberty. See, says the Gaul, how poor Italy is grown, how unwarlike the people of Rome is! The whole strength of their army consists in strangers (Tacitus, *Annals*, bk III).[325] But the greatest evil, and *that* which rendered the others irreparable, was the introduction of new laws, which altered the scope of the whole. That which formerly aimed at public good, was now wholly directed to the private interest and preservation of one person and his authority, | whose /131/ destruction would have been the greatest benefit to mankind that could be imagined, relating to temporal things. He was formerly a traitor that would hurt, oppress, or enslave the people; but now he is made the traitor that seeks to save and deliver them from the greatest misery and most shameful slavery that ever any people groaned under. The

[323] Prominent Roman families.
[324] Sejanus, Lucius Aelius; appointed prefect of praetorians under the emperor Tiberius in 14. Tigellinus, Ofonius Titus; caused many executions at Rome as prefect of praetorians under Nero.
[325] Tacitus, *Annals*, bk III, ch. 40.

least word or action towards doing good to the nation brought a man within the *lex majestatis*,[326] from whence there was no redemption. Whosoever either by birth or the qualities of his person was in a capacity of serving his country, was exposed to certain ruin. This *lex majestatis* did legally (if you call those decrees laws, which are extorted by the violence of a tyrant) establish mischief to the utter overthrow of all justice, virtue, liberty, glory, or felicity. He that made or obtained this law could soon be enabled thereby to give large rewards to the workers of iniquity. When all power was placed in him, he could create such judges as were at his devotion, or make them who were already judges so. He could keep such a number of lawyers, accusers, spies, and informers in his service, as destroyed all who for their virtues were thought enemies or otherwise able to hurt him. The histories of those times were continued relations of the services these men rendered to their princes. Former writers, says Tacitus (*Annals*, bk IV), might delight their readers with great and noble actions; we have nothing to relate but cruel commands, continual accusations, false friendships, and the destruction of the innocent. All this was under colour of law, performed by the perfidiousness of the lawyers and corruption of the law, introduced by their fraud to uphold the tyrant's power. This was ever covered with fair pretences. There never was a tyrant who did not govern by fraud. Tiberius was well versed in this necessary quality.

[132] His | custom was to cover new invented villainies with ancient names (Tacitus, *Annals*, bk IV). The same author in two or three short sentences fully describes the state of that monarchy.

First, by the multiplicity of the laws *in corruptissima republica plurimae leges*.[327]

Secondly, by the quality of the laws, for the interest of that one person *utque antehac flagitiis, ita tunc legibus laborabatur*.[328]

Thirdly, the effect thereof *non mos, non ius; deterrima quaeque impune ac multa honesta, exitio fuere*;[329] and in another place *ob virtutes certissimum exitium*.[330]

---

[326] 'law of majesty', i.e. on the treason of lese majesty.
[327] 'when the state was most corrupt, laws were most abundant', Tacitus, *Annals*, bk III, ch. 27.
[328] 'and where the country once suffered from its vices, it was now in peril from its laws', Tacitus, *Annals*, bk III, ch. 25.
[329] 'law and custom ceased to exist: villainy was immune, decency not rarely a sentence of death', Tacitus, *Annals*, bk III, ch. 28.
[330] 'and virtues caused the surest ruin', Tacitus, *Histories*, bk I, ch. 2.

Fourthly and lastly, by the persons employed and rewards given. Having showed that the way to honours and dignities were informing, accusing, betraying he adds *nam ut quid destrictior accusator, velut sacrosanctus erat*.[331] By this means Rome was brought into such a condition as you commend in England. The prince was absolute master of all. No man could be safe but by his mercy. No honour could be obtained but by his favour or favourites, and that could be obtained only by wickedness. Every man's house and table was a snare to him, often times his bed. Servants were set against their masters. Sons accused their fathers and were rewarded, as Vibius Serenus, who, being both accuser and witness against his father, obtained judgment against him and preferment for himself. Even senators were trepanners, as was seen in the case of Titius Sabinus, betrayed and destroyed by four of that order.[332] When some did move in the senate that accusers should not be rewarded, the prince | earnestly opposed /133/ it, complaining that thereby they would invalidate the laws and ruin the commonwealth, that it was better to take away the law than remove them that preserved it. By this means, says Tacitus (*Annals*, bk IV), accusers, a certain sort of men found out for the public destruction and never sufficiently restrained by punishments, are encouraged and allured by rewards. Now whosoever does in the constant series of his actions imitate these monsters, enemies to mankind, and to all that is good, has designs in all respects like unto theirs, that is, to destroy all liberty, virtue, or honesty, and all those who have love to their country or regard to justice, that the poor, weakened, and afflicted people, being deprived of those who might be their leaders, to recover their liberty may not be able to resist the force with which they are oppressed.

And having promised to speak of the kingdom of Israel upon this point, I will now add a few words concerning some of their kings and then conclude. God the lawgiver of Israel, by the hand of Moses and the law of the kingdom written in a book by Samuel, had so clearly declared his will, that it was not easy for wicked kings to invent any fine pretences to overthrow and invalidate them under colour of

---

[331] 'for the informer whose weapon never rested became quasi sacrosanct', Tacitus, *Annals*, bk IV, ch. 36.

[332] In 24 accused by his son of a plot against emperor Tiberius, who nevertheless took his side. Tacitus, *Annals*, bk IV, ch. 28. On Titius Sabinus see Tacitus, *Annals*, bk IV, chs. 68–70.

amendment. When therefore they resolved to reject the law as inconsistent with the manner in which they resolved to govern, it was necessary for them either to set up another worship directly contrary to what was prescribed in it; as Jeroboam did when he made the calves,[333] knowing that idolatry was so great a step to tyranny that they who had rendered their consciences subject to the will of the king in that would not contradict him in other matters; or, if they were not bold enough to attempt this course, they brought the people
[134] insensibly | so to neglect and forget the law of God, that not as much as a copy of it could be found in Joshua's time but providentially by those who repaired the temple. Men thus left, as without law, received such laws as were given by the kings, as were the statute of Omri, or else suffered themselves to be governed by will. The next work was to remove all such as were raised by God to recall people from idolatry to the observance of the law, as Elias and other prophets and holy men. They corrupted such as remained in authority. They who never wanted informers, false witnesses, men of Belial, with helping them to destroy innocent persons, they thereby struck a terror into others and so established their authority. Saul's example eminently shows the ways taken by good and evil princes. At the beginning of his reign, mean in his own eyes, he deserved to be reverenced by others. He sought the good of the people, favoured the best and most valiant amongst them, fought their battles against the idolatrous heathens, slew the witches, then wore the men of Belial against him. Samuel was his friend, God was his protector and counsellor. But when he fell from God, grew proud, disobedient, perfidious, cruel, and to have all the quality that make up a tyrant and an utter*ly* lost reprobate, he changes his whole course. That pride which made him disobey God, persuades him set up an interest of his own against his people, for whom God had ordained a better governor. His work was then to secure his own person and crown. He was tormented with suspicions and fears. He could not but hate those whom he feared, and cruelly desire to destroy those whom he feared and hated. The spirit of God would no longer dwell in such a
[135] breast. The evil one enters and vexes him. He | was as miserable as wicked. The men of Belial, who had been his enemies, became his friends, as fit instruments to advance such an interest as he had set

[333] I Kings 12:28–33.

140

up. The false, wicked, treacherous, malicious Doeg was his spy and the executioner of his fury,[334] who, though a type of Judas, does not so well answer the office of an English trepanner as that attributed by Moses Maimonides in his *More nevuknim* (part 3, ch. 22) to the devil, their master, *qui descendit et seducit ascendit et adversatur aut accusat*.[335] Rich, drunken, brutish Natal loved him. The prophet forsakes him. The wicked obey him. The godly flee and defend themselves from him or are destroyed by him. When he knew none could be affectionated to him but wicked persons, he was jealous of all that were good. The least kindness showed to David, the servant of the Lord, was looked on as a crime against him. Informers were ready to advertise him. The law was perverted. *Originally* no man could be put to death according to law but by the testimony of two witnesses. No action was to be punished as a crime but what was a sin against God, hurtful to the society of his people. The father was not to die for the son, nor the son for the father. But the new interest set up in the person of the king puts all out of joint. Singl*y* Doeg is accuser, witness, and executioner. The crime was only giving bread to a prophet in his necessity, and a sword to him that fought the battles of the Lord,[336] who also had the best title to it by having taken it from the fiercest and proudest enemy of God's people. The high-priest is put to death for it and the city of the priests destroyed. In all this the devil was his counsellor, the worst of men his instruments; and he that was acted by the one and made use of the other soon fell to destruction. In the time of David we hear of no act punished as a crime, which was only against the person or interest of the king. He reigned well and left the law to its right course. No spy, no informer, or corrupt judge is mentioned. The other | kings of Israel and Judah, /136/ though for the most part exceedingly wicked, did not often come to that height of iniquity *as* so to turn the law for the maintaining of their interest, as to punish, contrary to law, those acts which did prejudice only to themselves, in such cases as that of Joash and his servants. They were indeed put to death for slaying him, which is no more than ought to have been if they had killed another man. The cruel and wicked Athaliah brings in the very word treason[337] and,

---

[334] I Sam. 22:18–19.
[335] 'he descends and leads astray, [then] he ascends and attacks or accuses', Maimonides, *The guide of the perplexed*, bk III, ch. 22.
[336] I Sam. 22:13.   [337] II Chron. 23:13.

according to the custom of those who desire their crimes may go unpunished, applies it unto those who would do justice upon her. Jehoiada, little regarding this, commanded her to be dragged out of the temple and slain.[338] The kings of Israel drew the law more to favour them than the king of Judah. They had entirely left the law as to worship, so might the kings more easily introduce their own laws in civil matters. We do not rightly know what were the statutes of Omri, so much detested by the prophet. But the excesses of Ahab and his accursed wife give ground of a conjecture that the work of his idolatrous father was to strengthen the royal authority.[339] They who know they most deserve to be destroyed, take most care to preserve themselves. We often hear Israel rejected God when they desired a king, which shows a contrariety between God and a king. We do not find that the law of God distinguished the person of the king from others, so as to make that no crime or not to be punished in him, which is a crime and to be punished in others. Nor that any act or design against him was esteemed a crime unless it were such as was in the same degree criminal if it were against a common person. Much less can it be said, the names of God and the king were ever joined together in the law of God. That which swayed in Ahab's time was so corrupted by Omri or some of the idolatrous tyrants, his predecessors, that whensoever a mischief was to be done, they could colour it by putting the name of God and the king together, as if the

/137/ opposing of | the one had been an offence against the other. He has blasphemed God and the king, say the witnesses of Belial, his majesty's loyal subjects, when just and innocent Naboth was to be put to death.[340] It is usual amongst us to hear the same language from men of the same humour and temper. Many of them have said, he cannot be a good servant, who will not perjure himself for his master's service. And the practice of that wickedness is yet more frequent than the confession of it. Our venerable judges and lawyers do seldom

[338] II Chron. 23:14–15.

[339] From the biblical account relating to king Ahab, Omri's son and successor, it can be inferred that Omri was hard pressed by the Assyrians who wrested from him a few cities and extraterritorial rights in Samaria (I Kings 20:34). It can also be safely assumed that Ahab's marriage to Jezebel, daughter of Ethbaal, king of Phoenicia, was initiated by Omri with the aim of a political and economic alliance between the two countries (I Kings 16:31). This, together with the royal marriage between Ahab's daughter and Jehoram, king of Judah (II Kings 8:18), must have enhanced the military, political, and economic power of the northern kingdom of Israel.

[340] I Kings 21:13–14.

conspire to commit a wicked murder, but they profane the name of God to cover it with a pretence of law and justice. They follow the example of Ahab, Jezebel, and their adherents. When they had introduced a law contrary to the law of God, they executed it by the help of the men of Belial, false witnesses, and corrupt judges. And they murdered Naboth by the device of a whore and a witch[341] zealous to preserve the royal authority. These were the pillars upon which that monarchy stood. By their means the king, their detestable master, was made fat with blood and spoils. His power was by them enlarged and upheld, until God raised up an avenger to overthrow it.

Thus have I given you and myself the trouble of alleging once more these examples out of sacred and profane story, that you may see what a long series of evils, annexed one to another, is brought in by perverse princes, who, not contented with those snares which could be laid for innocent persons by spies, informers, or false witnesses, have never rested until they have perverted the very law itself, though the best that ever was given, endeavouring still to destroy all that was just in the rule or the administration of it, that they might govern according to lust under pretence of law. Whensoever any prince has endeavoured to set up an interest in his person or family, he has done the same. It proceeds not from the humour of one or a few of them, but *ex necessitate rei*.[342] Whosoever does aim at so corrupt an end as the fulfilling the lust, or upholding the power of a man or family to the prejudice of a nation, must follow the same way. | /138/

If you find that our law consists of such a multitude of customs, statutes, and judged cases, that no man can understand them; if the intricacies thereof are such as no man can comprehend them; if this corruption be maliciously introduced to bring the estates, lives, and liberties of all men in the land to depend upon the will of one or a few men; if thereby the intent of the law be entirely frustrated, so as that which was intended for the people's good, tends to their destruction; and if new laws are introduced which maintain the power of one or a few men in opposition to the good of the nation; if words, intentions, or actions in themselves not evil, or but slight errors, are made criminal and punished with the greatest rigour that can be deserved by the greatest crimes; if a corrupt son of men be found out and upheld

---

[341] I.e. Jezebel.
[342] 'out of the necessity of the situation'.

to increase these mischiefs; if the interpretation or execution of this corrupted law be put into their hands, that they may thereby vex, impoverish, oppress, and enslave the people, or destroy the best men amongst them; you may certainly conclude the authors of these works have designs in all respects answerable unto those who have walked in the like paths. But how fair soever the appearances of advantage by such practices may be, they are built upon a foundation that cannot stand, and therefore are not to be valued. They must fall and wither, such as trust in them must perish.

PHILALETHES: your discourse is not so clear but some scruples remain with me, and I shall not be satisfied until you solve them.

First, you show an ill opinion of the profession of lawyers, which has ever been esteemed honourable and exceeding*ly* beneficial to mankind.

Secondly, you make little difference between a magistrate and a private person. You distinguish not at all between an act intended or executed against him that is supreme and against any common per-
[139] son, as if there were no such thing as treason.|

Thirdly, you take no notice of the maxim *divide et impera*, which has been highly esteemed by all politic princes. This sort of lawyers who are useful ministers in sowing seeds of division and hatred between persons and families, by which rebellions are prevented, deserve to be esteemed by them.

Fourthly, though you acknowledge lawyers to be very useful in establishing the power of kings, you blame their counsel in favouring them, whereas I see nothing that a prince can desire but the establishment of his authority. Those counsels are certainly good which tend thereunto. Those persons are most to be favoured who most advance them. And I cannot imagine what can be required to justify those counsels more than the experience that those who have followed them have thereby gained what they desired.

EUNOMIUS: whatsoever I say against our lawyers, I no ways blame the profession or study of the law. I know the administration of justice to be one of the noblest works that can be done by man, and it is to be performed by those only who do study the law, which is the rule of it. God commands his people to apply their hearts to the knowledge of the law and teach it unto their children. Their kings, judges, and elders were to study it. David was exercised in it day and night. The chief and best men of that nation have in all ages done the like. The most virtuous amongst the heathen studied the laws in force amongst them. Pericles, Aristides, Phocion,[343] Cicero, the two Gracchi, and the two Catos, with a multitude of others whose virtues we admire, excelled in this science. But I do not see what advantage our mercenary lawyers can thence draw unto themselves. The one seeks justice, which is never divided from truth, the other perverts it for gain. He speaks for his client that pays him, whether truth or not, whatsoever may serve his purpose. He sells himself to defend causes, though never so unjust. And as one of the most supercilious | /140/ amongst them used to say (Sir Wadham Wyndham),[344] my client has my tongue, not my heart, and that they go not together. Those who deserve to be called lawyers ought in all places to be in the chief magistracies, to do justice for the good of the nations where they live for the punishment of evil-doers and the encouragement of such as do well, with the preservation of liberty and property. If there be anything called law which is unrighteous, they seek to abrogate it. They redress what is amiss, explain what is obscure, and supplement what is defective. But these execrable and mercenary wretches, wheresoever there is the least shadow of good government, either are utterly excluded, or very rarely admitted unto any share in magistracy. They are crafty in putting false colours upon truth, perverting justice, ensnaring the innocent, overthrowing liberty, corrupting what is sincere in the law, rendering that intricate and dubious which might be made clear; and generally for their own gain, or to please a wicked master, they are principal instruments in bringing all those evils upon a people, which all good lawyers or lawgivers endeavour to avoid. You need not therefore wonder if the profession of the one be esteemed honourable, the other infamous. Or that the first should be loved and reverenced as benefactors unto mankind, and these detested and despised, as growing fat only with the destruction and misery of others. There is, methinks, the same difference between those who study the law for a right end and these, as between Joshua, Gideon, David, Epaminondas, Maccabee, Camillus,[345] with all the

[343] Pericles, Athenian politician (495–429 BC), promoter of democracy. Aristides, Athenian 'strategos' (military leader) who took part in the battle of Marathon in 490 BC. Phocion, Athenian general, 402–318 BC.
[344] Wyndham, Wadham (1610–68), English lawyer.
[345] Epaminondas, Theban politician and military leader, d. 362 BC. Maccabee, Judas, Jewish leader against the Persian king Antioch, who re-established the Temple in 164 BC.

worthies of ancient or modern times (who have valiantly defended the people of God or their own countries, employing their swords only for the maintenance of justice and defence of the oppressed), [141] and the most | abominable pirates or thieves, who live by murders and rapine. You will easily pardon me if I distinguish between these two so different sorts of people who do *in* no way resemble each other.

To the second, there is a great difference between a magistrate and a common person, but it principally depends upon the manner in which he executes his office. If I follow the law of God I can make no difference between the punishment due to him if he transgress, and another man that does in like manner transgress against him. The same law which says: he that sheds man's blood, by man shall his blood be shed,[346] does neither exempt a magistrate from the punishment due for murder if he commit it, nor inflict anything beyond death upon a private man that kills him. We find no such thing as treason in God's law. We first hear of that word from Athaliah, Joram, and Jezebel. The tyrants of Rome and other places, when they had overthrown the power of the law, made edicts, and forcibly extorted them from the senate or other assemblies, whereby not only conspiracies against them, but any word or act that savoured of disaffection or disrespect unto them was made criminal. This alone subverted and destroyed all liberty, justice, virtue, and happiness in the empire. Though the consuls, praetors, and other inferior magistrates had then the full exercise of their power, *legesque, si maiestatis quaestio eximeretur, bono in usu*,[347] that alone filled the cities and provinces with terror, blood, and all the other mischiefs accompanying tyranny. Princes in other countries have ever sought to introduce the like, and where they have prevailed, they have established mischief by law so-called, and maintained it by force until the oppressed nations broke their yokes. There is another kind of treason, which is ever evil, comprehending many crimes, that is, conspiracies or [142] actions | against the true king or sovereign power of a nation. As all civil laws are made to preserve civil societies, he that endeavours to overthrow them must needs incur the greatest penalties denounced by them. This is a very common crime, but seldom are any others

---

[346] Gen. 9:6.
[347] 'the laws, apart from the process in cases of treason, were in proper force', Tacitus, *Annals*, bk IV, ch. 6.

guilty of it but he that wears the crown and those that wickedly assist him, overthrowing the political government of a nation to set up his own tyranny. Civil wars and sedition (says Machiavelli) are the distempers of a state, the introduction of a tyrant is the death of it.[348] He that does this is the worst of all men, and those that assist him in his wickedness are next unto him.

To the third, I do not forget your maxim *divide et impera,* and I know lawyers are very useful instruments for such work. But because that is one of the most detestable designs that ever was, by the devil, put into the heart of the worst of men, I thought they should not have been commended for advancing it. We are told kings are God's vicegerents, shepherds and fathers of their people. Now fathers desire to maintain union and friendship among their children, that they may be helpful to one another. Pittakes,[349] to invite his children to *unity*[350] and concord, showed them a bundle of arrows which they could not break whilst bound up together, but there was no strength in any one of them when divided. The same is true in a nation. He that desires to preserve it increases the power thereof by uniting all sorts of men in procuring things for the common good. He that divides it, weakens it; he that weakens it, as far as in him lies, destroys it. He is not therefore a father but an enemy. The like may be said of the shepherd. He keeps his flock together, that it may the better be fed and defended against enemies. Wolves and thieves would | have it scattered and divided, that they may catch and /143/ destroy such as wander alone without defence. He therefore that divides and scatters his flock is not a shepherd, but a thief or wolf. Everyone will confess that God's vicegerents should follow the precepts and example of Christ. Now, his great precept to his disciples is love one another. My peace, says he, I leave with you. Paul comprehends all christian graces under the word love (Cor. 13).[351] He cannot be a Christian that has it not and does not live in it. Satan ever was the sower of discord. He therefore that sows discord amongst the people cannot be the vicegerent of God, nor a Christian, but the child and servant of the devil. His children and servants you are whose work you do. And their assistants are like unto them. You

---

[348] Machiavelli, *Discourses,* bk 1, chs. 4–5.
[349] Pittakes of Mytilene on Lesbos, 650–570 BC, an aisymnetes from 590 to 580 BC.
[350] Due to the binding of the MS, this word is illegible.
[351] I Cor. 13:13.

must therefore necessarily confess that those kings are enemies to their people, wolves, thieves, and servants of the devil, and the lawyers, their ministers, are like unto them, or they can have no such design as to sow division amongst the people, that they may rule over them. And then the chief use of the lawyers falls to the ground.

To the fourth, besides the present satisfaction a prince may take in the success of his counsels, I think they are not to be praised unless they have some other qualities. At least permanence and justice are absolutely necessary. But I will speak more plainly. None can rightly rejoice in a felicity that is not permanent, that cannot be permanent. He that walks in these unjust ways, walks in enmity to God, whom he disobeys, and to man, whom he hurts. As he fulfils the law who loves God above all and his neighbour as himself, he does to the /144/ utmost of his power abrogate the law of God and all just and true | laws of man, who, through instigation of the devil, lives in a perpetual opposition to both.

Enmity against man grows from a contrariety of principles or of interest. Of principles, when they are irreconcilable in the root, that is, one in God, the other in the devil. Of interest, when one would have that which the other has, or keep that which the other would have; does not what the other would have him do, or makes him suffer what he would not suffer. But the greatest enmity is when men differ both in principle and interest, and when contrary principles lead into a contrary interest. It is men of principles, that is, of good principles, which men of ill principles are afraid of. Good principles keep men steady and constant in the pursuit of a good interest, that of the community. The most universal principle, the most important interest is a ground of the greatest and sharpest enmity, which grows from the contrariety discovered in them. The principle comprehends all civil and all moral things, the interest is important and irreconcilable, the enmity therefore is perpetual. The most important temporal interests of all honest men are: to preserve life, liberty, and estate; to be preserved from suffering evil, unless they deserve it by disobeying a known and just law; and to have a way open, by honest industry, to provide, everyone for his own family, according to his vocation. The utmost contrariety unto all this that can be imagined is, when, by the impulse or instigation of him who is author of the contrary principle, by one or more men the rule of justice is perverted and the administrators of it corrupted. When everything is made matter enough for a suit; all suits *being*[352] long, chargeable, and in the | issue uncertain. And when a vast number of lawyers, *[145]* accusers, informers, and trepanners are kept up and favoured to hinder justice, defraud, ensnare, or destroy all those who seek righteousness and would live innocently.

No man can take from another his spiritual interest, for that aiming at eternity is above the power of man. Nevertheless, those that are in authority can hinder such as live under them from the outward performance of spiritual duties, and the receiving of such helps and comforts, as one brother can impart unto another according to the measure of grace that he has received. Whosoever therefore does take from us the use of these does all that lies in him to deprive us of eternal as well as temporal felicity. He that does this is our greatest enemy. He destroys all liberty and property. He brings those who set up a government for their felicity into the lowest degree of shameful misery, that any man or nation can fall into, with this aggravation, that their misery is caused by him or them, who, being entrusted with power to do justice, ought more than any others industriously to preserve them from it. Whosoever therefore being set up to maintain the public interest, does create an interest to himself, which is to be upheld by these means, is the perpetual and irreconcilable enemy of all that nation, except the corrupt rabble amongst whom he divides the prey that he gains. It is essentially necessary to all true magistracy that it intend the good of the people. Those magistrates that perform their duty and office in seeking and procuring this, may justly be called fathers and shepherds. But maintaining an interest contrary to that of the people that entrusted them, they become enemies of that people and ought no longer to be looked upon as fathers or shepherds, which are titles of love and sweetness, but thieves, wolves, tyrants, the worst of all enemies. | Aristotle (*Politics*, bk v)[353] *[146]* briefly represents the difference between a tyrant and a lawful king. A tyrant, says he, seeks his own profit, a king that of those who are governed by him. According to Socrates[354] a king is not created, that he may carefully provide for himself, but for the happiness of those that create him. This agrees with Isidore.[355] That is the rule of

---

[352] MS: 'are'.
[353] Aristotle, *Politics*, 1310b ff.
[354] Plato, *Republic*, 343b.
[355] Isidore, bishop of Seville (600/1–36), *Etymologiae*, bk IX, ch. 3.

government, says he, which refers all to the profit of those who live under it. For he that changes the orderly discipline of government into the confusion of tyranny, seeking pleasures to himself by the labours of others, describes not a government but a tyranny. And in another place; tyranny refers all to its own profit; a kingdom seeks that of the subjects. This is so often confirmed by poets, philosophers, historians, prophets, fathers, heathens, Christians, ancient and modern people of all sorts, except tyrants and their flatterers, that we may well conclude it to be the voice of mankind, or of God speaking in man. And that those that speak or act to the contrary, seem to be degraded from the nature of men into that of savage or sottish beasts. Tyranny, being the centre where all corrupt and filthy interests do meet, must needs be hateful to God. And, being the greatest cause of misery unto man, hurtful to all except the rabble depending upon it, all good men must needs be averse unto those from whom they receive the greatest hurt. Whosoever therefore governs wickedly is hateful to God and man, and exposed to the wrath of both. That state cannot be permanent which is opposed to both. Nor have good men cause to despair of remedy. This evil is not incurable, since it may be cured *by the destruction of its authors,* as it often has been, both in Israel and other people, by the hand of God and man, | the sword of the Lord and of Gideon. I may safely rely upon what history relates, reason dictates, Scripture denounces, and the spirit explains in this case for the strengthening of my position that whatsoever government is unjust, cannot be permanent, since God that did hate it, does hate it; he that has punished it, will punish it; because that is ever evil and he is ever good. His hand is against all he hates, and all who love him will ever be ready instruments in his hand to execute his wrath upon his and their enemies.

[147]

If, lastly, there could be no friendship between the tyrant Saul and holy David, nor between the house of Saul and the house of David, neither in the letter, as David was to take from him the crown and glory which he enjoyed, nor in the figure, where he, as a type of Christ, was to destroy the Jewish church; first flourishing in gifts and graces, afterwards rebellions, decaying, and rejected; resembled in both by Saul, who first was amongst the prophets and after, on his fall, the spirit of the Lord departing from him, he is guided by the evil one. If Doeg, to the letter a court flatterer, an informer, a murderer of innocent persons, was certainly and perpetually an enemy unto all those who were just and good, there must be a perpetual enmity between those who walk in the tyrannous ways of Saul, assisted with Judas-like instruments, and all those who would enjoy the inheritance that God has given them, even their lives, liberties, properties, and benefits of a righteous law, in liberty of person and conscience. Though Saul may flourish for a while in his wickedness, his glory will in a short time vanish, and he, together with all his designs, must perish. The glory of a tyrant is like that of the fruits which are said to grow | near unto the lake where Sodom stood. /148/ They are beautiful to the eye, but are nothing save rottenness, poison, and noisome vapour, fit for nothing but to be thrown into the filthy lake from whence they sprung, which resembles tophet, prepared of old for kings. The advantages then, how great soever, that are gained by wicked means with the help of wicked ministers, bring those to destruction who rejoice in them. Which having finished, I think, I have performed the task I undertook, and, unless you have something to object, desire to betake myself unto my rest.

Tenth Dialogue

Ninth Court Maxim: Union with France and war with Holland is neces-
sary to uphold monarchy in England, or thus, a strict friendship is to be
held with the French that their customs may be introduced and the people
by their example brought to beggary and slavery quietly [356]

PHILALETHES: the king is fixed in this resolution as the whole course
of his actions do show ever since he came to the crown. The first he
did was absolutely to break the agreement made with the Span-
iard.[357]

Then soon followed the match with Portugal, the assaulting and
sacking *of* some of the Spanish plantations in the West Indies. And
[149] the evidence is completed in his selling Dunkirk to the king | of
France.[358]

EUNOMIUS: what advantage can be expected from France for all this?

PHILALETHES: the king of France well understands how great the

---

[356] MS: '[Brief abstracts and collections only]', inserted by the copyist.
[357] In July 1660 Charles II concluded the war with Spain. A month later, however, the
king of Portugal, who had been subject to king Philip of Spain but was now fighting
for independence, offered Charles his daughter Catherine of Braganza. After much
hesitation Charles accepted this offer and married in 1662, a choice that implied
friendship with Portugal and enmity with Spain.
[358] Dunkirk, which had been captured and annexed to England in 1658 by Cromwell's
army, was sold in 1662 by the government to Louis XIV because the costs of its
upkeep were very high and the public revenue was deficient. The sale let loose a
storm of indignation from the merchant community and Londoners in general,
thereby contributing to the growing unpopularity of the government in 1662.

power of money is in our court, and has disbursed large sums to some of our ministers, to his great advantage.[359] There is nothing so secret in our court, but by the next post it is known at Paris, and all businesses are represented to the king in such colours as most agree with the French interest. The king of France made peace with Spain at his match with the infanta thereof,[360] which so amazed the king of Portugal that all underhand assurances of assistance from France were not sufficient to satisfy him. Which put the queen mother of Portugal, who had the principal part of the government, to seek a match with England; and so both advance her daughter and provide for the security of her son's country. Specious pretences are made of advantage to England concerning trade: the East Indies and Tangier, beauty and virtue of the lady extoled; but that which gave success was a large sum of money given to the courtiers[361] and the powerful assistance of the king of France, who desired to uphold Portugal without breaking with Spain, and saw no hand could so well do it as England.[362]

The king's reasons for union with France I take to be principally these:

First, the government of France is the most absolute in these parts of the world, and we endeavour to bring ours to the same model.

Secondly, to bring in the vices of the French, to corrupt our young nobility, gentry, and people; and those are most favoured at court, that conform | to the French manners and fashions in all *[150]* things.

And lastly, the king's affairs being unsettled and uncertain at home, he sees no prince abroad so powerful, prosperous, and active,

---

[359] Charles II and his Lord Chancellor, Clarendon, were suspected of having persuaded the Privy Council into approval of the sale of Dunkirk with the aid of French bribes.

[360] The Franco-Spanish war which had lasted for thirty-seven years ended with the Peace of the Pyrenees of 1659. By this Louis XIV of France gained frontier provinces in both north and south, and a Spanish wife whose marriage opened the prospect of dynastic union in the future.

[361] Catherine of Braganza brought with her the richest dowry any bride had ever brought to England. It included £800,000 in cash, with Bombay and Tangier.

[362] In spite of the Peace of the Pyrenees of 1659, France continued in an indirect way to wear down the strength of its traditional enemy, Spain, by supporting the alliance between England and Portugal to the extent of paying the English troops sent there.

as the king of France. He has therefore so obliged him and espoused his interest that the fanatics say he depends on him.

EUNOMIUS: first, I think that prince who impairs his reputation, and draws on him the hatred of his people, to be always a loser, what collateral advantage soever he gains.

Secondly, if he would keep the king of France his friend, he should endeavour to gain his esteem and most carefully seek all advantages whereby to secure and revenge himself, if he prove his enemy.

Thirdly, there are many good heads in our nation that will throw off the court veils, show the people their true interest and who they are that advance or oppose it. The English nation ever contended with France for superiority, often with good success, and will horribly detest any that renders it dependent on and subservient to its interest. The delivering up *of* Dunkirk to him, one of the best places in the world for us, and now more necessary than at other times since Flanders is in danger to fall into the hands of the French or to be divided between them and the Hollanders, and the vanity of pretences of assistance from Tangier, all see.

Lastly, the king of France, *being* of much spirit, activity, and judgement, full of desire to advance his crown and people, will little esteem him that gave him Dunkirk for a little money which he could not hope to recover by force, though he had to the utmost employed [151] his great power. And having paid money for it, | can say: I owe you nothing.

PHILALETHES: but, notwithstanding all this, the king of France knows what the power of the English nation is. If the forces thereof were rightly employed, they might curb and oppose him more than any other. He will therefore endeavour to maintain that government in England, that family in the government, which will ever endeavour to bring it to the utmost weakness, effeminacy, and vileness, so as neither to be able to offend him or defend itself.

EUNOMIUS: if your design succeed of bringing the people to such poverty, misery, slavery, and baseness, the king of France will look on, perhaps, and when no virtue, vigour, or power is left in the nation, will make an easy conquest of it. *So you may live and die his slaves.*

Eleventh Dialogue

Tenth Court Maxim: What advantages the Court may draw from Spain and Holland or the United Provinces [363]

PHILALETHES: there is such a perpetual contrariety between the interests of Spain and France, that he that unites with France *must break with Spain*. It is easy to know how he should proceed with Spain as to the public. But courtiers may contrive that some hold correspondence with one, some with the other, that they may have constant pay and presents from both.

EUNOMIUS: England never had in the least any dependence on France or on any other power, since England, Spain, France, and | /152/ the best part of the known world was emancipated by the dissolution of the Roman empire. The interest of every nation that cannot pretend to a universal monarchy[364] or more limited superiority over its neighbours, is to keep any others from attaining it and maintain its own freedom and independency on any for protection, as it is best for any private man that cannot hope to be king to endeavour there shall be none. Freedom is the greatest advantage next to dominion. He that cannot command, ought to endeavour to preserve himself from being commanded. If he cannot gain power over others, to retain that over himself. England cannot pretend to such hopes of a

---

[363] MS: 'Brief collections only', inserted by copyist.
[364] Contempories called France the 'new universal monarchy' since its power and aspirations increased impressively under Louis XIV.

universal monarchy as France and Spain have long contended for. Therefore, it is best for England that no prince in Europe attain unto it. Though France must have many hard steps before it can arrive at such a monarchy as can deserve the name of universal, yet that king does at present enjoy many advantages that may reasonably give him higher expectations that way than any other prince in Europe. And, having a mind equal to his fortune, he is not like to omit any opportunity. England ought therefore rather to curb than advance the growth of that greatness that is already become formidable to all the states of Europe. The counsels of England's governors have heretofore been to change parties as often as either grew strong enough to be feared. This consideration excited[365] Henry VIII against Charles V, emperor, more than the quarrels about his wife, and the emperor sought to raise troubles in England, rather to divert England from */153/* seeking to restrain his power | than to revenge the disgrace of his aunt. The like reason moved queen Elizabeth to raise and foment troubles in Flanders, with charge and danger, to oppose the terrible power of Philip II of Spain.[366] France was then in civil wars; nothing was to be feared from thence. She and her council rather feared Spain rising to such a height as might prove irresistible.

All the best judging princes and states of Europe were swayed by the same reasons about the year 1628.[367] Though the power of the Austrian family reigning in Spain was somewhat abated by the war in Flanders,[368] the other branch in Germany, by the accession of Bohemia and other new-gained advantages,[369] grew so great as gave cause of fear lest that suspected family should raise itself higher than ever it had been. This set their heads on work to find ways of securing themselves from so great a danger. Ferdinand II invaded Italy, but his expedition, which was thought would have subdued Italy, ended in the sack of Mantua through the counsels of the Italian princes and

---

[365] Editorial hand has deleted the word 'invited' and has put 'excited' in its place.

[366] In 1584 Elizabeth I of England decided to support the Netherlands with a small army in their struggle against Spain.

[367] Sidney here comments on the Thirty Years war (1618–48).

[368] The Twelve Years truce with the Dutch republic had ended in 1621; the war continued till 1648.

[369] In 1619 the Estates of Bohemia deposed Ferdinand II (1578–1637), emperor of the Holy Roman empire (1619–37) and member of the Austrian branch of the Habsburg family, for fear of losing its protestant liberties. Frederick V then became king of Bohemia, but he was soon defeated by Ferdinand in the battle of the White Mountain in 1620, and Ferdinand retook possession of Bohemia.

states.[370] Envy and fear whetted their inventions to weaken the Austrian family at the root. They stirred up the princes of Germany as most obliged to think of defence, because nearest the danger of being oppressed. The kings of Bohemia and Denmark had made unsuccessful trials.[371] They search*ed* therefore into the remotest corners of the world to find king Gustavus of Sweden, whose valour and virtue was proportionable to so vast an undertaking.[372] Some ascribe all this to controversies in religion, but besides many reasons that persuade me to believe that even Urban VIII, | then pope, did at first /154/ favour the design of Gustavus, no man can continue in that opinion who considers that France, Venice, and Savoy, three popish states, were the contrivers and advancers of it. Though at the same time the king of France, by help from the king of England in taking La Rochelle, very near*ly* accomplished his design of rooting the Protestants out of France.[373] No humour of the times or accidents were the causes of these. It depended on causes that are perpetual and immutable. For there is a natural and therefore perpetual enmity between him that will command and him who would not obey him; as also between those who, each of them, seek to command the other. This united all these princes against the aspiring house of Austria, for the general good and liberty of all Europe. The like ought they to do against any family or state that set upon the like design of enslaving all the rest unto their wills.

[370] In 1629 France launched an invasion in Italy in order to assist the garrisons of the strategically important states of Mantua and Montferrat, who had been fighting against Spanish aggression since 1627. To meet this threat posed by the French, Philip IV of Spain asked Ferdinand II to send imperial troops, which he did. But in 1630 France launched a second invasion, thereby reducing the war in Mantua to a stalemate.

[371] Frederick's defeat in 1620 created an international body of support for his cause. The leader of this alliance, Christian IV of Denmark (1588–1648), invaded the empire in 1625 under pretence of defending the protestant cause, but his armies were routed by Ferdinand II and in 1629 Christian was forced to sign a peace treaty.

[372] In 1630 Gustav II Adolf invaded the empire. As the bulk of Ferdinand's forces were tied down in Mantua, the Swedish king faced less resistance than Christian IV had done, and he soon overran most of central Germany and conquered Bohemia in 1632.

[373] In 1628 Louis XIII took the huguenot stronghold of La Rochelle. Charles I had indeed signed a contract by which a ship of the royal navy and seven merchant vessels were lent to Louis, but the English on board were determined not to take part in an attack on La Rochelle and they only handed over their ships to the French after peace had been concluded between Louis and the Huguenots in 1629.

No man that has but the least insight into the affairs of Europe can choose but see that the French only at present are in a condition of attempting any great matter to the endangering of others. Their territory is much enlarged of late,[374] their frontiers admirably defended, the people numerous, the nobility so excellent in military valour and art by thirty years' experience that, perhaps, it may truly be said, they have more great and able commanders than all the rest of the world. Their king[375] is young, industrious, rich, endowed with many excellent qualities, content with moderate pleasures; applies his thoughts to redress the horrid corruptions and abuses crept into the government, ease the people's burdens, and advance the glory of *[155]* | his crown and nation. If you desire to imitate France, do it in these things that deserve praise, and not make those your patterns whose enormities he endeavours to correct and punish. Other great states of Europe being in a very contrary posture, shows the advantage he has over them and their concern to secure themselves. Not to see this is extreme stupidity. But to endeavour to increase the danger, rather than seek remedies against it, is the utmost excess of madness, which can be charged on no state I know (England alone excepted, which by what has lately passed in Portugal, West Indies, Dunkirk, and what is now in agitation with Holland, to the admiration of all the world, endeavour to set up a power, by which they are like*ly* shortly to be destroyed).

PHILALETHES: I deny not but it is good for England to keep the balance more equal between France and Spain. But we, knowing how uncertain all our affairs are at home by people being disaffected, officers corrupt, treasure exhausted, and that we want men, money, commanders, councillors, and everything, except spies, trepanners and bawds, think it necessary to look for support abroad. And the young, prosperous king of France is fitter to help us than the decaying monarchy of Spain. So it is good for the king and us to hold with France though good for England to watch and secure against him. Let other states look to the public interests of Europe, we endeavour to secure ourselves. We must serve the king of France that can help us and furnish us with money, whatever become of England.

---

[374] France acquired parts of Flanders, Luxembourg, and the Roussillon by the Treaty of the Pyrenees.
[375] I.e. Louis XIV.

EUNOMIUS: I do reverence the virtues that eminently show themselves in that noble-minded | prince that you put yourselves under /156/ for support. But I can commend the courage and strength of a lion; the swiftness, agility and fierceness of a tiger; yet will I not suffer them to enter into my sheepfold if I can keep them out. But if any such be near me I will be more careful for defence of my person and goods. It is truly said the vices of a prince are pernicious to his subjects and his virtues not less mischievous to his neighbours. Princes are ever birds of prey. Those endowed with noble spirits, like the eagle, preserve their own and seek their prey abroad and teach their young ones the use of their beaks and talons. Others that are base and cowardly, like dogs that devour the flocks they ought to defend, seek the easiest prey. They must have blood. That of foreign nations is not shed without danger. Their own subjects may be murdered safely by frauds or poisons, trepanners, perjured witnesses and juries, mercenary lawyers, corrupt judges; these instruments of wickedness can shed blood enough to allay the most raging thirst. All ancient and modern histories prove this truth. The Germans, Moors, Parthians, Sarmates, Dacians, Goths, *and* Indians feared the Roman banners when commanded by Trajan, Hadrian, Marcus Aurelius, Antoninus Pius, Theodosius, and other valiant and virtuous emperors. But at home all was serene and safe. Prisons opened, noble and virtuous captives set at liberty called home from their confinement in barren hands, preferred to honours; and the skins of corrupt judges were seen over the tribunal crosses and gibbets full of the broken limbs of delators, accusers, informers. But when the fearful, cruel, obscene Tiberius, mad Caligula, sottish, cowardly, gluttonous Claudius or Vitellius, and the filthy monsters Nero, Heliogabalus, and the like were masters of the Roman power, foreign nations feared nothing, but Rome itself overflowed with the innocent blood | of the /157/ best men. It was rare to see an eminent, virtuous man die in his bed. The histories of their times are nothing but relations of accusations and executions. Peter the Cruel, king of Castile, Ferdinand, the bastard of Aragon that reigned in Naples, and his bloody son, the wicked Louis Sforza of Milan, Charles IX and Henry III of France, and the like of the Scotch kings in England, were ever terrible to their own subjects but never feared by any foreigners.[376] On the

[376] Peter (1334–69), king of Castile and Leon from 1350. Ferdinand II (1452–94), king of Naples from 1458. Sforza, Louis (1452–1508), duke of Milan (1494–8). Charles IX (1550–74), king of France from 1560. Henry III (1551–89), king of France from 1574.

other side, Edward I and III and Henry V of England, Gustavus Adolphus and Carolus Gustavus of Sweden, Louis XII and Henry IV of France, were feared by none of their own subjects. But neighbouring nations trembled at the sight of their swords. And it is plain this present king of France walks in the steps of his grandfather[377] and the other of like or greater virtue, is feared by no subjects but such as have corrupted the government, oppressed the people, or embezzled the treasure of the crown and nation. He never had his hand in any subject's blood. His business is to ease their burdens and do them justice. No man suffered death for any state crime since the government came into his hands. If I were his subject, these qualities would make me love him. But, being of a nation France was ever a rival and an enemy to, and that has often shaken and sometime enjoyed the crown he now bears, I do extremely fear him, that he expects an occasion of absolutely enslaving us. If he support the Stuart family, it is not for love or alliance, but because he expects we shall be sooner destroyed by their fraud and ill-government than by his power. But granting that the king of France should really defend your court party a while against any foreign or domestic enemies, I desire to know who shall defend you against him. Nothing is more

[158] common in history than that | powerful princes have at last subdued the nations to themselves which they undertook to defend from others. If the king of France protect he will expect you shall be his servants. *Protectio trahit subjectionem.*[378] Louis Sforza died under the chains of the king of France, whom he had called into Italy as his protector.[379] England, to keep the balance even between France and Spain, should ever cleave to the weakest. England, when by its government thrown into rage and despairs, and the strength thereof destroyed, will be an easy prey to that power of France you endeavour to increase for your private ends and defence against the fanatics.

---

[377] I.e. Henry IV.
[378] 'Protection leads to subjection.'
[379] Louis Sforza died in a French prison in 1508.

Twelfth Dialogue

Eleventh Court Maxim: The United Provinces are ever to be esteemed enemies

PHILALETHES: next to those things of universal practice, our corrupting of servants to betray their masters, setting wives against their husbands, children against their parents, and employing spies and trepanners in all places; knowing that those that are divided among themselves can never hurt us; there is nothing we more rely upon than our bishops at home and foreign helps from the king of France. Your reasons make me suspect neither of these will long secure us from ruin. But I will proceed to the examining *of* other points of opinion and practice amongst us.

We look on the United Provinces as immortal, irreconcilable enemies, and by all ways imaginable we seek their ruin.

EUNOMIUS: is not the narrowness of their hand, seldom exercised in giving bribes, the chief cause of your enmity against them?

PHILALETHES: that may be something. But we also look on their power and riches, the security, happiness, | and prosperity they /159/ enjoy in a commonwealth, as a most pernicious example to England. Others leave their native countries, abounding in things necessary or delightful to man, to seek new seats in Holland, of all Europe the most unwholesome, unpleasant, unprovided, of all things requisite to the life of man; yet through good government and liberty of traffic so rich, powerful, and prosperous that no state in Europe dares singly contest with it. This example is so full and clear in our sight, that all our arguments for the splendour of a court and glory of a king as the only happiness to the nation are destroyed, and the people naturally inclined to liberty. For if those provinces encompassed with such difficulties oppugned with the vast power of Spain, and have with small helps attained so great prosperity, England, if so governed, may promise itself incomparably more, abounding in all they want, and, being free from all inconveniences they suffered or feared, apprehending no opposition but that of the Stuart family, which is left weak and naked the first moment we come to discover its reign inconsistent with our welfare. By destroying Holland we shall show the world that their prosperity is but a blaze soon going out.

Our next reason that fixes us in the desire of ruining the United Provinces is to make the prince of Orange master of them.[380] So shall we kill two birds with one stone: destroy them we hate and fear in Holland, and set up the title and power of the Orange family, that may help us to destroy our more hated and feared enemies at home. Queen Elizabeth assisted these provinces as thorns in the sides of the Spanish monarchy. But as soon as the Scotch line came into England, a new policy entered. King James, from his first coming to reign here, applied his thoughts to render himself absolute. He found little defence could be expected against the oppressed people [160] by buffoons and flatterers | with others who gained his favour by filthy ways not to be named. He applied himself to the corrupting and weakening of his subjects and to seek helps abroad. The house of Orange he thought not fit to be neglected. Prince Maurice's[381] valour and industry had increased his power and reputation, his ambition equalled the growth of either. Oldenbarnevelt[382] was a cruel eyesore to him. He therefore resolved to take him away, control strict amity

---

[380] After the death of William II in 1650, the Dutch republic was without a stadholder for twenty-two years because the States of most provinces opposed the promotion of his son William III.

[381] Maurice, prince of Orange, stadholder (1584–1625).

[382] Oldenbarnevelt, Johan van (1547–1619); Dutch statesman and architect of the Dutch republic. When Maurice in 1617 openly sided with the counter-remonstrants, who argued against the authority of the state in spiritual and doctrinal matters, Oldenbarnevelt sided with the remonstrants. Maurice eventually won the conflict and had Oldenbarnevelt arrested. After a long trial Oldenbarnevelt was condemned to death and beheaded in Den Haag on 13 May 1619. Disputable from a constitutional point of view, Oldenbarnevelt's conviction has often been regarded as a political murder.

with king James *and* asked his counsel about it, by Carleton his ambassador.[383] This virtuous king, the bishop's Solomon, advised neither to use sword *n*or poison; false witnesses and delegate judges would do his work under pretence of law and name of a trial more plausibly. This way was taken, and that wise and virtuous head, which had so long and so successfully laboured in the service of his country, was cut off, to facilitate his way who sought to oppress it. This and the rendition of Flushing and the Briel, wholly depending on the prince of Orange, were the two principal arts of that king towards the advancement of the house of Orange. King James and prince Maurice being dead, the same design went on in king Charles and Henry, prince of Orange.[384] King Charles married his daughter to him.[385] The conditions of their agreement were: that the king of England should assist him in making himself lord of the United Provinces and then he was to employ whole the power of them for the rendering him absolute master in England. But the troubles of Scotland and then of England gave king Charles *so* much work at home that he could not assist his ally, who, continuing but in the condition of a servant to the States, could little assist him against his own people in England and Scotland. That design therefore was wholly frustrated for their two lives. They are both dead, prince | /161/ William in the heat of youth and by the impulse of young councillors (Rehoboam's case), makes an attempt openly upon Amsterdam, strikes at the head city of the States, to seize.[386] His enterprise miscarries; he acknowledges his error, when he saw no better remedy, and much was imputed to his youth. By help of friends the business was composed, and when preparing much greater force for a second attempt, he dies, leaving a young son, which the king, his uncle, being now advanced, resolves to advance to the utmost of his power.

EUNOMIUS: I fully agree with your opinion that the king will endeavour to ruin the United Provinces and set up his nephew.[387] But some things in your discourse seem doubtful to me. What is that you call a

[383] Carleton, Dudley (1573–1632), English ambassador in the United Provinces (1616–21).
[384] Frederik Henry, prince of Orange, stadholder (1625–47).
[385] In fact it was his son William II of Orange, stadholder (1647–50), who married Mary Stuart, Charles's daughter, in 1641.
[386] William II attempted to seize Amsterdam in 1650 in order to substitute personal rule for the leading bourgeois oligarchy. He died the same year.
[387] I.e. William III of Orange, who in 1672 would become stadholder.

title in the prince of Orange? It appears not to me he has any. His ancestors were only servants to the States, and it depends on their will to employ him or not.

Secondly, how will his advancement ruin the States?

Thirdly, how will the king advance him? The meanest of them see the design and will oppose it to the utmost.

PHILALETHES: I believe not that the prince of Orange has any just title to the dominion of those provinces. The best servant may deserve a recompense, but can pretend no title to be master. Nor can the prince of Orange justify his endeavours for the oppressing them because his ancestors have been useful in defending them against Spain. They have done well and received a good reward, found safety, honour, riches, and power, beyond what any of the family ever enjoyed or could hope for if they had continued obedient to Spain. But to justify our attempts in favour of the prince of Orange, we make the service of his ancestors his title to their offices. And we [162] persuade men that prince | William, in attempting Amsterdam, had no ill intention against the town, but two or three magistrates that had personally affronted him, and that as a youth he sought revenge in a way not well to be excused. The house of Orange is low at present; and we find we may be mistaken as to that design and disappointed. And the Dutch, magistrates and people, will not be so easily taken with our fair words, *of* only restoring the young prince to the dignity deserved by the virtues of his ancestors, nor will trust to our promises of seeking no more if we attain that and for ought I see they are least of all moved by our threatenings. They say commonly *they have narrowly escaped ruin in the time of the three last princes*, and it were madness to expose themselves to the danger of a fourth trial, *for* the power of a prince and the subsistence of their commonwealth is inconsistent, that their liberty is their life. They think it much better to have a sharp contest with the king of England now, who seeks to advance his nephew to their ruin, than when he shall be of age in his own person to enter the quarrel. They have vast revenues, treasure, and credit, so as they are masters of all the money in their provinces. They are furnished with mariners and soldiers, sea-commanders, many great ships, and soon can build more. They have all provisions for war, fear not the king of Denmark, nor his union with England, whom they have once or twice saved from ruin, passing that bell to the Sound, when the king of Sweden his enemy held the castles, do what he could.[388] But their greatest confidence is in the justice of their cause, the defending their just rights and liberties | against them that wrongfully invade them. But we are not troubled at that. A well-armed bold thief has no reason to fear a weak /163/ disarmed passenger. In business of the world we see he that has craft and force and dares vigorously employ them, seldom fails of success in oppressing the just. But our fears spring from another root. We can lay no design so deep but somebody discovers it, let the colours we put upon it be never so fine and fair. Some or other throw them off, and show it to the world in its nakedness and turpitude. As long as we had only to deal with the youths of the Parliament, by the help of some well-fed tongues, our business went well. We made them believe the king thought of nothing less than war on Holland; or, if he did undertake it, that he was moved only by the complaints of his people, desire of restoring trade, and resolutions to comply ever with his Parliament by which they were obliged to serve His Majesty against all opposers with their persons and fortunes. We are ashamed of these pretences now. Women and children laugh at such stories. Everyone discovering that all the noise at the Parliament doors was by broken or breaking merchants, who, by pretending the loss of vast sums, sought excuses for the defrauding of their creditors, or such as having neither stock, industry, credit, *n*or understanding in trade to gain their livings in an honest way, desired to try piracy and rapine, seeking letters of mart for their justification. And, what is yet worse, everyone sees these were stirred up by us; examinations were taken, reports made by the king's creatures, and the poor cheated Parliament was made to do the king's work and furiously engage the nation in a | war under pretence of public good, which was designed /164/ only to advance the prince of Orange and that in the most destructive way to the nation imaginable, as thought the easiest and speediest way to impoverish and enslave it. So the people will utterly refuse to pay the tax levied to raise the sum voted *for* the king. And as the complement of all our disasters, the fanatics are fuller of spirit than formerly, and will not let slip so fair an opportunity of destroying us when engaged in a war with Holland. And may be, the king of

[388] In 1655 Charles X of Sweden violated the treaty of Roskilde and reopened war with Denmark. But when he attempted to seize Copenhagen in 1658, the Dutch republic intervened on behalf of Denmark and defeated a Swedish fleet in the Sound.

France has encouraged us to the war, that we may perish in it. We therefore proceed less violently in that war than was intended. We must therefore have recourse to fraud, make them believe the king intended not war on them, because we are not in a condition at present to undertake it.[389]

Secondly, great care must be had to sow seeds of division between them and the fanatics.

Thirdly, by gentle, long-drawn, ambiguous propositions lull them asleep, and divert them from using their present power against us, till we have strengthened the Orange factions and destroyed the fanatics.

Fourthly, by bribes and pretences we must divide the United Provinces.

And lastly, we must draw other princes into a league against them, and surprise them suddenly with great power when divided and *in* no way able to resist it.

EUNOMIUS: these are considerable advantages, but the difficulty is in obtaining *them*. These things are so easily discovered, that the pro-
[165] posal of them seems like that that is | usually said to children. The way to take birds is to lay salt on their tails. The *United* Provinces are governed by men of great understanding, long experience in business, and vigilant for the good of their country. They will never be brought into such snares as are discernible to children. There is no catching such old wary birds with chaff.

PHILALETHES: we have by wit and industry overcome great difficulties already, and hope to thrive still, by the same arts. When Sir George Booth's[390] plot in '59 came to nothing, and we had neither credit abroad nor force at home, we made the Scots and Presbyterians believe we had no other design than to accomplish the ends of the Covenant, that the king would leave all business to them, bestow all offices and honours amongst them, that the old cavaliers and all lewd persons should be discountenanced and none of them employed. By

---

[389] Sidney here comments on the build up of what was to be the second Anglo–Dutch war (1665–7). During the early session of Parliament in 1664, the English trading companies presented their complaints about Dutch competition. The Commons referred these grievances to a committee and on 21 April this reported that the king be requested to seek redress.

[390] Booth, George (1622–84); English politician who led an abortive royalist revolt against the commonwealth in 1659.

the like ways we led all their ministers and those of other sects like so many woodcocks into springes, twisted the sword out of the independent hands, and brought them all into such a condition that, giving a few baubles to the earl of Manchester and others as rewards for having broken their faith, lost their honour and renounced their religion, we could without danger burn their Covenant, which the king himself had taken, by the hand of the hangman.[391] At one blow we threw all the ministers out of their livings, which we had privately and publicly sworn and promised they should peacefully enjoy. We also hanged, disbanded, imprisoned, poisoned, or starved the most active of the soldiers, contrary to the Declaration at Breda, | which /166/ promised the continuance of the soldiers in the same pay and employments they then had, when the king was yet at Breda. If fanatics now rise, they must find heads and officers. By the like arts have we brought the Parliament to take away the Act for triennial parliaments,[392] and to make the Act about chimney money[393] for the king, a vast revenue they have given him, also the power of the militia[394] and by the Act for uniformity, and another against co*uncils* have they, to the utmost of their power, destroyed the seeds and roots of all spiritual and civil liberties, enslaved themselves and the nation by betraying their country. Our arts also thrive abroad. After all injuries imaginable to Spain, we have made that king believe our king to be his friend. And our ministers get great sums of money from him.

EUNOMIUS: you are so used to fraud, *that* nobody at length will trust you, and by suspicion of your pretences, be defended from your snares. You can cheat none but those that trust you, and if none will trust you, and you have no defence but fraud, you will be naked and so certainly ruined.

PHILALETHES: frauds are at last discovered, but if subtly contrived,

---

[391] In 1661 Parliament ordered the public burning of the Covenant.

[392] The Triennial Act was passed by the Long Parliament and was given reluctant assent by Charles I in 1641. It obliged the king to meet Parliament for a session of at least fifty days every three years and set up a procedure for the automatic summoning of Parliament if the king should disregard the Act. In 1664 the Act was amended. The repealed Act still stated that Parliament should meet at least once every three years, but left it entirely to the king to ensure this.

[393] The hearth tax (1662) was a direct tax of a levy imposed upon each hearth or stove in a house. It was intended as a source of permanent royal revenues.

[394] The Militia Acts of 1661 gave command of the militia to the king.

not discovered until they have their effect, and then the danger is over. We know the presbyterians, sectarians, ministers, and soldiers see well that they are cozened by the king's taking the Covenant and by his Declaration at Breda etcetera. But it is as beasts, who discover the snares in which they are taken when it is too late to escape. So the parliament men will in the end see that they have foolishly ruined [167] themselves. | But we have the power in our own hands, and well fixed the yoke on their necks, let them fret and rage as long as they will, though the people stone them for betraying their country, that shall never trouble us. We shall rejoice at it, least they should endeavour to expiate their former follies and crimes, and get reputation by some good actions for their country against us.

As to your next objection, I answer as Cesare Borgia to one that advised him to take hold, lest by too public and frequent perfidy, he should grow to that pass that nobody would trust him, for so he would necessarily perish. No such danger, said he, though I cheat and betray all I deal with, there are still fools enough that will trust me. The success answered his expectation. His whole life was a continued exercise of horrid lusts and cruelty, murdering men, ravishing women, polluting himself with boys, who, relying on his word, put themselves into his power. He still found those that trusted him increasing and prospering, until by an unhappy mistake of a bottle, he poisoned his father, the then pope, and himself, with what he had prepared for an entertainment of some hated cardinals. His father died presently and he was very sick.

The ways and ends of deceit are of such infinite variety, through different humours, designs, natures, passions, conditions, interests, and abilities of men, that no man that can well apply them need fear losing the opportunity of using the same weapons.

Eunomius: but proceed with your discourse concerning Holland.

Philalethes: we tell the Hollanders, the late rumours that gave grounds of jealousy were raised by the city of London, who, finding [168] the Parliament full of such heads as were easily set on fire, | brought a multitude of complaints of vast loss. And the young knights and burgesses, not accustomed to examine businesses, believed all, and to make themselves popular, would need once in their lives *to* show themselves sensible of the nation's concernment, and make those hasty votes that the decay of trade came by the usurpations, violence, and frauds of the Hollander; that the losses we had sustained by their means amounted to above four million seven hundred thousand pounds; desired his majesty to demand satisfaction, promising to assist him in case it were denied. His Majesty, professing always to follow their advice, could do no less than demand this sum, sending the two Houses to themselves in the country, lest they should hotly pursue what they had begun, showing plainly that what he did in this matter was only by the impulse of the Parliament, and not his own inclinations.

Secondly, we have a fair opportunity of stirring up strife between the Hollander and fanatics, that is, we say, what is past may be a good evidence of what is to be expected by Holland from the fanatic. When they had the power of England, their first work abroad was terrible war on Holland. Now they may expect worse for the irreconcilable hatred the fanatic bears them, for delivering up Okey, Corbet, and Barkstead.[395] As a testimony of this we allege that many of their sea-officers, that formerly would not serve the king, have greedily embraced the employment in this war against them.

Thirdly, we tell them the king is no boisterous undertaking prince, but as his father and grandfather, according to the maxims of his family, | seeks peace with all neighbours, turning his designs /169/ inward on his own people, that he may enjoy the fruits of his crown in peace. And his chief ministers and favourites, being no military men, will not put the king upon designs that suit not with their temper. And the cause of the war being to restore trade, none can be so ignorant as not to see that His Majesty endeavours to destroy it. So that they can do him no better service than to drive the English absolutely out of trade, bring London to that weakness and poverty as to render it supple and pliable to His Majesty's commands. For while they have trade they will be rich, and while rich, they will be proud and rebellious. To elucidate this business we can say many things to them, which they for their own interest will keep secret, and which we are obliged to deny and forswear, when charged on us by the fanatic.

---

[395] Okey, Corbet, and Barkstead were English regicides who, at the Restoration, forfeited life and estate. They contrived to escape to Germany, but when they went to visit some friends in Holland in 1662, they were captured in Delft by the English ambassador in Holland, George Downing, who had obtained from the States General permission to seize any regicides he found in Dutch territory. Immediately sent to England, they were executed on 19 April 1662.

And we hope to find easy ways for accomplishing the fourth. Some of the Orange faction have crept into all their councils, and these depend upon us for help. That we call the Orange faction is only a plausible name given those that seek the ruin of that commonwealth and so enslave their country.[396] Downing is a fit instrument for this work.[397] He has learned the arts of an inquisitive spy. He has reason to like those arts, by which from a beggarly boy he is raised to riches and power. He is grown to understand the diseases and sores that are in the States government. The weaker provinces also look [170] with an envious eye on the greatness and power of | Holland, which is of great advantage to us and adds much to the Orange faction, and all those that cannot get, or will not seek, a livelihood by honest means, are ready to set up a tyrant who will need such ministers as they are. They pretend gratitude to the noble house of Orange, call them their defenders and deliverers, whereas that family was defended and delivered by the Hollanders from ruin, and advanced to far greater honour, power, and riches than they ever before enjoyed or could reasonably hope for. The constitution of their government has one defect, which we hope to improve to their ruin. No providence or town acknowledges any superior. They have particular interests contrary to their neighbours, and sometimes hardly consistent with the welfare of the whole commonwealth. We sharpen the passions that rise from hence, increase their jealousies of each other, tell the weaker by our means they shall attain their ends, which they can hope for in no other way. Thus setting up a private interest in each, we hope to set up a faction, contrary to the welfare of the whole, and make ourselves heads of it, to dissolve the union by which they subsist, and then they fall into our hands.

The last point is not of more difficulty. The states, concerned in the growth or ruin of the United Provinces, or that can do anything for or against them, are France, Spain, England, Sweden, Denmark, Poland, and Portugal. France has of late had many sharp contests with them, though no war, and this high-spirited king of France will

---

[396] The Orangists in the Dutch republic desired the restoration of the stadholdership and the end of oligarchical rule by the States of the provinces.
[397] Downing, George (1623–84), English ambassador in The Hague, had close contacts with the Orange faction and paid some of them with money from the English government. The main objective of this cooperation was to enhance the interests of the prince of Orange, William III.

not endure to see his designs crossed by the | narrow, dirty territory *[171]* of a new-born commonwealth. He knows he can never much increase his power at land until master of the sea. Nor will he think his own kingdom has its due form till, by reuniting to his crown Flanders, Brabant, and the Rhine on that side serve again to defend his frontiers. The United Provinces are the greatest obstacles to both these designs; they are not to be contested with at sea, and are able very powerfully to hinder his progress by land. They must be brought lower. England only can do it, and he will to the utmost assist our king if he undertake it. Spain bears them an immortal hatred, and will favour them that endeavour to suppress them. He will think it easier work to recover the country out of the prince of Orange's hands than out of theirs. Sweden looks on them as those that chiefly hindered the conquests of Carolus Gustavus, and brought him into great straits. So they will join with their enemies to revenge themselves on them, which they can never do by their own power. Denmark is averse to them. That king owing them too much, hopes to pay, by their ruin, a debt heavy enough to destroy him. The contests between Portugal and them about Brazil in America and several places in Africa and Asia will engage that king in a league against them.[398] When all these by our means combine together, and the Orange faction in their own bowels assault them at home, they will soon be brought to nothing.

EUNOMIUS: I see yet difficulties in your designs and weakness in your arguments, which I shall render evident to you. You may spare your pains of raising jealousies between the Hollander and fanatic. Both parties know their | interests as inseparable, as that of the *[172]* houses of the Stuarts and Orange, the common enemies of both. They must necessarily join to preserve each other when their enemies join to destroy them both. The last war was not brought on by a contrariety of interests, nor was act of counsel; but both found themselves unaware involved in it by a fatality that none could understand. The effects of it were so pernicious to both, that they were endangered and we destroyed by it. Such an experience does sufficiently show the error of the undertaking and deter both parties from the like for the future. And the delivery of Okey, Corbet, and Barkstead is not to be imputed to the States General, who were surprised

---

[398] The Portuguese drove the Dutch out of Brazil in 1654.

and cheated by Downing.[399] That is to be imputed only to him, with some of the Orange faction and a corrupt secretary. The nation gave from the beginning evident marks of abhorring so barbarous a treachery.

And your fair words will not accomplish your third end, because nobody will believe you. You know their power, and your treasures are exhausted by the fraud of your officers. The whole nation begins to discover the tyranny of the government. You have not men fit for counsel or action, officers, soldiers, mariners, money, victuals, ammunition, and all sorts of provisions are wanting. All things at home or abroad are unsafe, so it will appear less strange, that you desire to retire out of the strait, whereinto you had giddily and fool-ishly brought yourselves. The States General know all those things, and that you pretend gentleness and retreat only to gain a fitter occa-sion more *effectively*[400] to exercise your malice and set up the Orange family. So may you be brought now to the hard necessity of a [173] war, | with danger of utter ruin, or patch up a peace with much infamy after all your great boasting.

You are not like*ly* to succeed better in your fourth point. Your designs are discovered and the strength of such designs lies only in secrecy. If war be deferred, Holland can provide greater force, dis-cover and weed out from among them the suspected friends to you and traitors to their own country. As for the link of union between the United Provinces, I think they have reason to wish it were stronger. Their constitutions seem to have a more particular regard to the preservation of the liberties and privileges of each town and province than to the welfare of the whole. However, having so long resisted the arts and power of Spain, France, and the subtle princes of the house of Orange, little is to be feared from them. Who knows not that the kings of Spain for thirty years have endeavoured to set up the house of Orange, that the country might fall into their power, when the strength of it was once overthrown by a tyrant? Many underhand treaties and offers have been made, many plots contrived, spies employed, treasures spent to this end. And do you hope after all this, by means of a little treacherous scout, to accomplish what all

---

[399] It is said that the States General were unaware that any regicides were in Dutch ter-ritory when they gave George Downing permission to seize regicides; and that they secretly intended to favour the escape of any who might be in danger. Downing, however, kept the States to their promise.

[400] MS: 'effectually'.

these have never been able to compass? You are so detested, hated, and despised by them, that, though not perfectly agreeing among themselves, they will unite unanimously against you. It is true their commonwealth seems to be a vast building of loose stones, which not well cemented, threatens ruin. But their delight in liberty and prosperity, their desire to maintain it, | has kept them unanimous in /174/ defence against all enemies, though some did think a little accident might disorder and dissolve it.

And though probably the kings you mention would willingly see the United Provinces brought low, I see as little reason to believe you can advantage your designs against them by a foreign league as by any other way. For though they desire their power to be abated, yet not that it should be united to that of England. And the king of France knows that in losing the benefit of trade with Holland, by which all the maritime provinces receive great advantages and his own revenues much increase, those provinces might be discontented with him, and his revenue much diminished. Judge then what likelihood there can be that an English war on Holland should be carried on principally by his power and treasure, as you expect. And that the king of England only should reap all the advantages of the war.

As for France and Spain, their interests are so irreconcilable, that if France takes one side, Spain always takes the other. As for your advantage hoped for from Sweden and Denmark, those two kings have far sharper controversies one with the other, than with the United Provinces. Denmark desires to recover what was lately lost, Sweden to keep what it has gained or enlarge their conquests. This engages them in perpetual machinations one against the other. Will they, think you, wave their own interests to advance yours and the prince of Orange's? Will the king of Denmark hazard his tottering crown in a war against them, that lately preserved it from falling to the ground? Lose his benefit of trade with the United Provinces? And give his own subjects opportunity of throwing off the lately imposed yoke, by turning his mercenary soldiers against himself for want of | pay from him? Norway, the other part of his kingdom, the /175/ Hollanders are masters of a good part of the revenues of it, have the hearts of that people. The whole nation does particularly subsist by traffic with them. Will he wave all this and in compliment to you help you to destroy those that preserved him and his country? And think you to draw Sweden into the same snare? Have you found their

counsels so weak, light, imprudent as to neglect their own interest to follow yours; to lose their traffic with Holland, which is great and helps them off with all their commodities? Who shall pay the customs of Riga, Reval, and Stockholm (which are more than three-quarters of the revenue of that crown) if the Hollanders send no more ships thither? If Denmark should break with the Hollander at your persuasion, would not the Swedes enter into a stricter union with them on that occasion? Have not they as much command of the Sound as Denmark, when destitute of relief from Holland? Besides, the present powers of these two kingdoms are so well known, that no men or money can reasonably be expected from either, and then what would their league with you profit you? As to their shutting the Sound, a burgomaster of Amsterdam said well not long since that Amsterdam kept the keys of the Sound, meaning the power at sea. The success verified what he had said, for in the year 1658 their fleet, that went with the first succour to Copenhagen, in spite of the two castles then both in the Swedes' hands and their king then in Cronenburg, notwithstanding the opposition also of a fleet of Swedish ships equal almost in number to theirs and commanded by the gal-
[176] lant Wrangel, they | passed through and succoured Copenhagen. Men skilled in those matters say the Swedish fleet might with better advantage have fought them in the open sea than relied upon the help of those two castles on each side *of* the Sound. Or, though this passage should be shut, none I think will pretend with cannons to shut that of the Belt, which is twenty miles broad, convenient for passage, and where no ships can lie to hinder it.

And your hope of keeping them from trade by means of a league with Denmark and Sweden is as frivolous as the rest. For Prussia and Poland plentifully furnish them with pitch, fur, masts, hemp, flax, corn, and all other commodities which are afforded by the other countries except iron and copper. So that, unless you can bring Poland and the elector of Brandenburg into the league, nothing is done. And the king of Poland, who has lost half his country and by foreign force and intestine troubles *is* in danger of losing the rest, is not like*ly* to engage in others' quarrels and lose the advantage of increasing his own trade, if the other kings of Sweden and Denmark, by not suffering the Hollanders to trade in their countries, should cast them wholly upon him. As for Portugal, that now wants the support of others, and therefore is not like*ly* to assist you.

PHILALETHES: I desire you to tell me, what then you do believe is the design of the king in this war, who you think began it, and what will be the end of it.

EUNOMIUS: there is difficulty in these questions, but I will satisfy you as well as I can. We have already agreed that the king endeavours to ruin the United Provinces by establishing the power of the prince of Orange; that the merchants | and Parliament are both stirred up /177/ by him to move for a war and the steps made towards it are marks of the obedient Parliament's compliance with his commands. Nevertheless, the business of Guinea succeeding very contrary to expectations[401] and other obstructions occurring, the king endeavours to continue the peace. The lightness and uncertainty of court counsels begets this variety of proceeding. Except some general maxims of getting as much money, doing as much mischief, and oppressing the people as much as they can, there is a perpetual uncertainty in all their counsels and actions. The king did desire war, and now seeks to avoid it, expecting a more favourable season to execute what he intends for the house of Orange.

But to satisfy your demands, the French, that have a great power in our court, have this advantage above all princes in Europe: the king of Spain wasting himself in hopeless enterprises against Portugal, the other branch of the Austrian line is involved in a terrible war against the Turks; so, if England and Holland, the two other great powers of Europe, be engaged in a war, he may quietly see all these emulous powers ruining themselves. So may he come to give law to them all. These two nations, England and Holland, being intent on war, the king of France will gain all the traffic, and increase his power at sea as fast as either of ours can diminish. So he sits on a sure rock, beholding the danger of those that suffer storms at sea. The bravados of the king and his ministers against the Dutch proceeded from hopes in France, but, finding their dangers increased by the boldness of the Hollanders, that they thought would fear them, and that the promised assistance | was small and far off, whilst the want /178/ of us was great and present, they are willing to retire. And the king, by gaining money from the Parliament on pretence of this war, may

---

[401] In July 1664 a fleet of the English East Africa Company seized Dutch strongholds on the coast of Guinea, but later that year the Dutch defeated the English garrisons and retook their possessions.

furnish himself to keep up an army to oppress England. In a while it may be feared that those who were desirous to buy their peace, will hardly be content to sell it.

In fine, the king seeking the ruin of the English trade and people, and the ruin of the Holland commonwealth, these two nations may see their joint interest against him and Orange, and unite in counsels and action; joining their hands, hearts, and heads to extirpate the two detested families of Stuart and Orange, who, like serpents, as soon as they recover a little vigour, tear out the bow*el* of them that cherished them. The opposition between us and them, their concernment and ours, is universal and irreconcilable. Their safety is our destruction, our safety is their destruction. We desire to be governed by good laws, possess our goods in safety, with the full enjoyment of our civil and spiritual liberties. We seek to increase our fortunes by honest industry, advance our persons and families by virtue and the service of our country, and by merit gain that which truly deserves the name of honour. All this is contrary to the interest and maxim of tyrants, who, with their own inherit all manners of vices, pride, avarice, cruelty, lust, and perfidy as qualities inseparable from their blood. These rare kingly qualities cannot be freely exercised, until their power be unlimited and the misery of those under it inexpressi-
[179] ble. | Those who see and well consider this, will to the utmost lay out themselves and all they have to secure a multitude of innocents by the overthrow of a few guilty heads.

PHILALETHES: you make a very severe conclusion of your discourse, but I will not think it unjust, till we farther examine other maxims, much esteemed amongst us.

EUNOMIUS: I hope God will give us another opportunity for this ere long. But now the night calls us to our rest.

Thirteenth Dialogue

Twelfth Court Maxim: Spain, Germany, Italy, and the catholic Princes are nothing to our court

PHILALETHES: in our last conference we discussed, as far as was requisite, the maxims and interests of our court, as they related to France and the United Provinces. It is hardly worth our pains to consider how the king and his ministers stand affected to other states, being little important to us. We only shall make use of them as occasion is offered. We look on Spain as decaying, fear it not, and hope for nothing but money to our chief ministers, that we may do them no hurt on Portugal's side. Denmark is our friend, but cannot help us. Sweden, we suspect, is ill-affected to us, but cannot hurt us. The princes of Germany are considerable only to such as attempt something in their country, which is far from our thoughts. We know the king, by interesting himself for the businesses of that country, might gain advantages to the nation, and easily unite all the Protestants of the world into one body and make himself their head. And that great | and good work might be a foundation for effecting oth- /180/
ers, pleasing to God and man. But for the attaining *of* such ends, we must have a frugal court, justice must be administered, men of virtue and valour advanced and employed, military discipline restored to subjects; and then we, who by our court get money enough to live in the height of splendour and pleasure, must apply ourselves to such as are very contrary to our complexion, requiring

177

much sweat and blood. All these things are extremely contrary to our designs.

The bishops tell us it is good to undertake no war for the advancement of the Protestants' religion but that against conventicles carried on by justices of the peace and constables. We believe them, and leave all those fine things that are for the public good, advancement of the cause of Christ in the world, and diminishing the power of antichrist, to the fanatics, who, by reading the Bible, fill their heads with speculations which please them. But if we harkened to them, we should have troubles and remorse of conscience and be disturbed in all our designs for a pleasant life; put upon frugality, honest industry, justice, and temperance. But we utterly renounce all this manner of life and everything that leads or belongs to it. This reason persuaded us to think no more of Germany than if it were overwhelmed with the sea.

Nor consider we Italy much more when we can do little, unless by the help of Germany. And they who govern there think little of us. The last king thought that by favouring the papists in England, and

[181] giving them an opportunity of destroying all the Protestants | in Ireland, he had merited great assistance from Rome and all other popish princes.[402]

But all that was obtained was a sum of money. And unless we restore the Irish to their estates and power in government and restore a full exercise of the popish religion in Ireland and England, we have little hope of advantage from Rome.

EUNOMIUS: if these be your only obstacles, they are easily removed. You may justly expect all assistance from the catholic princes, that they can pretend to who are the chief pillars of their cause. For His Majesty by his gracious proclamation in 1662 fully showed his desires to favour them. In his speech to the Parliament not long after he acknowledged himself much obliged to them for their services done to himself and his father (of which certainly the greatest was the killing of above two hundred thousand Protestants in Ireland, men, women, and children), which necessarily obliged him to favour

---

[402] In 1641 the Old English Catholics rose in arms against the protestant settlers in Ulster and killed many of them. Contemporaries in England wrongly believed that a wholesale massacre of Protestants was planned and carried out as part of the rising, and that the rebels were authorized to do this by king Charles I in order to restore Roman Catholicism in Ireland.

them.[403] The court also is now full of popish priests, friars, and jesu-its, who are so publicly favoured, that it is thought, the poor fanatics might so far have sheltered themselves under their wings that those strict laws for uniformity and against conventicles should have found strong opposition, least thereby the papists might have been trou-bled. Nor had they ever passed, as is believed by understanding men, unless the papists had been assured beforehand the execution thereof should not hurt them.

This was farther evidenced in managing the business between the Protestants and papists of Ireland before the commissioners at Lon-don,[404] where Sir Nicholas Plunket in His Majesty's | presence did /182/ rightly admonish Audley Mervin[405] of his mistake in calling the Irish rebels, showing plainly that the name of rebel did belong to the Eng-lish Protestants, who have opposed His Majesty's commands and interest, and the Irish were his loyal subjects, who obeyed and exe-cuted his commands. Sir Nicholas spoke not upon report, he himself was the very man who in '41 with the Lord Gormanston and two or three more laid the plot by the late king's own command, and received instructions for the execution of it from His Majesty's own mouth at London as the chief of the Irish have often confessed. This queen mother had many conferences with him about it, when it was feared, if his visits to His Majesty by the back-stairs had been too fre-quent, it might have given occasion of jealousy. And His Majesty that now is, in his letter signed by secretary Bennet,[406] commanded the commissioners to restore to the earl of Antrim his estate, which testified the said earl did nothing but by command and for the serv-ice of his father, it being notorious unto all Europe that the Antrim

---

[403] In December 1662 Charles II issued a declaration defending himself, among other things, against undue tolerance of Catholics. The tone of the pronouncement, how-ever, was one of approval of his catholic subjects, and in February 1663 Charles again defended himself in a speech in Parliament.

[404] In 1662 Parliament passed the Act of Settlement which vested in the crown all the Irish lands involved in the Cromwellian confiscation, with the exception of church and college lands and the lands of 'innocents'. The execution of the bill was entrusted to a body of seven commissioners called the court of claims.

[405] Mervin (or Mervyn), Audley (d. 1675); fought the Irish rebels, kept to the royalist party till Cromwell's arrival in Ireland in 1649. He was one of the commissioners for Charles II. Nicholas Plunket compiled and authored a contemporary account of the affairs in Ireland in 1641.

[406] Bennet, Henry (1618–85), earl of Arlington (since 1660); was made secretary of state in 1662.

was head of the Old Irish that slew all the English in the North.[407] They could loyally and valiantly, without any distinction of age or sex, hang, kill, burn, drown all who being Protestants and innocent had merited His Majesty's displeasure. This was one of the acts for which the last king lost his head, and I think it is certain, His Majesty that now is, by approving such a work and rewarding the chief actor, deserves more from the Romish party than Charles IX of France did by the massacre of Paris and wars against the Huguenots, or Philip II of Spain could pretend to when | he designed in England and acted in the Low Countries, since the number of the slain in Ireland does much exceed the other two; with this important circumstance, to widen the difference, that some interests of state may have concurred with the hatred of the protestant religion in incensing the kings of France and Spain against those their subjects after dangerous wars raised by them. Whereas the English in Ireland, living in peace and obedience to the government, no *indictment*[408] could be made against them but for their religion. And if any detract from the king's merit because all the Protestants in Ireland were not destroyed, and the like executions were not done in England and Scotland, it may be answered to the first, if they will have a little patience, they may see that work completed as soon as Ormonde, Muskerry, Plunket,[409] and others, who were both the contrivers and executors of the last design, have fully ripened that which is now on foot for the destruction of those that remain. As for the second omission, no exception can be taken at his late majesty, for everyone knows he wanted power, not will, as himself is said often to have expressed. They have no discontent at Rome, because they see not all done presently as to the open exercise of popery in England etcetera. The counsels of that court have been prudently and subtly managed. If they should see His

[183]

---

407 MacDonnell, Randal, second earl of Antrim (1609–82); prominent Roman Catholic royalist during the English civil war who in 1643 was captured while carrying papers that concerned a planned rising in Scotland with support from confederate Irish Roman Catholics. At the Restoration he was imprisoned in the Tower on a charge of treasonable correspondence, but in 1663 both Charles II and the queen mother successfully intervened in the proceedings to restore Antrim to his estates.
408 MS: 'cocception' (?).
409 Ormonde, James Butler, first duke of (1610–88); leading agent of English royal authority in Ireland and lieutenant general in the English army from the outbreak of the Irish rebellion in 1641 till 1647. MacCarthy, Donogh (1594–1665), first viscount of Muskerry; general of the Irish forces of Munster for Charles I, and active in the Irish rebellion.

Majesty's zeal so far transport him, as by too hasty and violent proceedings that way to expose himself to danger for the catholic cause, they are so tender of his safety, they would be the first that should allay such a dangerous heat, and teach him to temporize. It is reported *that* when the king was at Cullen, he offered publicly to profess the catholic religion if he might have | some allowance from [184] Rome for his present subsistence. Pope Innocent X said *he would not buy souls*. And the duke of York, giving testimony of the like thoughts, the king of Spain gave a sea command in a letter to the pope saying, *el Duque de York es católico*. And the Parliament now is pliable and obedient, all penal laws are now taken off from papists, so the work may be done with ease.

PHILALETHES: there is much strength in your reasons, but there is one thing that spoils all. The crafty priests have observed we use two kinds of discourse, the one when we would gain advantage, the other when we have gained it. They remember the brave words given to the two last popes to get money, which, once obtained, was employed in uses very different from the intention of those that gave it. Cardinal Albizzi told the pope Sir Kenelm Digby thought to cheat His Holiness, promised everything they demanded in behalf of Catholics in England and Ireland, but could perform nothing. So the pope gave him arms which he sold for ten thousand crowns, which was all he got.[410]

EUNOMIUS: the English of this is, you having often cheated them, they will trust you no more.

PHILALETHES: that is too true.

EUNOMIUS: if they will not trust you for such little cheats to get money, how can you expect the Protestants should trust you, that have so often been bitterly betrayed by you to their utter destruction, if God had not wonderfully assisted them? Can you expect they should ever give credit more to your oaths, promises, or declarations? And if both parties, protestant and | papist, disbelieve you, [185]

---

[410] Digby, Kenelm (1603–65); was sent to the pope in 1645 by the catholic committee sitting at Paris to collect money for the royal cause. Despite his reputation with papal authorities of being useless for advancing the pope's cause, which was to pave the way for the free exercise of catholicism in Ireland, Digby obtained 20,000 crowns from the pope.

they will despise you and hate you also, which is as plain a way to your destruction as your enemies can wish.

Fourteenth Dialogue

Thirteenth Court Maxim: The king's designs are at home. He has reason to suspect men of virtue, valour, and reputation, and he is obliged to destroy them he suspects

PHILALETHES: our king leaves great designs abroad to such hardy, boisterous princes as the Swedes, who can go into no place not better than the cold rocks where they are born. Our king is well at home, and is to secure himself from enemies there. If he seek his people's good, he must put himself and ministers on troublesome and dangerous enterprises for the good of the nation, live frugally, have beggarly officers and attendants. And our king knows the art of government better than so, and lives in pomp and pleasure, and his favourites and ministers also with him. He loves his people as men their farms for the rent got by them, or as a butcher his ox, in hopes of what he shall make of his carcass. His business is so to tie his ox, that he may not kick or push him, that is, to kill him. So our business is not to gain the love of the people, but to take from them the power of hurting us, though they hate us and then let their hatred be as great as they please. No man's hatred hurts if there be no power to execute it. The hatred of the people often vents itself in curses, or at most in some mad tumult. The first does no hurt. The second usually ends in the ruin of the author. But the hatred of the people is dreadful when governed by prudent councils, and the authority of some principal persons, experienced in businesses of war and peace. These | are the *[186]* men we fear. Conspiracies are ever carried on by such as these. Such hands threw Edward II and Richard II from the throne they unworthily possessed. This consideration obliged Tiberius to poison the noble Germanicus, whose noble birth, flourishing youth, admirable virtue, supreme valour, and the reputation gained by these qualities and many victories were unpardonable crimes. Multitudes were slaughtered by Nero for like reasons. And Tacitus, speaking of Domitian's hatred to Julius Agricola (in his life), says, *causa periculi non crimen ullum aut querela laesi cuiusquam, sed infensus virtutibus princeps.* By his virtues he merited poison from his jealous master.[411]

EUNOMIUS: whoever marks the court government will find that great industry is used to destroy the best men. But first, do you hate them because good, or because against you?

Secondly, have you the same desire to destroy them that are evil, if they be against you?

Thirdly, is this a new maxim, or the prosecution of an old received one?

Fourthly, what ways conduce to this?
Satisfy me in these points, and I will give you my opinion upon your whole discourse.

PHILALETHES: we do not destroy these men because virtuous and good, but because against us. Yet it comes to the same thing. For all that are virtuous and good are against us. And there is a difference in our proceedings, against those that are good and those that are evil, though equally against us. For we know enmity against us is natural and inherent in all that are good. So, having no hopes to gain them, we have no other thoughts but to remove them. But the vicious and evil can only have such hatred to us as rise from some accidental discontent or passion which may be removed. They that are | one in principle with us, will grow friends to us. Therefore we trouble not them, unless in extraordinary cases.

To the second, it is certain all good persons are against us, and it is possible some evil ones, for private interest or discontent, may be so too, as sometimes two competitors for a crown are equally wicked, yet are engaged to seek the destruction of each other. This made it

[187]

---

[411] 'There was no indictment to account for his danger, no complaint from any victim of wrongdoing: merely an emperor unfriendly to high qualities', Tacitus, *Agricola*, ch. 41. Agricola, Julius (40–93), Roman general and governor of Roman Britain (77–84). His death was not caused by Domitian.

necessary for king Charles to poison his father; and for king James to solicit the execution of his mother and to poison prince Henry, whose virtues he feared; and for his mother to kill her husband, for dragging her adulterer Rizzio from her table and killing him.[412] To the third, this is no late invention. All active princes have taken this course: Nero, Caligula, Domitian, and a multitude of others. In Turkey it is a matter of course for him that comes to the government to kill all his brothers and nephews, as Nero killed his mother, brother, and wife; and Herod his wife and sons. This wise practice was never better observed by any, except the Ottoman family, than by that of the Stuarts. Buchanan's history dedicated to king James[413] shows how well his ancestors understood the arts of reigning, by taking away the principal persons for nobility, power, and virtue. He observes that there were few of that family, yea hardly any, that did not slay his father, son, or brother, or was not slain by one of the like relations, and very often, they suffered from one what they had acted on others, for the hastening of them out of the world. He that now observes what kind of persons our prisons are full of, will easily discover who it is the king fears and hates, though he has had no occasion yet to take away any of his own blood.

By the late laws against conventicles,[414] praying | and preaching /188/ are made capital crimes, whilst all profaneness, blasphemy, and lewdness are commended. Many have been taken away for their virtue and goodness, though other pretences have been found. No testimony for this is equal to that of Vane. He must be made a sacrifice, as solicitor Finch well said, for the good of the nation, which had not another man equal to him in virtue, prudence, courage, industry, reputation, and godliness. Tacitus says that Nero having butchered a multitude that were eminent in these hated, dangerous qualities, in killing Thrasea Paetus and Barea Soranus, thought to destroy virtue itself (Tacitus, *Annals*, bk xv).[415] Nor can it be imagined our king had any other desire when he cut off Vane's head, than to destroy, as in

---

[412] In 1566 David Rizzio, secretary and confident of queen Mary of Scotland, was murdered at the instigation of Henry Stuart, earl of Darnley. Darnley was killed in an explosion in 1567. The other accusations are unfounded.

[413] Buchanan, *History of Scotland*.

[414] The Conventicle Act passed Parliament on 17 May 1664. Aimed to prevent ejected clergy from holding their own separate services with members of their previous congregations, it prohibited religious meetings of more than five people (except families) which did not conform to Prayer Book regulations.

[415] Tacitus, *Annals*, bk xvi, ch. 21.

its root, all virtue, wisdom, and godliness, since those, who were eminent in any of those qualities, looked on him as their master, and seemed to have learnt all they knew or practised by his precepts or example. This was a stroke that showed how carefully he treads the steps of his ancestors. Such blood as this does most strongly cement the foundations of his throne. And when we have mixed with it that of some of his nearest followers, we shall not fear that any storms raised by others that pray and read the Bible shall be able to shake it.

Fourthly, as to the ways for this end, they are to be chosen, according to the prudence of the king and his ministers, with reference to the nature and temper of the nation and present state of affairs. If we followed our own course, we should take examples from the duke of Alva, who, finding many thousands in prisons in Flanders, to make short work, killed them all, and in a few weeks filled the same with as many more Bible readers. So Herod slew all the Sanhedrin. Dionysius all the senate of Syracuse. Agathocles at once slew eight hundred [189] of the most worthy persons in | the same place. But the humour of our nation so abhors these apparent cruelties, that we are forced to find other expedients more slow, but as sure. We for the most part take care to have some pretence of law, which seldom fails us. For our lawyers have tricks enough by interpretations, equivocations, and variety of cases to render our law so uncertain and intricate, as to bend it which way they please. And the judges and lawyers that depend on us, will ever turn it that way which conduces to our interest. Which was signally verified in Sir Henry Vane's case, who was suffered to cite Bracton, Littleton, and Coke, with ancient and later statutes, as much as he pleased, they cared not for all that, but, according to command from His Majesty, condemned him to die. And lest these judges, that are so loyal and obedient to the king as to hang whom he pleases, how worthy and innocent soever, should endanger themselves thereby, His Majesty has pleased to draw this supple Parliament to make new laws which will fully answer our purpose. Especially that for treason and conventicles, the first of which is of so large extent, comprehending all words against the government that hardly any man can be free unless he resolve not to speak at all; and lest any should be so cautious, as to avoid these snares, we have by the lawyers in the House caused them to be drawn so ambiguously, that none can know whether he come within the penalty or not.

Lastly, lest through oversight there should be any place left for an

escape, the act concerning conventicles will stop all gaps. For those
we suspect will be preaching and praying, and though that act
appoint not the utmost penalties, unless to those that pertinaciously
persist in calling upon God in spite of the king, yet there is enough to
give | us a pretence to secure them all, or at least whom we list. The /190/
matter thus prepared the execution is easy. We give honours and
rewards to accusers and informers, fill all houses with spies, set division in all families. We can everywhere almost find or make some so
corrupt, as to be our friends, and discover what is done by the rest. If
the wife be inclined to gallantry, or the son debauched, we know they
are ours. If they do not of themselves fall into these courses, we have
baits to allure them. By this means, few can so conceal themselves
but we know what they say in their chambers or beds. We send trepanners everywhere. Out of their reports we frame accusations. And
as we have judges, sheriffs, lawyers, and juries at our devotion, we
can make anything pass for a crime, and every crime capital.

EUNOMIUS: *I desire to know* what other ways have you of remov-
ing suspected persons, and then will I give you my opinion of the
whole.

PHILALETHES: I exclude not sword and poison when either seems
necessary. Else the customs of the Stuart family has forborne it. In
'41 it was found expedient to destroy all the Protestants in Ireland;
accusers, informers, judges, and juries could not do our work, which
obliged the late king to downright killing. And they did not often use
poison, unless on those of their own blood, where they could find no
pretence for a trial at law. King James could not publicly accuse
prince Henry for having more wit, spirit, and goodness, than he
could wish; nor king Charles accuse his father of living longer than
agreed with his convenience; so both secured themselves by poison.
If queen Mary Stuart had this way rid herself of her hated husband,
she might | have avoided all the miseries that fell upon her from her /191/
subjects about it. So her father, James IV, might have removed his
father, James III, by poison, and not have raised a party that gave
him battle, killed him, and then pronounced him *jure caesum*, says
Buchanan.[416] As for Jezebel's way of killing Naboth, if there be any
difference in murders, there is more atrocity in that performed by

---

[416] Buchanan, *History of Scotland*, bk XII.

false oaths and corrupt judgements than by those acted openly by the sword. Thus having performed my work, I desire you to begin yours, to say what in government obliges to use these means, and what is like*ly* to be our success in using them.

EUNOMIUS: you truly say your court fears and hates all good and virtuous men, which evidently shows the evil of your government. All things depend on their causes. Fruits are suitable to their rent. An evil tree cannot bring forth good fruit, nor a good ill, so you may judge rightly of the tree by the fruit. Acts of justice, virtue, goodness proceed from good principles. The exercise of frauds, rapine, perfidy, and cruelty comes from a corrupt root. And everything loves what is like to itself and the principle in which it lives, and hates the contrary. The utter contrariety between good and evil causes an irreconcilable enmity between the followers of each. A good man hates that that is evil, an evil man loves that that is evil and hates all that is good. And he that hates his brother is a murderer in heart, that is, desires to destroy him. The nature of everything is to destroy all that is contrary to itself and its principle. Everything desires to propagate its own principle by the destruction of the contrary, and is
[192] stirred on to action by fear of being destroyed by | its contrary. The nature of everything is discovered by its love or aversion to that which is suitable or contrary to it. And there is such a proposition between the way and the end of all actions and intentions, that the end is still discovered by the way that is taken to it. If your principle were good, rooted in godliness and virtue, you would discover and acknowledge a similitude to your principle in all good and godly men, and cherish it, as assured that all such aim at the same end with you and strengthen you by unanimously joining for the same ends, the advancing of all goodness and virtue, and destroying all wickedness and the favours thereof. You would not then fear their meetings who only read, expound Scriptures, and call upon God. This is a certain evidence of your contrary ends, and of your being acted by a contrary principle. You suspect none whose speeches are full of blasphemy and lives infamous by all manner of impiety. The greatest vices are testimonies of loyalty. Prisons are full of the most godly persons in the nation, your palace receptacles of the most wicked and vile men in the nation. If you show any dislike to debauchery, it is only by such pitiful ways, as a proclamation against drinking healths,

or an act for observation of the sabbath, which is said to have been by the king's order, thrown into a place, that by its foulness well resembled the hearts of them that framed it. The penalty of not observing these commands is His Majesty's displeasure, and everyone sees that none enjoys his favour but they that live most contrary to them. So is he *suarum legum auctor idem ac subversor*;[417] like his taking the covenant, obliging himself by oath in the | presence of God and man for *[193]* accomplishing the ends of it, and then causing it to be burnt by the hand of the hangman. When they would seem to do anything for the discountenancing of profaneness, it is in such a ridiculous manner, as discovers their hypocrisy to all men. But when the godly are to be persecuted, all craft and care is used, all rigour and cruelty is exercised in the execution of their wicked laws and contrivances, which shows to all the world a perfect agreement between their heads and hearts, hands and tongues. Against profaneness there is nothing but frivolous neglected words. But against preaching and praying the highest atrocity of punishment is threatened, and the utmost rigour is used in the prosecution. This contrariety between good and evil men was always the same as between God and the devil. When good men are in power, they are always hated by the wicked. When wicked men are in power the utmost of their rage is exercised against the godly. Joshua, Caleb, nor any of a good spirit hated or oppressed Moses; but Korah, Dathan, and Abiram,[418] men of pride and ambition, set themselves against him. David never feared Saul, till the spirit of God was departed from him. Then the spirit of the devil entered, and he evidences it in the persecution of the godly and murder of the priests. The whole series of the kings of Israel and Judah shows that the godly endeavoured to destroy wicked and idolatrous persons; but if wicked, they thirsted perpetually after the blood of the godly. Josias slew the priests of Baal, Ahab and Jezebel the true prophets of God. Hast thou found me and my enemy,[419] said that bloody idolatrous tyrant to holy Elias. And when his palace was full of lying prophets that he favoured, he confessed there was another but he hated him. This quarrel began with the fall of man, and will never end | till the powers of sin and death be destroyed and swal- *[194]* lowed up in that victory, which the son of Mary shall have over all

---

[417]'The maker and breaker of his own enactments'. Tacitus, *Annals*, bk III, ch. 28.
[418]Rebels against Moses and Aaron. Num. 16:1–33.
[419]I Kings 21:20.

his enemies on earth and in hell. The devil, by whose impulse Ahab acted, taught him to know the spirit of God. When the rites of Bacchus, Ceres, Venus, Priapus, etcetera were publicly celebrated, the poor Christians were driven into deserts and caves to call upon God. When wicked idolaters possessed the throne and tribunals, all places were more polluted with the blood of the holiest Christians than by the obscenities of the governing princes. The like method has ever been followed by those which professed the name of Christ in unright counsels. They ever persecuted the sincere lovers of the truth. The Arian fury raged a while.[420] The Roman tyranny has had a longer reign. And now the English prelacy endeavour to build a new throne out of the broken pieces of tottering Roman *babel*.[421] Those that are completely wicked endeavour to destroy moral virtue, the shadow of godliness. Hierocles, in *Carminibus Pythagoricis*, says moral philosophy cleanses the mind from all pollution of passions, and prepares it to receive the dull illuminations; so Dionysius Areopagitus, *De hierarchia ecclesiastica*, of three parts of christian progress to it, purgation, perfection, union.[422]

I may then conclude my discourse with this. The most impious persons in the world have been most furiously bent upon the destruction of the godly, and show themselves thereby most detestably wicked. Their hatred is heightened and sharpened by their father and master the devil. Now your court, above all places in the known world abounding in impiety, profaneness, lewdness, and vice, it is no wonder that by contrariety of principle it is so bitterly bent upon the [195] destruction of all that have anything of virtue or godliness. |

To your second demand, as to the success and end of such practices, by the end such designs have had in all ages, I may answer, the mischief you have contrived for others will fall on your own guilty heads, as ever on the like attempters it did. Though I know not how long you may be continued for a punishment of the sins and exercise of the graces of God's people, I dare say your end will be destruction, as truth itself has assured us. No weapon that is formed against the truly righteous shall prosper. That which makes me hope your end

---

[420] Arianism was a heresy of the christian church in the fourth century and was named after its originator Arius. It denied the divinity of Christ.

[421] Due to the binding of the MS, this word is uncertain.

[422] Hierocles of Alexandria (d. 431/2), neoplatonist. Dionysius Areopagitus, first bishop of Athens, created by the apostle Paul.

near, is that the measure of your iniquity seems to be full, the harvest ripe, and when a separation is made between the wheat and you, you will be fit for the fire. The blood of the saints also cries aloud against you, and God will not long delay his appointed vengeance.

Fifteenth Dialogue

Fourteenth Court Maxim: handling this question by way of conclusion to the whole discourse: Whether monarchical government be simply and universally unlawful

EUNOMIUS: It appears you hate and fear none so much as virtuous and godly men. You suspect no meetings so much as those that are for the most godly ends. And consequently, you endeavour to hinder the things and destroy the persons you hate and fear. Your fear and hatred against them for being good and godly, does denominate you to be contrary; since none hate or desire to destroy any but such who are contrary to themselves. Nor can this blood be washed off by pre-
[196] tending you persecute them as seditious, nor | as godly, since your rage is evident against those who can be accused of no crime but godliness. And your laws are not against those who meet seditiously and tumultuously, but such as have no other end but preaching and praying. This is sedition to you. The poor Quakers, that desire nothing but to be sufferers for conscience sake, renouncing all force, deserve your hatred, because they call upon God, as Daniel did though the king forbad it.[423] There is nothing I less wonder at in your proceedings than this. You have reason to fear that spirit, whose gifts godly men do enjoy, may be a link of union amongst them to your destruction. You know their division was your establishment. And the frauds by which it was wrought being now detected, it is probable you can keep what you have by no other but the same arts by which

[423]Daniel 6: 5–24.

you gained it. And as the division amongst the honest party was the cause of your prosperity, their union will easily bring you to destruction. Joining in prayer and holy exercises does not only make them know one another, but increases their love to each other and faith in Christ, their head. This you call sedition. These are the pestilent fanatics, that must be destroyed to secure the peace of your tyranny and wickedness. And as herein you follow the steps of all the wickedest tyrants since the world began, you must be content with such titles, for nothing is more reasonable *than* that everyone have a name agreeable to his actions.[424]

Your second question concerning monarchy in general requires a long discourse, but I will draw it into as narrow a compass as I can | /197/ without being obscure or leaving the proofs imperfect. I dare not say all monarchy is absolutely unlawful, for monarchy in the largest sense, as signifying a government where one man has a pre-eminence above others, may be distinguished into many sorts, which differ not only in degree, as where that one man has more or less power, but in specie or kind, as good and bad, just and unjust, which we will examine according to the rules of Scripture, reason, and human authors.

I find three sorts of monarchy in Scripture:

First, that of Moses, Joshua, Gideon, Samuel, and other judges. Secondly, that described *in* Deuteronomy, chapter 17. Thirdly, that in the eighth and tenth chapters of Samuel I.

The first is that where one man beloved of God, guided by his spirit, full of faith, wisdom and holiness, raised by God to be chief among his people for the accomplishing of some great work, as bringing them out of Egypt, giving them a law, driving out accursed nations, delivering *them* from tyrants, and the like, is simply good. And happy were that people that enjoyed such evident marks of the presence of God amongst them, and care of them in raising up such men to protect and deliver them. This is not kingship, but far from it. Gideon would not reign over them, nor should his sons. The Lord shall rule over you, said he (Judges 8:23). This was a theocracy. So when Samuel ruled, they desired a king. Samuel therefore was not a king, and that desiring a king was a rejecting of the Lord their king, and not Samuel.

The second kind of monarchy is kingship, not simply good or

---

[424]MS: '[chapter of monarchy in general begins here]', inserted by copyist.

bad, but capable of being so restrained, as to be in some degree useful, from which if it break loose and exceed its due limits, it grows
pernicious. The necessary qualifications to make this government
[198] good is that the man be chosen by the Lord, that he | be one of our
brethren, and that he exalt not himself above his brethren when king;
and that he depart not from the law of God to the right hand or to
the left (Deuteronomy, ch. 17). Kings naturally fall into pride, lust,
and covetousness. Here is a check upon those growing vices. The
multiplying of horses, wives, riches is forbidden. Josephus (*Jewish
antiquities*, bk IV, ch. 6), paraphrasing on this place, says Moses told
them the form of government God constituted among them was
best, and that they ought to be contented to have God for their king.
But if they would have a king, he should be one that excels in wisdom, justice, and piety, with power of acting nothing without counsel and consent of the high-priests and elders, etcetera. If he attempt
it, they were to forbid him.

The third and last sort of monarchy is simply and universally evil.
They would have a king like the other nations round about them.
This demand was a renouncing of God, as their head, Lord and king.
They have not rejected thee but me, said the Lord to Samuel. They
were a people chosen out from amongst the nations, enjoying felicity
and liberty and a law and government constituted by God himself.
This pleased them not. They are not content only to be of the idolatrous religion of their neighbours, but must have their form of government too, to show how strict a union there is between idolatry and
tyranny. They would be like them in the misery and shame of slavery, as well as in the filth and pollution of idolatry. The devil sets up
idolatry, that is the worship of himself under several names and figures, in opposition to the worship of the true God. And when men
are brought into that snare, he can easily draw them to set up tyrants
[199] in opposition to the government God had set up. | He doubted not,
but when they had set up one to be their head who might be his lieutenant or vicegerent, he would uphold his interest and worship
amongst them. *To all other evils done by them, they added this of asking
a king.* Nevertheless, harken to their voice, says God to Samuel, that
they may bear the punishment of their sin and folly. But first protest
to them and tell them this shall be the manner of their king. If you
will have such a one as the other nations about you have, he will do as
the kings of those other nations do. And when you shall cry unto me

by reason of your oppressions under him, I will not hear you. The success answered the prediction in every point. The kings they had chosen answered the devil's expectations and accomplished his designs. Following the example of their neighbours, they led the people into idolatry, and from thence into destruction. They soon found their error. But God, as he had threatened, denied the remedy. They groaned under even Solomon's yoke, but knew not how to break it. On his death they hoped for more tolerable conditions from his son, but found him as much more harsh than his father as less wise. They thought the fault was only in the person, and by changing him hoped for his ease. They knew the right of constituting or rejecting kings remained in them, and therefore sought for that felicity under Jeroboam, which was denied by the house of David. But this was like the vanity of a man in a fever who trembles and tosses himself in his bed, hoping for ease by change of place, not considering that the disease is seated in his blood, not in his bed. They imputed their miseries to Solomon and Rehoboam, not to the king or government itself. And, seeking to deliver to themselves from those, cast their necks under the feet of one that was worse. In rejecting God and his rule they lost their wisdom and strength, and then, | like /200/ birds in snares, the more they strove for liberty, the more were they entangled in unavoidable slavery. If any object, the Israelites were never so powerful and rich as under David and Solomon, as appears by their magnificence, and vast treasures, I answer, the Israelites having sinned grievously in asking a king, God in wrath harkened to their voice, and the continuance of those kings over them was the continuance of his wrath and judgements upon them. And though they cried unto him for deliverance, he would not hear them, as he had fore-threatened them.

Whoever thinks kings given as a punishment, should prove a blessing to them, accuses God of want of wisdom in appointing that which could have an effect so different from his word and intention. But in the midst of judgement God remembered mercy, raising up one man after his own heart to be their king, and for the accomplishing of his own counsels, kept a lamp still burning in the house of David till they had filled up the measure of their iniquity, and then they were utterly overthrown by Nebuchadnezzar. But besides the assurance that whatsoever God gives as punishment can never prove a blessing, it will appear that all those evils are to be imputed to the government itself. Laws are made and governments constituted as remedies to human frailty and depravity. Those laws only are good which lead to and encourage virtue, and punish vice. Whoever is composed of flesh and blood is to be suspected of iniquity. Man in honour, at his best, is as the beast that perishes. He cannot always resist temptations to evil. In a commonwealth, therefore, well-constituted laws govern, not men. Though the magistrate be wicked, the constitution is to be such that his exorbitant lusts may be restrained and his crimes punished. Where all is out of order, the weakness or [201] wickedness of a man is the destruction of a nation. All that is | said of the magnificence of Solomon or others only shows they verified what Samuel by the command of God did denounce unto that people. Their kings enriched themselves by the oppression of the nation. The felicity of the Israelites could as little be inferred from the riches of their kings, as any man can truly say the people of England is now happy because the Stuart family, with their creatures and parasites, live in the height of splendour and luxury. The contrary may be most rightly concluded. For as the riches of the thief is the poverty of the passenger robbed by him, the plenty of the king, who has nothing but what he tears from the subject, is their want and misery. That which looked like prosperity under Saul, in some success against the Philistines, Ishmaelites, and others for the accomplishing of God's just judgements on them (God having not utterly rejected them, though they had rejected him) was of small duration, and at length the chiefest of them, with their king and his sons, fell down slain upon Mount Gilboa. Their best king, David, had the most successful reign. Yet even that was accompanied with many dreadful testimonies of God's wrath. What numbers of people were slain in the civil wars between him and the house of Saul? The yet more fierce and unnatural war between him and his son Absolom destroyed twenty thousand of them. When Saul and his sons were dead, God sent three years' famine for the cruelties exercised upon the Gibeonites by Saul and his bloody house. And the angel of the Lord slew seventy thousand of the people for king David's sin in numbering them. The whole story of the kings of Israel and Judea is a continuation of tragical cruelties, acted by or upon them and the people under them. The conclusion was: the ten tribes were led into that captivity, whence to this day they never returned. And Judah was utterly ruined under Zedekiah, and the city and temple of Jerusalem turned.

PHILALETHES:[425] but why should the people be | punished for the [202] sins of the king? I have sinned, but these sheep, what have they done?, says David on his having numbered the people (II Samuel 24:17). Let thy hand be against me and my father's house.

EUNOMIUS:[426] the Scripture shows us three ways of untying this knot, whereby people have made themselves guilty of the king's sins.

First, by asking and establishing a king, he became their creature and servant, and they became guilty of his crimes.

Secondly, the guilt of their kings was more fixed on them, because they punished him not according to their law, which commands them to spare no idolater whatever without any exception of persons.

Thirdly, they aggravated both these sins by following their example in wickedness. Jeroboam, Ahab, Jehu, and others being leaders unto idolatry and others' sins, drew a total destruction on themselves and houses. The people who were next in guilt, must have their part in the punishment too, though not utterly destroyed, till there was no remedy (II Chronicles 36:16). What a weight of blood and guilt does England groan under on this account? Our fathers on a frivolous pretence of a far-fetched consanguinity, placed that family in the throne, which of all that pass under the name of Christian was most infamously polluted with blood. And though they have ever since added sin unto sin, and sold themselves to do all manner of evil, favouring superstition and idolatry and filling all the land with innocent blood, our madness has been such as not to have been taught by experience, that is the mistress even of fools. Burnt children dread the fire, but we, more childish than children, though often scorched and burnt, do again cast ourselves into the fire like moths and gnats, delighting in the flame | that consumes us. Yea, to [203] our shameful destructive folly we add the crimes of faithlessness and ingratitude unto God, who, having through the abundance of his goodness broken the unworthy yoke laid on our necks, brought vengeance upon one impious head and *has* given us the opportunity of expelling and extirpating that wicked race. We could never be contented till we returned again into Egypt, the house of our bondage. God had delivered us from slavery and showed us that he would be our king; and we recall from exile one of that detested race as if

---

[425] MS: 'Objection. But why ...'   [426] MS: 'Answer. The Scripture ...'

the war which destroyed so many thousands of men had been only to drive foreign countries, where, if possible, he might learn more vicious and wicked customs than what had been taught him by his father and the histories of his family, suffering those to be sacrificed to his lust and rage, who had been the most worthy and successful instruments in our deliverance. We set up an idol and dance about it, though we know it to be most filthily polluted with innocent blood. We take no notice of this. Whilst the sword of the Lord hangs over our heads, we live carelessly and secure as the Canaanites when Joshua was ready to fall upon them. We promise ourselves peace, but there will be, can be, no true peace till by the blood of the wicked murderers a propitiation be made for the blood of the righteous that has been shed by them.

I pray you, pardon this digression. I speak this in the anguish of my spirit, broken through the abundance of my sorrow, sighing for the iniquity of my people, praying to God that his wrath may not overflow the whole world; but that he would save those who are free from these great offences and such as, through a slack or fearful con- [204] nivance, have made themselves in some degree guilty, and | repay the whole by a speedy vengeance on the heads of the principal actors or abettors, and destroy the root of that poisonous plant, which never brings forth any fruit but impiety, filthiness, perfidy, cruelty, oppression, and idolatry.

PHILALETHES: I cannot much complain of your digression. And if you have said as much as you think fit on that subject, and the three several sorts of monarchy mentioned in Scripture, I desire you to proceed to speak of those sorts of monarchy you find in the world not mentioned in Scripture, whether amongst Christians or others; examining by the way which are to be justified and which not; or how far each one may be just or tolerable. And then we shall easily see, to which species or kind of monarchy, that amongst us does belong.

EUNOMIUS: those that speak of monarchy in general and the rights belonging to a king as a king, seem to misspend their time, as comprehending those governments under one rule, which so far differ in kind and degree, that it is hard to find two in the whole world exactly the same, in the rights that belong to him that is the chief. The prelates infer a right in one king to do what is done by any other king, as if, because Nero killed his mother, king Charles might poison his father, and because Saul killed the priests and destroyed the city of the prophets, therefore the present tyrant may fire London and drive all the better sort of ministers out of their livings, obliging them either to leave their integrity and abjure the covenant by them sworn, as he has done for an example to them, or else to starve and perish in prisons, taking also upon him to murder | the best of them, as he /205/ pleases. But first I shall speak of monarchy, then of the monarch.

Monarchy in general is distinguished into regal and despotical. Despotical government is exercised over slaves. The good of the governor is principally intended. If any consideration be had of the good of the governed, it enters by accident, for the governor's sake, as a man feeds his horse well, not for love to his horse, but himself, that he may be strong and able to serve him; or as a man fats his sheep to kill for his profit. On which account the great Turk is content that his Bassas or governors of several provinces of his empire may enrich themselves by tyrannizing over the people and robbing strangers, that so he may take away their lives and treasures together, at his pleasure, on one pretence or another.

There are three sorts of slaves.

First, slaves by nature that have the shapes of men, but in their spirits little differ from beasts, being base, stupid, sottish, guided wholly by sense, like beasts, utterly void of all political or moral knowledge, unable to govern themselves. These must have a master, and wholly depend upon his will.

The second sort are those who by nature are free like other men, but by some fault forfeit their liberty and so become slaves by breach of the law to which they had agreed, incurring the penalty appointed by it. This kind of slavery is now common in France, Italy, and Spain, where men are condemned to the galleys for offences that in other places are punished with death. These deserve their chains. Whole nations also may forfeit their liberty by cruelty, perfidy, and injustice, giving right of war against themselves, and being conquered, become slaves. According | to this law prisoners so taken in /206/ war are sold. This is right of conquest, which though generally rejected by some as unjust, grounded only on force, I think is sometimes most just. For as there are just causes of war, he that is conqueror in such a war does justly enjoy the fruits of his victory. When

I make a just war, I have a right to kill him that opposes me, and that man whom I may kill is so much mine, that, if for my profit, I may save him for my use as my servant.

The third sort of slaves are such as by violence, oppression, or fraud are unjustly brought into servitude. These are rather *servientes* than *servi*.[427] This is condemned by Solomon, as that posture of a state wherein, through the iniquity of the ruler, servants are set on horsebacks, while princes go afoot on the earth. Base-spirited men, void of all virtues, are exalted, and the truly noble in understanding and goodness depressed. These ever have a right of recovering their liberty, which no time can take from them. The continuance of the injury increases it. Their lord has no title to his dominion over them but force, and they may justly repel force with force, retaliating upon[428] him what they have suffered from him, and punish him with bondage or death.

The second sort of monarchy, that is, legal, differs from this in all respects. A free man governs free men according to law. The good of the governed is aimed at principally; the good of the governor comes in accidentally as a reward of his virtue if he do well administer the government, if evilly, he is to be punished. The same law of justice and reason that allows reward for virtue, denounces punishment for vice.

/207/ Secondly, the laws prescribed to him to govern by | have the force of a pact between the governor and governed. He, falsifying his trust in breaking the pact, can pretend to no benefit by it, but incurs the penalty of his infidelity.

Thirdly, the end for which these governors are constituted being the good of the governed, if the governor employ his power to their hurt, the constitution is void, and he that was first in the government becomes the last, by that eternal rule of justice that the delinquent is ever inferior to him whom he has offended.

But it is high time now to speak of the monarch, and first of him that is lord, or has the despotical government. He that will rule men so, must show that he is above them in nature and virtue, and free from the vices they have, if he will be so much above them in power. For if no better than they, they are as fit to govern him as he them. It

---

[427] 'enslaved rather than slaves'.

[428] Editorial hand has deleted the words 'inflicted on' and has put the words 'retaliating upon' in their place.

is ridiculous to give him a political pre-eminence, that naturally has none. That that is contrary to nature is ever evil. *Par in parem non habet imperium.*[429] He that is but equal to others ought not to rule over them. God directed the Jews to choose one that excelled others, at first setting up of kings. The lot fell on him that for outward appearances in height and beauty excelled them all, which suited with their vanity in desiring a king, like the rest of the nations. So him the Lord has chosen, says Samuel, there is not one like him amongst all the people (I Samuel 10:24). But when God had pity on them who for a false show of good, suffered true and real evil by his reign with whom at first they were so pleased, not regarding the countenance or stature, *He* rejected Eliab and Abinahab,[430] and chose him who for industry, valour, justice, and piety, the true virtues of a king, far excelled all the Israelites of that age. In the third election God carried the point higher, appointing one | who for wis- /208/ dom, the highest virtue for government, excelled all before or after him.

Either of these two kinds of despotical government may be just if the governed be so qualified, as to deserve such a condition, or governors have such virtues as give a just title to such pre-eminence over them.

PHILALETHES: I see you prepare for the third kind of despotical government, but before you come to it, what think you of the point of birth, which methinks gives the most undeniable right over others? And what think you of riches?

EUNOMIUS: I did not forget birth and riches, but willingly omitted them as not concerning the matter of our discourse. For we examine not the reasons why men are exalted, but why they should be exalted, from rules of justice and reason. Whilst we continue within these limits it is hard to tell how riches or birth can enter into consideration. We call riches gifts of fortune (as in Cebes's stoic table)[431] because we know not why God disposes of them to such and such. It is plain, they are often enjoyed by them that have nothing else, that

---

[429] 'Equals can have no right over each other.' Bracton, *On the laws and customs of England*, fol. 5, p. 33.
[430] Eliab and Abinahab: I Sam. 16:7–8.
[431] *Cebetis Thebani tabula, qua vitae humanae prudenter instituendae ratio continetur*, often printed together with Epictetus's *Enchiridion*. See the 1585 Plantin edition as an example. The 'table' in the text refers to the *tabula*.

has the least appearance of good. No man therefore for them is to be called to the government of mankind, which requires the highest excellency in the person, for the most noble and difficult work that can be undertaken by man.

The like may be said of birth. It is evident to all, there is hardly any sort of men nature does more sparingly impart her most precious endowments of body and mind to, than those of highest birth. And nothing is more contrary to reason and nature than that men should be placed in those great offices, who are naturally most unable to perform the duties belonging to them. Any child, says Solomon, is bet-/209/ ter than an old | foolish king who will not be advised. I am sure I may thence conclude, an ancient wise man is far better than a foolish young boy, though the son of a king. A wise man will seek one fitly qualified for the end and purpose he intends by him. If I have great weights to carry, I seek men that have strong backs and shoulders. If I want counsel I go to them that excel in wisdom. It were madness to ask physics of a man because he is a good soldier, or give the command of an army to another because he is a good physician or lawyer. Riches or birth, being but accidental advantages, can never give any natural privilege. Again, the honour of birth belongs to those that descend from good and wise men; not to those that descend from tyrants, who are the worst and maddest of all mankind. The particular advantage any man can expect among a people, by his ancestors, is by being the heir of such as have done great good to that people. But such as come from those who have oppressed, injured, betrayed, and exercised unjust dominion over that people, can of all mankind least pretend to any such prerogative. Nor can they have title by their riches, for take from them what is given them, or what they extort from the nation, there is none poorer than they. If a fool govern fools, it is unequal, and they are as the blind leading the blind, and both will fall into the ditch.

The last kind of despotical government is naturally, universally, and eternally unjust, detestable and abominable, that men naturally endowed with gifts, fit to govern themselves, and live for and unto God, their country, and themselves, should by fraud or violence be brought to live to and for another man equal to or worse than them-/210/ selves, | when they have no way forfeited the liberty to which they were born. This in Aristotle's terms is the highest and worst tyranny, comprehending all that is vicious, wicked, and shameful. To attempt it is a wicked madness. He that executes it is a monster, an enemy to mankind. All men are obliged to join hearts and hands to destroy him. Therefore, says he, great honours were not anciently appointed for such as killed public thieves and murderers, but tyrants who are the greatest thieves and wickedest murderers.[432]

We now come to the second sort of monarchy, *that which is* legal, which I will also divide into three sorts:

First, when a man of admirable valour, justice, and wisdom rises up amongst a free people, excelling every one and all together, so that they willingly submit to be governed by him, as excelling in all those virtues which conduce to the ends for which government is constituted; to wit, the felicity and perfection of the governed. Socrates, describing the duty and person of a king, says he must excel in valour, industry, and knowledge in military affairs, that he may protect and defend them from wolves and thieves, administering justice, protecting the innocent, punishing evil doers; and by his precepts and example draw the people to virtue, and so to be good and happy.[433]

Lastly, the felicity and perfection of man consisting in the knowledge of and union with God, he cannot be a king whose soul is not illuminated by God, filled with the knowledge of divine things, that he may be a leader of the people to their chiefest and highest good. This is such a king Seneca speaks of, *rex est qui metuit nihil, Rex | est [211] qui cupiet nihil,*[434] that is, for himself and of temporal things. This is not an empty speculation of whatever was, nor will be, though I might grant it without prejudice to the end I aim at. For if no man can be found so above all others in a nation, in virtue and those qualities that conduce to the ends for which governments are constituted, there is none who, according to the rules of nature, reason, and justice, can pretend to such a superiority over all others in the government. But the place of king is above all others, therefore none can be a king according to the rules of nature, reason, and justice. Whoever therefore assumes to himself any such power, breaks all those bonds, renders himself an enemy to mankind, and obliges all that are friends to reason and justice to destroy such a monster, who, having the shape of a man, has nothing else of humanity. But some stories

---

[432] Reference to Aristotle, *Politics*, bk v, chs. 10–11.
[433] Reference to Plato, *Alcibiades*, bk 1, 133–5.
[434] Seneca, *Thyestes*, 388–90. See n. 80 above.

acquaint us with such persons that have excelled all, and so had a natural supremacy over a people, and *were* just as willingly submitted to by them for their good. It is said that in Peru a man and woman found a people, living in beastly barbarity, cruelty and idolatry, without society, law, or rule, killing and eating one another. They told them they were sent by God to do them good, teach them to build houses, make cloths, sow corn, enter into society, give them laws.[435]

Thus having performed my undertaking, if you have nothing farther to object we may put a period to this discourse.

Finis.

---

[435] See n. 19 above.

Index of biblical quotations

Index of proper names

Index of subjects

Cambridge Texts in the History of Political Thought

Titles published in the series thus far

Aristotle *The Politics* (edited by Stephen Everson)

Arnold *Culture and anarchy and other writings* (edited by Stefan Collini)

Austin *The Province of Jurisprudence Determined* (edited by Wilfrid E. Rumble)

Bakunin *Statism and Anarchy* (edited by Marshall Shatz)

Baxter *A Holy Commonwealth* (edited by William Lamont)

Beccaria *On Crimes and Punishments and other writings* (edited by Richard Bellamy)

Bentham *A Fragment on Government* (introduction by Ross Harrison)

Bernstein *The Preconditions of Socialism* (edited by Henry Tudor)

Bodin *On Sovereignty* (edited by Julian H. Franklin)

Bossuet *Politics Drawn from the Very Words of Holy Scripture* (edited by Patrick Riley)

Burke *Pre-Revolutionary Writings* (edited by Ian Harris)

Christine de Pizan *The Book of the Body Politic* (edited by Kate Langdon Forhan)

Cicero *On Duties* (edited by M. T. Griffin and E. M. Atkins)

Constant *Political Writings* (edited by Biancamaria Fontana)

Diderot *Political Writings* (edited by John Hope Mason and Robert Wokler)

The Dutch Revolt (edited by Martin van Gelderen)

Early German Romantic Political Writings (edited by Frederick C. Beiser)

Early Greek Political Thought from Homer to the Sophists (edited by Michael Gagarin and Paul Woodruff)

Ferguson *An Essay on the History of Civil Society* (edited by Fania Oz-Salzberger)

Filmer *Patriarcha and Other Writings* (edited by Johann P. Sommerville)

Fourier *The Theory of the Four Movements* (edited by Gareth Stedman Jones and Ian Patterson)

Gramsci *Pre-prison Writings* (edited by Richard Bellamy)

Guicciardini *Dialogue on the Government of Florence* (edited by Alison Brown)

Harrington *A Commonwealth of Oceana* and *A System of Politics* (edited by J. G. A. Pocock)

Hegel *Elements of the Philosophy of Right* (edited by Allen W. Wood and H. B. Nisbet)

Hobbes *Leviathan* (edited by Richard Tuck)

Hobhouse *Liberalism and Other Writings* (edited by James Meadowcroft)

Hooker *Of the Laws of Ecclesiastical Polity* (edited by A. S. McGrade)